PLATO THE MYTH MAKER

PLATO
the
MYTH
MAKER

Luc Brisson

TRANSLATED, EDITED, AND WITH AN INTRODUCTION BY
Gerard Naddaf

THE UNIVERSITY OF CHICAGO PRESS
CHICAGO AND LONDON

Luc Brisson is directeur de recherche at the Centre National de
Recherche Scientific and is vice president of the International Plato
Society. Among his many publications are *Inventing the Universe* and
Introduction à la philosophie du mythe. Gerard Naddaf is associate
professor of philosophy at York University.

The University of Chicago Press, Chicago 60637
The University of Chicago Press, Ltd., London
© 1998 by The University of Chicago
All rights reserved. Published 1998
07 06 05 04 03 02 01 00 99 98   5 4 3 2 1

ISBN (cloth): 0-226-07518-4

Originally published as *Platon, Les mots et les mythes:
Comment et pourquoi Platon nomma le mythe?*
© Éditions La Découverte, Paris, 1994.

The University of Chicago Press gratefully acknowledges a
subvention from the government of France, through the Ministry of
Culture, in partial support of the costs of translating this volume.

Library of Congress Cataloging-in-Publication Data

Brisson, Luc.
    [Platon, les mots et les mythes. English]
    Plato the myth maker / Luc Brisson : translated, edited, and with
an introduction by Gerard Naddaf.
        p.   cm.
    Includes bibliographical references and index.
    ISBN 0-226-07518-4 (alk. paper)
    1. Plato.   2. Myth.   I. Naddaf, Gerard, 1950–   .   II. Title.
    B398.M8B55   1999
    184—dc21   98-8641
                                                                CIP

♾ The paper used in this publication meets the minimum
requirements of the American National Standard for Information
Sciences—Permanence of Paper for Printed Library Materials,
ANSI Z39.48-1992.

CONTENTS

What is a Myth?

The word "myth" is notoriously difficult to define. No one definition has been universally accepted.[1] This lack of definition is symptomatic of a real problem associated with the meaning of the word "myth."

Claude Lévi-Strauss's famous contention that a myth will always be recognized as such independently of the particular circumstances in which it originated does not in itself constitute a definition of myth. This simply amounts to saying that *x* is a myth. Indeed, we all think we know what is meant by a myth; a myth is something like a Greek myth we would say. In sum, to say that *x* is a myth is tantamount to saying that *x* is a myth just like *y* in ancient Greece. This is not a mere coincidence, for the words and concepts of myth and mythology were in fact coined by the Greeks. While it is true that what came to be called "myth" (at least in a popular sense of a false or unbelievable story or fiction) set the standard for numerous generations, it is not clear how this occurred. Until Plato the vocabulary *(muthos/logos)* hardly distinguishes between a "true" account and a "legendary" account. This is a point which is too often ignored,[2] and it deserves a closer examination.

Muthos / logos prior to Plato

The basic meaning of the word *muthos* (the Greek word from which the word "myth" is derived) seems to have been "something one says," whence *muthos* has the sense of "word," "saying," "advice," or "story" in Homer.[3] The word *muthos* is never employed or associated, in Homer, in the popular and pejorative sense of a false or unbelievable story or fiction. When *muthos* is employed in the sense of story—e.g., "Listen to the story *(muthon akousas)* of the wanderings" at *Od.* 3.94; 4.324[4]—it is without dis-

tinction of true or false, like the later *logos*. The other uses of *muthos* in
Homer (mostly in the plural) are also employed in a sort of neutral sense
to reflect something one says.[5] This is also the case with the only two examples of *logos* in Homer. Both are in the plural and both are employed
synonymously with *muthos* or *muthoi* (*Il.* 15.392; *Od.* 1.56 = "deceptive
language," *logoi aimulioi*).

There is no change in the meaning of *muthos* in Hesiod. In fact, in
Hesiod as in Homer, *muthoi* and *logoi* are still interchangeable. Thus we
are informed at *Works and Days* 194 that *muthoi* (words) can be crooked
(skolioi) and at *Theogony* 890 that *logoi* (words) can be deceptive *(aimulioi)*.[6] This is consistent with his statement at *Theogony* 24, that the Muses
know both true and false speech *(muthos)*. This lack of innovation may
explain why Hesiod relates the *logos* and not the *muthos* of the gold, silver,
bronze, and iron ages at *Works and Days* 106.[7]

The famous *muthos/logos* dichotomy is still nonexistent—at least from
a linguistic standpoint—in the works where we would most expect to find
it, that is, those of the first philosophers whom we conventionally call the
Presocratics.[8] In fact, *muthos* (there are less than a dozen occurrences of
this word) is still employed—rather ironically, from our perspective—as a
synonym for *logos*.

Xenophanes (c. 570–470), who is best known as the first to vigorously
denounce the old traditional theology, that is, the mythology, of Homer
and Hesiod and to replace it with a new "rational" theology, uses the plu-
rals *muthoi* and *logoi* almost synonymously in the same phrase: "first it is
necessary for righteous men to praise god with auspicious stories *(euphē-
mois muthois)* and pure words *(katharoisi logois)*."[9] Parmenides (c. 515–
450), for his part, terms the ultimate account of truth both a *muthos
(monos d'eti muthos hodoio leipetai)*[10] and a *logos (en tōi soi pauō piston logon
ēde noēma amphis alētheiēs)*.[11] And while Empedocles (c. 492–32) describes
his most truthful account as a god–given *muthos (theou para muthon akousas)*,[12] he equally attributes the truthfulness of his account to a *logos (su
d'akoue logou stolon ouk apatēlon)*.[13]

These examples from the Presocratics do not, therefore, diverge from
the original meaning of the Greek *muthos*.[14]

Pindar (c. 518–438) appears to have been the first to contrast *muthos*
to *logos* with respect to traditional stories about the gods. Indeed, at *Olympian Ode* 1.28–29 (476 B.C.), Pindar employs *muthoi* and *pseudea* (lies)
interchangeably to contrast ignoble stories about the gods to his own *logos
alathēs* ("language of truth"; "historic truth"?). And at *Nemean Ode*
7.21–25, *muthoi* and *pseudea* are employed synonymously with respect

to the charm of Homer's narrative and contrasted with *alatheia*. On the other hand, he still terms his own version of traditional stories a *logos* (e.g., *Ol.* 7.21; *N.* 1.34). In sum, there is still an ambiguity here.

A similar contrast appears shortly after in Herodotus (c. 480–425). Although the Father of History only employs the word *muthos* twice in the nine books of his *Histories*, on both occasions it signifies what is not believable as opposed to what is believable. In the first instance at 2.23, Herodotus states that to explain the Nile's origin as due to the mythical river Ocean is to give credence to what cannot be seen or known and is thus to tell a "myth" *(es aphanes ton muthon)*. In the second instance at 2.45, he describes one of Heracles' exploits in Egypt as "a very silly story" *(euēthēs muthos)*. In both cases, what he describes as a "myth" is related to a supernatural phenomenon which conflicts with observed facts as opposed to his own accounts, which he characterizes as *logoi,* that is, as true (see, e.g., 2.25). However, the fact remains that Herodotus does not identify all traditional stories or tales as *muthoi* or untrue[15] (indeed, despite the numerous traditional stories, the word only appears twice), and in some instances these stories are called *hiroi logoi* or "sacred traditions" (see, e.g., 2.48, 51, 62). Herodotus is thus no less ambiguous than Pindar. Indeed, it would be rash to conclude from these few examples in Pindar and Herodotus that *muthos* refers to a precise subject matter.

Thucydides (c. 460–400), for his part, never employs the word *muthos,* but he is the first to employ the derivative *muthōdēs* to designate what lacks credulity or historical value; what cannot meet his own high standards; what cannot be scrupulously verified; and thus what pertains to legend (1.21, 22). The oral tradition, the tradition based on memory, the one upon which Herodotus so much depended for the source of his *Histories,* is only worthy of contempt for the author of the *Peloponnesian War.* But again, there is nothing to indicate that Thucycides has a "precise" subject matter in view.

There is thus little, if any, evidence prior to Plato which could lead one to conclude that there was a clear opposition between *muthos* and *logos.*[16] However, none of this means that *logos* was not employed earlier on in the sense of a "rational" discourse.[17] Indeed, this is already clearly the case with Heraclitus (c. 540–480), although it is possible that prior to him the word *logos* was already employed in this sense.[18] The primary reason for which *logos* was able to perform this function is found in the root of the word. *Logos* is derived from the root **leg-*. The fundamental meaning of this root is that of "gathering," "picking up," "choosing."[19] In sum, *legein* was not originally a saying verb,[20] but a word which translated the activity and laws of the mind.[21] If *legein* was later to become a saying verb, this was due to its figurative meaning of "recounting, telling over, reckoning up"— one of the essential aspects of the verb "say."[22] However, contrary to *legein*, *logos* retained in Attic Greek the rational values of the root **leg-* with the meanings "account, reason" and applied them to the concept of speech.[23] This explains why one can reduce the numerous meanings that *logos* was to take to two: speech and reason. The subjection of the first to the second explains why *logos* could, and did, take on the sense of a "rational discourse," that is, a discourse which is argumentative and open to criticism, a discourse which can be logically and/or empirically verified.

In the final analysis, however, the famous *muthos*/*logos* dichotomy is not clearly attested prior to Plato, although the germs may be discerned in some authors.

Muthos / Logos in Plato

As Brisson so aptly demonstrates, it was Plato himself who established the meaning of *muthos* once and for all both in its primary sense and in its broad or derivative sense. In its primary sense, as Brisson observes, Plato employs myth *(muthos)* to designate essentially what we automatically associate with the traditional myths of ancient Greece and indeed when we say *x* is a myth just like *y* in ancient Greece (of which Homeric epic is the paradigm). As Brisson notes, when Plato employs the word *muthos* in the primary sense he both describes it and criticizes it. He describes it as a particular kind of discursive practice and he criticizes it from the perspective of a superior kind of discursive practice: philosophy. In its broad or derivative sense (that is, its metaphorical sense), Plato, as Brisson observes, employs *muthos* to designate unfalsifiable information (whence the expression *eikōs muthos,* "likely story," in the *Timaeus*) as opposed to information which can be verified, that is, information which is preoccupied with truth or *logos.*

What Plato understands by *muthos* is much more than simply a "traditional tale" or fiction, which is "unbelievable" (the initial reaction to the "primary sense" of the word noted above). As Brisson discovers, a contextual analysis of Plato's use of the term *muthos* reveals that what Plato understands by myth is synonymous with what an ethnologist and others would call "oral literature." This is a richly rewarding discovery and one which essentially dismantles Marcel Detienne's general thesis, according to which there is no coherent theory of myth in Plato.

For an ethnologist, myth (which is inseparable from oral literature and tradition) is a message (or set of messages) that a social group considers to have received from its ancestors and that it transmits orally from generation to generation.[24] Brisson ingeniously demonstrates, in detail, to what degree Plato's famous Atlantis myth (albeit a pastiche) conforms to the ethnologist's general definition and how most of the occurrences of the word *muthos* in Plato must be understood in the context of such a message. Before examining how the Atlantis story conforms to a *muthos,* something must be said about myth and oral literature.

If myth is a message which is transmitted orally from generation to generation, then myth is a phenomenon associated with an oral culture or tradition.[25] But while it is generally true that myths are transmitted orally, it is also true that in the Greek oral tradition,[26] myths were communicated in the form of poetry.[27] Poetry is a form of spoken discourse which is "contrived" by an oral poet to assure that the message/myth will be retained in memory by the community.[28] This explains why Plato considers the poet not only as a myth-teller but also as a myth-maker, indeed, as the myth-maker par excellence.[29] In the ancient Greek tradition as it is abundantly evidenced by Plato, it is the great poets, Homer and Hesiod, who are seen as the primary "creators" of "oral tradition" and, by extension, of "myth." This fact necessitates a closer look at the relation between poetry and oral literature in the Greek tradition.

Poetry and Oral Literature

There now seems to be some consensus that Homeric poetry (the *Iliad* and the *Odyssey*) was not the work of a single author but rather that it grew out of centuries of oral performance by numerous Greek bards.[30] This consensus is due essentially to the work of Milman Parry and his successors, notably Albert Lord (the so-called "formulaic school").[31] Parry thesis was based on the critical connection between "formulaic diction" and the possibility that Homer was an oral bard rather than a literate writer. He demonstrated how the omnipresent verbal repetitions constitute an exceptional system of economy and scope within the technically demanding epic meter.[32] It was the extraordinary meticulousness of the system which led Parry to the conclusion that Homeric poetry must have been the product of a long series of bards working within an inherited tradition. The mnemonic technique (which helped them make, perform, and pass down the oral tradition) must have been the product of composition by oral improvisation[33] and must have taken generations to develop and refine.[34]

Moreover, according to Parry and the formulaic school, oral poetry can not exist outside the context of performance.[35] And since the bard was performing for an audience, the audience and the occasion affected the formulaic style of the performance.[36] It was thus the audience and the occasion which determined which formulaic phrases would be included in the performance and which not, although the metrical needs of the poet dictated, in the final analysis, which formulae would be retrieved from the stockpile to meet the occasion. This entails that the oral poet does not memorize,[37] but composes, so to speak, in the heat of the moment, reacting to the audience and the context.[38] Although no two performances were identical (the sine qua non of improvisation and, of course, orality), there was no room for originality and individuality, since the poet was restricted to reiterating tradition according to rigid metrical formula.[39]

Parry's thesis also accounts both for the distinctive linguistic phenomena of Homeric style and for the epics' numerous historical inconsistencies.[40] Indeed, while most agree that oral tradition (and thus the formulaic technique) to which Homer refers originated in the Mycenean period (1,400–1,100 B.C.),[41] most equally agree that the diverse elements derive from various periods (indeed, it appears difficult to argue to the contrary).[42] This, in turn, suggests that what counted was not "accuracy" but rather a performance that was captivating and yet conceivably in conformity with the oral tradition (something Plato's Atlantis story seems to confirm). In sum, although new information and new experience were continually grafted on the inherited models (something to which Plato would be opposed), they were framed (or perceived) not as conscious "innovations" but as "contemporary decisions," that is, as though they were words or acts of ancestors (something Plato seems to confirm).[43]

Orality and Literacy

The oral-formulaic thesis is not without its detractors. One of the main criticisms of it is that the poetic tradition as it is portrayed by Parry and his school is too mechanical or deterministic; the poet appears to be in a linguistic/structural straightjacket that leaves no room for poetic individuality and originality.[44] Although there is a consensus (as noted above) that the Homeric epics are the product of a long oral tradition, many argue that the Homeric epics are too long, complex, and masterful to have been the result of mere improvisation on the spur of the moment. There are two main variations on this claim. Some argue that the monumentality of the poems entails that writing was employed (as if to say, that it is no coincidence that these exceptional works appear with the advent of writing sometime in eighth-century Greece); others, including proponents of the oral-formulaic school, argue that the oral technique was advanced enough to account for this monumentality, although the poems were obviously put into writing some generations after their creation.

Proponents of the later group put the accent on the notion that memorization of oral poetry—whatever the length—is not incompatible with improvisation. Thus Rosalind Thomas, a major defender of innovation in oral poetry, gives a number of (non-Greek) examples of oral poets practicing in private before a performance (as Critias appears to do in preparation for his recital of the Atlantis story, as we will see below), and she sees these as a clear indication of memorization and reflection on the part of the oral poet—the sine qua non for an original and lengthy oral epic.[45] Geoffrey Kirk, a strong defender of the formulaic school (but equally of the thematic method in composition), argues that verbatim repetition (and thus memorization) was possible because of both formulae and thematic structure and that the poems were thus orally created by two monumental poets in their present form about 700 B.C. and then transmitted more or less verbatim by "reproductive singers" before they were finally written down in the sixth century.[46] Most recently, Gregory Nagy, another proponent of the formulaic school, has proposed a more compelling theory. He begins with the Parry/Lord thesis that composition and performance are aspects of the same process (composition-in-performance), but he adds a third aspect, diffusion, to this interaction. He argues that while it is clear that the Homeric poems reflect a social setting datable to the eighth century, there is no evidence to prove that writing was necessary for the process of composition and performance (he also argues that the materials did not exist for dictation), although there is evidence for diffusion. He believes that the versions of the poems later put into writing became more popular than the others (and, hence, became progressively less changeable) in the course of their diffusion. He connects the diffusion and its consequences with Panhellenic festivals, and in particular with the Panathenaia, a religious festival (which I discuss, in context, below) at Athens which had a long history in connection with the performance of the Homeric epics.[47]

Proponents of the first group are most certainly in the majority, although this appears to represent a sudden turn-around.[48] Maurice Bowra contends that Homer was an oral poet who then learned the art of writing.[49] Albert Lord argues that since an orally composed poem cannot be transmitted orally without major changes, and since the powers of oral poets are destroyed if and when they learn to write, then Homer must have *dictated* the epics.[50] Adam Parry contends that while it is proven that the *Iliad* and the *Odyssey* were designed for oral performance, we do not know that they were composed orally.[51] He argues that the monumentality of the poems entails that the technology of writing was involved (contra Kirk), and also that writing, at this time, would *not* have affected the bard's "thoughts or mode of expression" (contra Lord).[52] In sum, Homer may have written the poems himself without the constraints of an audience.[53] Eric Havelock (another strong champion of the formulaic school) has a position similar to that of Adam Parry. He believes that the Homeric texts are an accurate record of orality and that they were written down by Homer himself. In fact, Havelock sees Homer as a reader as well as a writer who composed his texts from already written episodes.[54] However, Homer was not writing for a reading audience, but for a listening audience.[55] It was only generations later (in the fourth century) that public literacy developed in ancient Greece. This explains not only how the Greek oral tradition was able to be preserved, but also why it was accepted and thus remained so popular. Moreover, "formulaic technique" not only enabled the poets (or rhapsodists) to continue to teach orally the poems, but it also enabled the population at large to memorize the poems verbatim and thus to retain their proper control over each recital.[56] However, it was not just a question of memorizing and controlling, but also of actively participating in the performance, of reliving the experience of the past.[57] Jack Goody, an influential non-classicist, contends that the Homeric epics were already influenced by Mycenean and Near Eastern forms of writing and thus that the formulaic argument is not a guarantee (contra the proponents of the formulaic school in general) of their orality.[58] Goody also argues (contra Havelock) that lengthy verbatim recall *without* writing is difficult, in reality, to defend; what we see is an absence of such verbatim recall, and this, in fact, explains variation in oral tradition.[59]

However, all this raises another fundamental and controversial issue: to what degree did the technology of writing influence our way of thinking? This is no less controversial than the historical debate revolving around the linguistic origin of the Homeric epics. Indeed, there is a certain overlap.

The Cognitive Effects of Literacy

One of the primary students of the cognitive effects of literacy has been Eric Havelock. Havelock's work has been extremely influential, in particular, outside the world of classical scholarship,[60] although it has also very much influenced the French structuralists in the classical tradition, including Brisson. Since the focus of much of Havelock's work is associated with Plato's opposition to Homer and oral tradition, it is important to put Havelock's thesis in context.

Havelock's whole theory of "primary orality" originates from his interpretation of the Homeric epics as an "accurate record of orality."[61] He believes (as noted above) that the "main" purpose of oral tradition in nonliterate societies is to preserve the collective knowledge of the group and to pass it on from generation to generation (a thesis which is confirmed in other quarters and, more importantly, by Plato). In order for this to ensue, this knowledge has to be memorable and memorizable. He argues that in nonliterate societies in general, *only* what is expressed as a narrative of action is memorizable, and the *only* linguistic statements which can be expressed as a narrative of action are "poetized statements."[62] Since oral poetry entails an "endless series of actions,"[63] Havelock contends that it is thus impossible in Homeric Greek to make timeless or universal statements (with or without abstract subjects), including propositions using the verb "to be" *(einai)*,[64] such as "the angles of a triangle are equivalent to two right angles" or "God is good or perfect," so typical of Plato's "rational" theology (as we shall see below).

Havelock argues that the invention of the Greek alphabet, which he dates to about 700 B.C.)[65] radically changed all this over a relatively short period of time. "The alphabet, making available a visualized record which was complete, in place of an acoustic one, abolished the need for memorization and hence rhythm. Rhythm had hitherto placed severe limitations upon the verbal arrangements of what might be said, or thought. More than that, the need to remember had used up a degree of brain-power— of psychic energy—which now was no longer needed. The statement need not be memorized. It could lie around as an artifact, to be read when needed; no penalty for forgetting—that is, so far as preservation was concerned. The mental energies thus released, by this economy of memory, have probably been extensive, contributing to an immense expansion of knowledge available to the human mind."[66]

Words ("visible artifacts") were now available for more intense scrutiny than is orally possible, and this encourages personal awareness.[67] Visualizing a text enables "backward scanning" and reflection on how the subject matter is organized.[68] In sum, the introduction of the visual element into language gradually brought about new modes of thought and new compositional tools, including topicalization and the development of logical categories.

The first consequence of writing was to record orality on a scale never previously realized.[69] The creation of written records then drew the attention of some literate Greeks for whom the written word became an "object" clearly differentiated from the reader and writer.[70] Since written statements have structure then, what they represent is quickly perceived as also having structure—that is, as being an ordered cosmos.[71] The existence of written words now makes abstraction (including propositional statements using abstract nouns and the true copula) possible.[72] The new language is worded "so as to replace agents by impersonal forces and the acts of agents performed upon other agents by statements of relationships between impersonal entities."[73] The new language of *logos* replaces the old language of *muthos,* and it is fully exploited by the Presocratics. Of course, although human consciousness was radically and permanently transformed in ancient Greece, it still remained essentially an oral culture until Plato, and this, according to Havelock, largely explains Plato's attitude toward poetry. Indeed Plato was the first great exponent of an entirely new kind of consciousness.

Why may we ask did this not occur elsewhere, since literacy was certainly not restricted to the Greeks? Havelock argues that this "revolution" could not have occurred elsewhere without the type of alphabet invented by the Greeks.[74] Although the Greeks borrowed from the Phoenician system of writing, which employed only consonants, they radically transformed the alphabet by adding vowel signs. Doing so took the guesswork out of determining the meaning of written texts.[75] It took, so to speak, the guesswork out of their meaning. The Greek alphabet provided us with a "visual representation of linguistic noise that was both economical and exhaustive" and that could "be combined in such a way as to accurately represent any linguistic noise."[76] With the Phoenician system the reader had to determine which vowels and thus which words were meant. The Phoenician system was thus an imperfect representation of speech sounds (this, of course, holds for other systems, including the cuneiform syllabaries) and because of its intrinsic vagueness, it tends "to deal with action and thought in typical situations and use a style which is formulaic and repetitive."[77] Further, it tends to represent a culture which is more likely to focus on religion and myth.[78] On the other hand, the Greek alphabet demands relatively little instruction to master (a point of which Plato appears very much aware; see *Laws* 810a) and so literacy became accessible to almost anyone.[79] If none of this happened elsewhere, is was simply because it could not have occurred without the true alphabet.[80]

Literacy and Politics

It should be no surprise that while Havelock's primary thesis that Greek literacy actually restructured consciousness is not without its supporters (and Brisson is certainly among them), it has also garnered a good deal of valid criticism. Indeed, Havelock claims (or, at least, appears to claim) that by simply adding vowels to the consonant symbols borrowed from the Phoenicians, the Greeks discharged a surge of psychic energy which radically and permanently transformed human consciousness. This is tantamount to claiming that "Greek alphabetic literacy" was the *sole* cause of "logical thought"[81]—indeed, of the so-called "Greek miracle" and everything we associate with it. While it may be true that literacy is a "necessary cause," it is difficult to see how it could be the "sufficient cause." The advent of the *polis* certainly antedates the introduction of the alphabet, and, as Jean-Pierre Vernant has shown "with the *polis,* social life and human relations took on a new form, and the Greeks were *fully aware* [my italics] of its originality."[82] And he convincingly argues that the major distinguishing feature of the *polis* is speech, that is, speech *(logos)* associated with "open debate, discussion and argument."[83] In brief, there is a reciprocal relation between politics and speech *(logos)*. Geoffrey Lloyd is equally convinced of this. In a series of studies (inspired by Vernant and others),[84] he attempts to show that it was the institutions of the *polis* which primarily explain the peculiar development of Greek thought and science: "The institutions [of the *polis*] created an audience of people who had extensive experience of evaluating evidence and arguments in the context of legal and political debates, and it is the audience which is crucial to the deployment of the particular style of reasoning characteristic of early Greek speculative thought."[85] The spirit of secular competition (economically driven) so typical of Greek political life is already evident in Hesiod (*Works and Days* 25–26), and it would be at least premature to see this as already the consequence of writing. Indeed, Hesiod's whole approach in the *Works and Days* may be perceived as a critical and open discussion. Further, it is important to note that in addition to a government which was open and secular, there was no established priestly class and no centralized bureaucracy prior to the advent of literacy.

But to what degree would Greek speculative thought have developed without literacy? There can be little doubt that literacy strengthened the preexisting social tendencies. It is highly unlikely that laws would have been codified without writing. And, according to Oswyn Murray, the codification of laws should be seen "as the first step towards the breakdown of traditional aristocracies."[86] This is also indicative of the fact that "lawgivers" were already perceived as secular experts *(sophoi)* with a quasi-divine power[87]—a fact of which Plato was well aware. Marcel Detienne, for his part, shows that writing was already deployed for political ends around 650.[88] In sum, although most decisions were still made by public debate and without the aid of writing, writing was paramount in the movement toward more sophisticated constitutions (something Plato was keenly aware of, as we will see below).

Moreover, would historical inquiry (and/or critical historiography) have been possible without writing? Would the inconsistencies between the past and the present have been noticed without a permanently recorded version of the past to consult?[89] Do not written records foster the development of "critical evaluation" and thus an "accumulation of scepticism" in general?

Literacy and Politics in Anaximander

The evidence is that the capacity for critical thought developed within generations after the advent of writing, but not, strictly speaking, in the form of critical historiography. The scepticism generated by the inherent inconsistencies between the past and the present first gave birth to philosophy and science. And the first philosopher, at least the first to have written a book (in prose) of some sort, is Anaximander of Miletus (c. 575).[90] His cosmological model is indicative of the new rational or natural approach (as opposed to mythical approach) to the origin and development of the present order of things, that is, an *historia* (or investigation) of the *peri phuseōs* type. The Milesian claims, after beginning with a rational cosmogony, that the earth is at rest at the center of the celestial sphere. The reason he gives for this is that the earth being equidistant from all the points of the celestial circumference, there is no reason for it to move up rather than down, or left rather than right. In sum, the Milesian's reasoning behind both the position of the earth and structure of the universe appears to be mathematical. Detienne contends (or seems to contend) that Anaximander's cosmological model requires a sketch, and a sketch could not have been done without the aid of writing, and, therefore, that the Milesian's models (and reasoning) are dependent on writing. Detienne also sees this sketch as the impetus behind the claim that Anaximander was the "first" with the audacity to draw *(graphai)* the inhabited world on a tablet.[91] More importantly, Detienne implies that without the impact of writing the geometrical and isonomical vision so indicative of Anaximander (and Plato) would not have occurred.[92] In sum, writing and not politics, or at least writing more so than politics, is a necessary condition for the critical and argumentative approach associated with Greek thought. However, during Anaximander's time monumental temple-building was common practice, and the Greek architects, relying on a practice they inherited from Ancient Egypt, made models and sketches of the monuments both before and during construction.[93] This is not to claim that writing was unimportant, only that writing need not be employed to account for Anaximander's models. The reasoning behind the models is another matter. Further, it can be argued that Anaximander's cosmological model is not only eminently mathematical but also that it reflects the socio-political conditions of his time.[94] This is not only reflected in the socio-political terminology employed to describe the cosmological model strictly speaking, but equally in his famous fragment which describes how the present order of things is maintained.[95] In conjunction with this, it is noteworthy that Anaximander is also characterized as a legislator, and legislation and writing go hand-in-hand.[96]

Anaximander is also the first to explain that humanity had a real beginning in time: it emanated from a sort of primordial slime which was activated by the heat of the sun after the initial formation of the universe—a thesis which was adopted by virtually all of his successors including both the Presocratics and Plato.[97] And, in conjunction with this, there is some evidence that Anaximander was the first to postulate a rational explanation of the evolution of society (with the Nile as its possible source) with the support both of genealogies and of an idea of human progress—a thesis which was again adopted by a number of his successors, including Plato.[98] This suggests, I believe, that Anaximander also had an interest in contemporary and recent history and thus in "critical" historiography. The testimony (noted above) that Anaximander was the "first" with the audacity to draw *(graphai)* the inhabited world on a tablet would appear to support the idea.[99] His later compatriot, Hecataeus (c. 500), who some call "the father of Greek historiography" because of his critical work, *Genealogies,* is explicitly said to have improved upon Anaximander's map and geographical description following his extensive travels.[100] And Xenophanes of Colophon (c. 570–470), a virtual contemporary with Anaximander, is credited with having composed epics on the foundation of Colophon and Elea. More important, and not unrelated, Xenophanes is well known for his theory of human progress and his own extensive travels.[101]

Is there any reason to doubt that Anaximander also traveled extensively? Certainly, the doxographical tradition leads us to believe that he visited Egypt (as Hecataeus certainly did). Travel, in general, was an important factor (albeit not on a par with writing or politics) in exposing the Greeks to other systems of belief and to a sense that the universe, humanity, and society had a much longer past than previously thought. And it may help us to understand Anaximander's synoptical (and systematic) account of the origin and development of the universe, humanity, and society—and of how this order is (or is to be in the political context) maintained. In this respect, his *historia* would be a direct challenge to Hesiod's *Theogony,* which also seeks to explain how the present order of things emerged and can be maintained. There is no reason to believe that Anaximander would not have heard a performance of Hesiod's mythical account (or have even consulted a written version of the famous poem), and there is also no reason to believe that Anaximander would not have read aloud his own version. And the fact that he felt it important enough to compose his ideas for others to read or to hear is indicative of the importance he placed on the technology of writing and public debate. From Anaximander to Plato, each and every philosopher made use of the technology of writing, and each and every philosopher was aware of the *historia* or investigations of their predecessors. Indeed, there is a continuing tradition of assimilation and criticism. Each *historia* is analyzed, criticized, and enriched. In sum, whether or not writing was initially just an aide-mémoire, it is evident that it soon became a sine qua non for reflective analysis (albeit not for free exchange of ideas: that is a given, a sine qua non for political existence), for the content is far too complex to digest in a single performance.[102] And since debate was part of the performance, there is no reason to believe that the philosopher would not alter his initial ideas.[103] More importantly, since the Presocratics were almost all legislators and statesman, public performances may have played a more important role than previously thought.

What is Literacy?

There is a consensus, even among antagonists, that Greek society remained essentially an oral society at least to the time of Plato.[104] This does not mean that literacy was not widespread but rather that writing was not the normal means of communication if speech were possible. Indeed, there is a good deal of evidence that written texts (in general) were composed to be read aloud before an audience, and this is not surprising considering that written texts, literary ones in particular, would obviously have a restricted circulation. More importantly, as Rosalind Thomas and others have correctly noted, an educated man was essentially one who could speak well in public (as the advent of the sophists so well attests) and, therefore, there was no need to read books.[105] It was the fact that Greece remained essentially an oral society which explains, as Havelock notes, Plato's attitude toward the poets. Whether Plato was "the first great exponent of an entirely new kind of consciousness," as Havelock contends, is another matter.

Plato on Writing

In the *Cratylus,* Plato contends that the various consonants and vowels of the alphabet (although not in the context of writing) are naturally suited to "represent" certain ideas (e.g., the vowel *O* is held to be naturally suited to represent roundness). In sum, we are dealing with a mimetic theory of natural representation, a theory that Plato contends applies not only to language but also to art.[106] This explains, at least in part, Plato's objection to art (and by extension poetry) in *Republic* X. It is a representation of a representation; in brief, a deception.[107] This is also his position in the *Phaedrus,* where the written word enters into the picture for the first time. Plato now contends that the written word is only a copy of the spoken word.[108] Or more precisely, it is an image of "the living and breathing word" (*Phdr.* 276a). Writing like painting deals with "lifeless" products. Just as figures in a painting appear like human beings and yet remain silent if you interrogate them, so written words seem to manifest intelligence, but if you ask them a question they remain silent like painted figures.[109]

This is the essence of the Egyptian King Thamus' reproach to the God Theuth, the inventor of writing, in the famous passage in the *Phaedrus.* Writing is not "a recipe for memory and wisdom," as Theuth claimed, but a recipe for forgetfulness and a semblance of wisdom. Because of it, men will no longer recall things from within themselves (i.e., their souls) but from the external marks of others.[110] Writing will cause men to cease to exercise their memory and thus will destroy memory as a power of recollection and as a repository for knowledge and, by extension, for oral tradition.[111] Knowledge (and oral tradition) is only possible in the context of an oral exchange of question and answer between a master and apprentice, what Plato calls the art of dialectic.[112] This is corroborated in the famous *Letter* VII: "Knowledge is not something that can be put into words like other sciences; but after a long-continued intercourse between teacher and pupil, in joint pursuit of the subject, suddenly, like light flashing forth when a fire is kindled, it is born in the soul and straightway nourishes itself" (341c; trans. Glen Morrow). Dialectical teaching is thus a social process. It requires a live exchange of ideas in the quest for truth.[113]

Plato's attitude toward writing is nonetheless ambiguous.[114] While he claims that writing actually weakens the memory rather than enhances it, as Havelock argues, could Plato have seriously thought that he could have organized a Socratic dialogue, let alone the more complex later dialogues, without the aid of writing? Did he never take notes to help organize his thoughts? Did written words never reach out to him when scanning notes (of written texts) with the mind's eye? Did he not see a written text as an aide-mémoire which would incite discussion with or without the presence of its author? There are, I believe, a number of examples of this.

At the outset of the *Theaetetus,* Terpsion asks Euclides if he can relate to him the conversation which took place between Socrates and the young Theaetetus as it was related to him by Socrates. Euclides replies that he cannot recall Socrates' account from memory, but he does have a "written account" since he took "written notes" *(hupomnēmata)* of Socrates' account (*Tht.* 143a-c). The written account is somewhat accurate because whenever he was in doubt on a particular point (that is, could not remember it), he would ask Socrates for a clarification and then correct the previous version. The "written version" was composed not as it was related by Socrates to Euclides, that is, in the form of an indirect speech and narrative, but in the form of "direct speech."[115] The composition, which will be read aloud by a slave, will enable Euclides and Terpsion to become spectators and listeners (indeed, active participants!) in a brilliant exchange of ideas (epistemological in the present context) thanks to (and in spite of) the written format. I will return to this in the context of the Atlantis story further on (*Critias* 108b–c).

Further, Plato's reflection on the alphabet, in particular with respect to the various combination of letters, was paramount in inventing various epistemological and conceptual approaches.[116] He employs letters on a number of occasions to conduct epistemological experiments. In the *Statesman* 277e–78e, he employs letters to help explain how paradigms work in his dialectical method. He believes that the study of letters can help us become better dialecticians. Much of his epistemological theory in the *Theaetetus* is based on an analysis of letters. Indeed he says (*Tht.* 206b) that a knowledge of the basic elements of language, that is, letters, reveals clearer knowledge than that of the complex elements. In the *Sophist* 263b, he employs letters of the alphabet to show the texture of philosophical discourse, that is, how some forms blend together and others not (the vowels being likened to the five most important Forms). In the *Timaeus* 48b–c, an analysis of letters brings us closer to understanding the basic elements of which the universe is composed. In the *Philebus* 17a–18b, Plato's theory of phonetic writing is the starting point (and model) for his philosophical investigation into the problem of the one and the many. And in the *Cratylus,* as we saw above, the relation between language and reality is analyzed from the perspective of letters.

More importantly, Plato was well aware of the importance of writing in the "historical" progress of civilization.[117] In his sort of Presocratic description of the development of society after a legendary flood[118] in *Laws* III,[119] writing does not only explain the transition from *muthos* to *logos,* from "oral tradition" to "critical historiography," but equally and perhaps more importantly, it is the sine qua non for legislation and thus for the future city of the *Laws.* The survivors of the flood were, of course, illiterate and uncivilized mountain dwellers[120] who lived a simplified existence for thousands of years *(muriakis muria etē).*[121] In fact, the only arts they possessed were pottery and weaving, which Plato associates with elementary forms of cooking and clothing[122]—any form of metallurgy and the tools associated with it having disappeared (*Laws* III 678d–e, 679d). Because of their simplicity *(euētheia),* these people were not only good *(agathos),* but they believed whatever they heard *(ēkouon).* However, they lived without *sophia* (*Laws* III 679c).

Plato describes the political system associated with these mountain dwellers, or Cyclopes, as an autocracy *(politeia dunasteia, Laws* III 680b). The inhabitants lived in separate, scattered households ruled by the eldest member of the family (680d–e). Each household lived according to customs *(ethē),* that is, traditional laws *(patrioi nomoi),* because writing *(grammata)* and thus legislators *(nomothetai)* did not yet exist (680a). At some point in time, several households came together in the foothills, developed agriculture, and surrounded themselves with a stone wall to protect themselves from the wild animals (680e–81a; see also *Laws* VI 781e–82d). At first each household lived according to their respective customs, but eventually representatives are chosen among the households to propose customs *(nomima)* which were in the common interest. Plato calls these representatives "lawgivers" *(nomothetai,* 681d) and contends that this is the origin of legislation *(nomothesia,* 681c). In this new situation, the former leaders constitute a sort of aristocracy (or even a kingship, 681d). The next stage in this gradual evolution occurs when a number of these societies settled on the plains and built cities *(poleis).* This resulted, over time, in the appearance of all forms *(panta eidē)* of political systems *(poleteiai).*

Plato believes that this could only have occurred well after the flood had been forgotten (682b), and he situates the famous siege of Troy and its aftermath in this period which, of course, lasted for some time (681e–82e, 683a).

Now when Plato refers to the siege of Troy and, in particular, its aftermath, he describes it as if it were historical fact, although he employs the word *muthos* (682a8).[123] The story originates, of course, with the poets and, with the help of the Muses, "they often hit on how things really happen" (682a).[124] But it is only in the fourth and final stage of his description—that is, in his discussion of the Dorian League—that he explicitly states that he is now dealing with "historical fact."[125] However, one would expect, because legislation and thus writing have been around for some time (in fact, aristocracy, which appears at the end of the second stage, should also entail writing since it is the result of legislation), that written documents on the Trojan war would have been available. He does mention that one of the first discoveries was by Palamedes, who is often associated with the invention of writing (677d).[126] Of course, Plato is well aware that writing existed in Egypt for thousands of years, and, given that he sees the various stages as lasting for vast periods of time (although there will *always* be some mountain dwellers and thus autocracies), it is not impossible that he believed in diffusion. Plato may have thought (to his credit) that writing was initially employed for codifying laws and only later for recording oral tradition. On the other hand, the Egyptian priest tells Solon that the Greeks, contrary to the Egyptians, are always young *(aei paides),* because no sooner does their civilization reach a certain point and it is destroyed by natural catastrophes (*Tim.* 22b). The Egyptian priest could back up his claim with written records, whereas the Greeks were incapable of this. Indeed, he explicitly associates writing with one of the basic necessities of civilization (*Tim.* 23a).

The Egyptian priest's claim is consistent with Plato's account in the *Critias* 110a. Here he informs us that it is only after the basic necessities of life have been provided that human beings have enough leisure time *(scholē)* to begin mythology *(muthologia)* and research *(anazētēsis)* into the past *(tōn palaiōn).*[127] From the fact that the so-called basic necessities of life were already provided for during the aristocratic stage, that is, toward the end of the second stage mentioned above, or, at the latest, during the third stage when all types of political constitutions began to flourish, it follows that writing and oral tradition have existed for a significant period of time. Now if writing was initially invented for the codification of custom (or at least is connected with it), then this implies (or seems to imply) that for Plato the advent of "oral tradition" is coeval with that of writing. I will return to the relation between writing and oral tradition further on. I would now like to get back to the relation between writing and legislation (or writing as the sine qua non for legislation).

It is only in the fourth and final stage of his analysis of the development of society that Plato proposes as a model for his "second best" *(hē mia deuterōs)* constitution the same principle of *metriotēs,* moderation, that he demonstrates to have been behind the success of Sparta (*Laws* III 691c–92a), Persia (694a–b), and Athens (698b–f) at diverse moments of their histories. But this principle of *metriotēs* can only be maintained in the context of a mixed constitution, that is, where there is a judicious balance between the warp and the woof, between the authority of the ruler and the liberty of the subjects: in sum, a combination of what Plato calls the two mother-constitutions of monarchy and democracy, of which Persia and Athens were the best examples (693d–e; see also *Laws* VI 756e, 759b). Since both the rulers and subjects must see the political *metrion* as distinct from their personal wishes, the *nomoi* or laws will be the real sovereign of such a state, for they express the conditions of the common good.[128]

Although Plato still considers pure *nous* as superior to a code of laws (*Laws* IX 875c),[129] he states that people would refuse "to believe that anyone could ever be worthy of such authority, to desire and be able to govern with virtue and science" (*Pol.* 301d).[130] On the other hand, he believes that society would endorse a code of "written laws" drawn up by a true statesman if founded on experience and public approval (*Pol.* 300b). The legislator may then travel abroad (as Solon) leaving "written directions" (since "verbal directions" may be forgotten) to follow in case of something unexpected. This is also Plato's position in the *Laws.* The original legislator will focus essentially on a general code of laws and will then abdicate (although available for consultation as long as he is alive). The future administrators of the laws will then work out the details through "experience." After every detail is thought to have been worked out, the laws must become immutable *(akinēta),* like the laws governing the movements of the heavenly bodies (*Laws* V 822a5). The upshot to this is that, without writing and thus the alphabet, what Plato sees as political salvation, a code of "written laws," would have been impossible.

In conjunction with this, it is not surprising that Plato insists that the future citizens of the state must learn to read *(anagnōnai)* and to write *(graphai)* when they are children (*Laws* VII 810b). Reading and writing will help them to "memorize" the code of "written laws."[131] But reading and writing will also assure that there is *no* room for "improvisation," that the legislator will have total control. Indeed, Plato insists that these written laws must be set to music—a music which, like the laws themselves, must *never* be changed—and not only sung but also danced to in chorus[132] with the accompaniment of the lyre (*Laws* VII 812a–e).[133] Participation should be compulsory for all. In other words, the written laws must be poetized and therefore performed in a fashion reminiscent of Homeric oral poetry.[134] However, Plato's position here is also reminiscent of Solon, a major figure for Plato in what follows.

Solon, interestingly, is both a poet and a writer and, in both instances, a poet and a writer working in the area of legislation. According to Plutarch (*Lives, Solon* 3.5), Solon undertook to publish his laws in the form of [heroic] verse, that is, the Homeric hexameter.[135] Plato seems to confirm this at *Timaeus* 21b, when Critias says that he and his comrades sang Solon's poems in their youth. In fact, he contends that Solon would have been the greatest poet of all (and remembered as such) had he published the Atlantis story in poetic form; and this would most certainly have been the case had he not been confronted with civil unrest on his return from Egypt, where he "heard" the story (21c–d).[136]

The Atlantis Story

This brings us back to the famous Atlantis story, the model for Plato's—and Brisson's—notion of oral tradition and thus myth. If a myth is a message that a social group considers to have received from its ancestors and that it transmits orally from generation to generation, then the Atlantis story, as Brisson demonstrates, most certainly conforms to this definition. But to what degree did literacy actually affect Plato's account of the story? Indeed, what is the role of literacy in the communication of the story?

Plato seems to imply that without writing, Solon and thus the Greeks would have remained ignorant of the great event. Indeed, although the Egyptian priest knew the story by heart and transmitted it orally to Solon without "reading" it, his oral account is nonetheless based on a written record, that is, sacred writings, which he must have consulted on a number of occasions. The fact that the priest tells Solon that Saïs (where the written record is kept) was founded 1,000 years after primeval Athens does not (contra Brisson) necessarily entail that the story was transmitted orally for 1,000 years before it was recorded in writing. Since Egypt survived the natural catastrophes that destroyed Atlantis and primeval Athens, one would expect that the written version from Saïs would have been recorded from another written version from elsewhere in Egypt, that is, unless we

are to assume that both Egypt and primeval Athens were themselves ignorant of writing, and this, I believe, is highly improbable. In fact, the priest
explicitly states that he still has a "written" record of the *nomoi* of primeval
Athens (*Tim.* 23e–24a). This is how he can be so certain that the socio-
political structure and laws of Egypt are modeled on those of primeval
Athens (24a–c). On the other hand, Plato explicitly informs us that the
version Solon heard from the Saïs priest was orally transmitted for several
generations (20e).[137] However, what is interesting here is the fact that although Critias had not heard the Atlantis story since he was a child, he
insists that it had such an impression on him that only after one night of
recall, he retrieved virtually all of the story,[138] that is, he could give a detailed account and not just the main points (26b).[139]

Does this mean that Plato believed that the oral version could dispense
altogether with the written version? Though it is improbable, there is a
temptation to believe that Plato would not advocate a written version.
More important is the question of the form the oral and/or written version
would have to take. The account of the Atlantis story in the *Timaeus* and
the *Critias* is in prose form, and not poetic form. Consequently, are we to
assume that Plato believed (as did Herodotus and Thucydides) that prose
was more effective than poetry for the transmission of what was worthy of
memory? This is tempting until we recall that Plato explicitly says that had
Solon put the Atlantis story in verse after hearing it from the Egyptian
priest, he would have become the most famous poet of all (21c–d). In fact,
if Solon's laws, as those of Plato's Magnesia, were meant to be performed,
then there is no reason to believe that Plato did not intend the Atlantis
story to be poetized and thus performed along the same lines as the Homeric epic tradition. Indeed, Plato seems to want it to compete directly with
Homer's great epic. After all, the occasion for the meeting between Socrates
and his interlocutors is a poetic competition, albeit not just any competition, but the Great Panathenaia, that is, the religious festivals (at Athens!)
in honor of Athena, and these had a long history in connection with the
performance of the Homeric epics (*Tim.* 21a),[140] a competition which, as
Brisson notes, was apparently codified by Solon himself.[141] And, as we saw
above, the audience actively participated in the performances, and, in doing so, reactualized and reexperienced the past. In conjunction with this,
what is primeval Athens if not the political constitution of the *Republic*
(and its corresponding *nomoi,* written or unwritten) engaged in the "concrete" world of war and negotiations, that is, in action![142] Consequently,
the "performance" of the Atlantis story, which is destined to assure the
continuity of the community in its memory, must be considered as a direct

challenge to the Homeric tradition.[143] But what does Plato find so reprehensible in Homeric poetry?

What Plato contests most about the oral tradition associated with Homer (and Hesiod) is that it grossly misrepresents the true nature of the gods and heroes. These poets represent them as being jealous, vengeful, quarrelsome, adulterous, etc., whereas it is imperative that the gods and heroes encourage virtue of the highest order. It is worth remembering here that the reason Plato is so preoccupied with the moral and "theological" side of the poets is because the tradition they endorse provides the ordinary Greeks with their code of value and hence behavior. However, the full effect of this can only be appreciated when one considers, as we saw above, that poetry entails performance and that the audience was emotionally, fully engaged in this rather contagious experience. In these events, the communal past was reenacted, indeed, "ritually" performed by the community in a rather trance-like state.

As Plato makes abundantly clear in the *Ion* (535a–e), when the rhapsode recites epic poetry, he has a stunning effect on his spectators. By throwing himself into the part of the character whom he portrays, he stirs up the emotions of the spectators, who visibly participate in his performance.[144] However, the poetic experience was not restricted to rhapsodic competitions during religious festivals. Poetry, and in particular the poetry of Homer, dominated Greek education and culture.[145] As Niceratus states in Xenophon's *Symposium* (3.5–6), his father, being concerned to make him a good man *(agathos anēr),* made him memorize the works of Homer, which he now knows by heart. Plato, for his part, remarks in the *Laws* VII 810 that if there was a debate, it tended to focus on the most effective way of teaching poetry to children: should the entire works or just the most outstanding passages be committed to memory?[146] More importantly, school children had to study the poetry of Homer (and others) not, at least from Plato's perspective, for its aesthetic qualities but for its ethical content.[147] Plato lists some of the more distressing ways the role models, the gods and heros, are portrayed by the poets at *Republic* II 377c–III 392c. And it is clear that the interlocutors in the opening book of the *Republic,* with the possible exception of Thrasymachus, are very much products of poetic culture.[148] Moreover, he makes it clear that poetic education entailed performance. The school children, like the rhapsode, threw themselves into the story and presented the speeches with the sounds and gestures of an actor (*Rep.* X 605c–608b). This is what Plato terms *mimēsis* as opposed to *diēgēsis,* that is, indirect speech or narration (*Rep.* III 392d). If Plato sees *diēgēsis* as less harmful than *mimēsis,* it is because in the case of *diēgēsis* there is no confusion between the narrator and what is said (393d–94b), whereas in the case of *mimēsis* the narrator delivers the speech as if he were someone else. That is, he assimilates himself through his expression *(lexis)* to the point that he represents or personifies *(mimeisthai)* the character speaking in thoughts and feelings.

Although Plato believes that, with respect to poetry and myth-telling, it is impossible to separate narration from representation or "performance" (*Rep.* III 394b–c), it is not for this reason that he believes that the poets must be banned from the ideal city. They must be banished from the ideal city because poetry and myth-telling engage in "multiple representations" (*polla mimēsetai,* 395a2; cf. 397e), and they are incapable of doing otherwise.[149] Further, since Plato assumes that one can become like the characters one performs, then it would be bad for the future guardians to take part in representations or "performances" other than those suitable to their profession (395c–e). In conjunction with this, he reminds us that it was agreed from the outset that each citizen should perform one and only one job in order to do it well (*Rep.* II 370a).[150] This is equivalent to stating that the citizens in general and the guardians in particular must remain as god-like as possible, that is, avoid transforming their proper character into that of others and exhibit only the qualities that would be considered suitable to their proper profession—qualities such as, in the case of guardians, courage, self-control, piety, and freedom (*Rep.* III 395c). Since Plato feels that it is neither possible nor desirable to eliminate *mimēsis* completely, he naturally opts for the simple style of expression which represents the good man (398b).[151] However, the poet and the myth-teller must not only imitate the expression of the good man, but they must also conform their language to the *tupoi,* or molds,[152] regarding the gods (398b).[153]

The molds *(tupoi)* that the poet must follow when composing mythical discourses *(muthoi)* relative to the gods *(peri theologias)* are the *tupoi* that the founder of the city or philosopher would have determined following his contemplation of the intelligible world.[154] Indeed, when Plato tells us that the *tupoi* that must be followed with respect to God *(theos)* must represent God as he really is (*hoios tunkhanei ho theos ōn,* 379a7–9), he means by this that the traditional gods must conform to an "ideal model," that is, an "intelligible form." This may explain why these *tupoi* are later called laws *(nomoi)*[155]—laws from which the poets must not deviate. Plato gives us two examples of these which are indicative of his position: (1) God is absolutely good and therefore can only be the cause of good things;[156] (2) God is absolutely perfect and therefore is immutable.[157]

It is obvious that these molds are derived directly from an analysis of the intelligible form of God. Indeed, God (or the gods) is described as good (*agathos,* 379b1, c2), cause of good (*aition tōn agathōn,* 380c9–10), beneficial because good (*ōphelimon to agathon,* 379b12), true (*alēthēs,* 382e11), simple (*haplous,* 380d5), perfect (*aristos,* 381c8), absolutely perfect (*pantēi arista echei,* 381b4), absolutely perfect and true (*komidēi . . . haplous kai alēthēs,* 382e10), most beautiful and best (*kallistos kai aristos,* 381c8), and immutable (*hekastos autōn menei haplōs en tēi hautou morphēi,* 381c9). In sum, gods can be truly or falsely represented because they are *nooumena* (intelligible entities) and not *horōmena* (visible entities).[158] Indeed, it is in apprehending intelligible entities that the mind *(nous)* is most capable of attaining truth *(alētheia).*[159]

Because Plato is of the opinion that we should try, in our activity, to become as godlike as possible,[160] one would think that the expressive, that is, mimetic, aspect of poetry and myth-telling should also be able to conform to the philosopher's model and corresponding *tupoi* with regard to God. However, if the poets are effectively banned from the ideal state, then the founders of the city *(oikistai poleōs),* that is, the philosophers, would not only have to provide the *tupoi* to be followed but equally would have to compose the *muthoi* that would correspond to these.[161] They would be responsible for both the content *(logos)* and the form *(lexis)* of the *muthoi,* and in particular the *muthoi* with respect to the gods. This explains why Plato contends that there are "true *muthoi.*" They are true insofar as they conform to the *tupoi* which, for their part, are derived from a direct apprehension of the intelligible forms.[162]

This brings us back again to the Atlantis story. In accordance with the oral tradition, Plato does his best to make the Atlantis story sound as real as possible. And the greatest testimony to his success resides in the fact that the uninitiated are convinced of its reality. Indeed, it is no less famous than Homer's Trojan war. Plato most certainly aided his cause by explicitly stating that his story, his *muthos,* was absolutely true (*Tim.* 20d7–8, 21a4–6, 26e6). There are a number of possible reasons for this. First, the story is based on an oral tradition with a sacred written confirmation. Second, the narrator (and thus the story) is "divinely inspired." Third, the story takes place in a setting (a religious festival) which guarantees its sanctity and thus its truth. Fourth, in conformity with oral tradition, the performance is perceived by the community as true. Fifth, the narrator's discourse is a faithful representation of the *aristē politeia* of the *Republic,* which Socrates would now like to see in action (*Tim.* 19c, 26c–d). In other words, the behavior of the heroes, the primeval Athenians, is modeled on that of the "philosophers kings," the perfect *tupoi,* and thus constitutes a sort of moving likeness of eternity. This is something both the poets and sophists would be incapable of performing (19d–e).

However, Plato has another important fact at his disposal. The Athenians did not have an epic (let alone a great epic) which treated the city's glorious history.[163] Indeed, they did not possess a coherent genealogy that linked them to their autochthonous ancestors. As Plato himself makes abundantly clear, Erechtheus, Erichthonios, Cecrops, and Erysichthon are no more than names (*Crit.* 110a–b); the Athenians are ignorant of their heroic deeds, in part, because they are almost totally ignored by Homeric tradition.[164] So what would be a better occasion to perform his epic than during the Panathenaia, a New Year's Festival instituted according to tradition by Erichthonios himself (which may go back to the Mycenean period) and celebrating the foundation of Athens and its first king, Erechtheus, the child and protégé of Athena?[165] The excitement that such a performance would have incited can only be measured, I believe, by the degree to which it has fascinated readers since its conception. This is oral tradition at its absolute best!

The story relates an extraordinary event—a war fought 9,000 years before by an earlier Athens against a great and aggressive power based on an island called Atlantis. Socrates' ideal city will be shown to exist in the primeval Athens, which, by providential coincidence, has a socio-political structure and institutions similar to those of the ideal state. In the story, primeval Athens will defeat the Atlanteans and will restore freedom to the Mediterranean, but will subsequently be destroyed in a great natural catastrophe—a typical feature of both rational and mythical accounts of the *peri phuseōs* type—which will also engulf Atlantis.

It is agreed that Critias will relate the *whole* story, but *not* immediately. Before proceeding, one must know the origin of these well-bred men, these Athenians of old, in order to determine why they behaved in such a distinguished manner (see below). This explains why Critias' story (and thus Socrates' request) is prefaced by Timaeus' account of the origin and nature of the universe and humanity, that is, a cosmogony and an anthropogony, the two initial stages of any *peri phuseōs* account.[166]

It is impossible to know why the primeval Athenians behaved in such an admirable way, that is, the true behavior of man in the city, without knowing first the nature *(phusis)* of man. And since the latter is dependent on the nature *(phusis)* of the universe, a cosmogony is obviously the starting point as in every *peri phuseōs* account, rational or mythical.[167] This explains why the real aim of the *Timaeus* is not physical (albeit a preeminent cosmological work) but ethical and political.[168] That is, the *phusis* of the universe must lead to the *phusis* of man, which will permit one to know exactly the appropriate type of human behavior in society. In sum, if I know the nature of man, then I should know the "meaning of life."

It should not be surprising that, if Plato's *peri phuseōs* account thus begins with a description (and a reminder) of the paradigm of the ideal city (*Tim.* 17b–19a), then this political model, in conformity with the general outline of *peri phuseōs* accounts, is later reflected in both the cosmological and anthropological models. Indeed, since the anthropological model (which all agree is a paradigm of the one employed in the *Republic*)[169] is explicitly stated to be modeled on the cosmological (*Tim.* 41d–44d, 69c, 90d), this is sufficient evidence of the analogy and thus the intimate relation between the three. In fact, the demiurge in the *Timaeus* behaves like the "founder of a city" or a "philosopher-king" (the word *dēmiourgos* also means magistrate). This is the case at almost every level, for example, in his choice of the form of the ideal living creature as the model for the cosmos (30b–31b), in exercising persuasion to come to terms with the recalcitrant elements or precosmic stuff (47e–48a), in issuing ordinances to subordinates (42d–e), or again in the distribution of the different parts of the human soul according to the different parts of the body (69e–70a, 70d–e).[170] In sum, and again in conformity with *peri phuseōs* accounts, the order and raison d'être of the universe are described in terms which reflect the basic ethical and political ideology of the *Republic*. Thus, after his discourse on the physical constitution of man, which follows that of the universe, Plato explains the general principles of education (86b–90d), the sine qua non of man's salvation which, for all intents and purposes, are modeled on those of the *Republic*. In the final analysis, there must be a perfect equilibrium between the movements of the soul and those of the body and, within the human soul, a perfect equilibrium between its parts, with a preeminence given to the intellect. This can be assured if the intellect contemplates the movements of the celestial bodies, for they provide the model for its well-being—albeit (once again) a model in conformity with a socio-political model.

The appropriate type of human behavior will correspond to the education the primeval Athenians will have initially received from Hephaestus and Athena.[171] In fact, at *Critias* 109d we are told that Hephaestus and Athena not only taught them the order of their polity but actually created from the soil this race of good men.[172] Of course, Plato is here following the Athenian tradition (indeed the civic tradition in general) in giving to the founder, indeed to the whole collectivity *(andres Athēnaioi)*, an origin that is not only autochthonous but also divine:[173] they are the children, so to speak, of Hephaestus and Athena (*Crit.* 109d). But Plato does not stop here. Primeval Athens is not only given a divine origin, but the polity advocated by Hephaestus and Athena (and modeled on that of the *Republic*) is identical with that of the *Republic*.[174] In sum, primeval Athens is nothing less than a perfect reflection of the intelligible model, a moving likeness of eternity, and this means that what we have here is not a true politogony, that is, a historical or rational description of the development of society, as in *Laws* III or in many of the Presocratic accounts as noted above, but something strangely akin to the old cosmogonical myths. This deserves a short clarification in the context of the oral tradition espoused by Homer and Hesiod.

Social Behavior in Homer and Hesiod

A cosmogonical myth is a traditional explanation about how the world order (natural and social) originated for the social group. The world order is seen as the result of the intervention of supernatural beings in an otherworld in a remote past which is different from the one in which the social group lives. The world order is generally understood in terms of the "social reality" of the otherworld. This "social reality" is perceived as the outcome of a series of conflicts and/or agreements between gods. It is a sort of mirror in which the society narrating the myth observes itself and measures its stability. And the fact that this tradition is "performed" by the community only enhances its persuasive power.

Ironically, the Homeric tradition has not bequeathed us a cosmogonical myth strictly speaking, although it is clear that the social reality of Homeric society, in particular, the heroic aspect, is a mirror of divine or Olympian society, which, in turn, mirrors the society (albeit with some confusion) in which the community narrating the tradition resides. Indeed, the epics are not, as we saw, without a good deal of historical authenticity, which explains why even someone as rational as Thucydides did not doubt the existence of the Achaean Greek siege of Troy. On the other hand, the poems represent an age in which deities intervened openly in human life, in a way which later they did not. Not surprisingly, although to Plato's regret, the deities are portrayed as anthropomorphic beings who not only behave like humans but actually speak and interact with them. They love, feel anger, suffer, and are mutually related as husbands and wives, parents and children. In sum, the deities are portrayed as persons and not abstractions. Nor is their sexual activity confined to themselves; the heroes are demigods because one of their parents (or grandparents) are divine. The struggles of the heroes, therefore, move their divine parents to action.

The heroes are the human social elite who are expected to live up to an exacting value system. Not to live up to this code of value meant disgrace, public shame.[175] What they strive for is *aretē* or excellence, for excellence is what a hero needs to protect and enhance his *moira* of *timē* (portion of honor)—and *timē* is everything! Thus, *aretē* and *timē* go hand in hand. Indeed, it was the denial of *timē* or honor due to the preeminent warrior, Achilles, which was behind his wrath: the theme of the *Iliad*. Agamemnon, as the commander-in-chief, deprived the renowned Achilles of his previous portion or share of booty *(geras)* and thus his *moira* of *timē*.[176] This initial distribution was done, however, in accordance with sacred customs or conventions of the society.[177] This is a perfect example of how social disorder erupts. It was, after all, a breach of rules which was the main cause of the Trojan war in general. Paris violated perhaps the most sacred custom of all: guest-host friendship *(xenia)*, when he stole Helen from Menelaus during such a visit. It was also a breach of rules that was behind the war between the Olympians and the Titans, as we shall see below.

The deities, in conformity with their human traits, are evaluated on the same scale as the heroes although they have more *aretē* (excellence), *timē* (honor), and *biē* (strength, *Il.* 9.498) and, of course, are immortal. The heroes, albeit demi-gods, are restricted to seeking immortality through glorious fame or reputation *(kleos)*.

Since what distinguishes one god from another is, as for the heroes, their *moira* of *timē*,[178] and, since respect for this is the essence of social order, it should be no surprise that human/heroic society and divine society are perceived as having a similar socio-political structure in Homer. Just as the deities assemble and sit in council in Olympus (*Il.* 1.97f., 220–22, 531f.), so do the heroes/humans assemble and sit in council.[179] Just as Zeus is considered king of the gods,[180] so Agamemnon is king of men.[181] But although Zeus can be persuaded and even reviled, his word cannot be effectively challenged.[182] Agamemnon, on the other hand, can be both persuaded and effectively challenged.[183] However, the fact remains that the way decisions are made in the human realm is perceived as conforming to the general order of the universe, for the official scepter *(skeptron)* and customs *(themistes)* are seen as a gift from Zeus.[184] Therefore decisions or judgments *(dikai)* can be considered as straight or crooked insofar as they conform to sacred customs.

However, while there is quite obviously a strict code of behavior (the sine qua non of social cohesion) based on sacred tradition which must be followed, what stands out in the Homeric epics (and, of course, this is Plato's primary reproach) is the rather devious and perverse behavior of the gods, a perverse behavior which is not only seen as mirroring human action but as providing its primary motivation: "Zeus (or any divinity) made me do it!"[185]

Just what type of world are we dealing with? There are, most certainly, a number of contradictions here. Zeus is, after all, the protector of social order, and to ignore this is to invite an Achillean type of divine wrath.[186] Yet he appears to endorse, indeed actively participate in, rather extreme asocial behavior. There are at least two levels to this antisocial way of life which must be distinguished.

On the one hand, the gods appear to sanction devious actions which occur outside their boundaries, including murder, rape and theft. In this respect, as Burkert notes, "religion appears as the very model of behavior":[187] Thou shalt not do x if there is a danger of offending, but if there is no danger of offending, x is permitted. Nowhere is this more evident than during one of those notorious pirate expeditions—an occupation which in early times, according to Thucydides, was perceived as rather honorable (1.5). Odysseus' imaginary account of his life in Crete (*Od.* 14.199f.) gives us a vivid description of these rather gruesome encounters in which murder, rape, and theft were the order of the day. Even though Odysseus was captured during one such adventure in Egypt, when he pleads for his life the Egyptian king actually protects him for fear of inviting "the wrath of Zeus, the stranger's god, who above all others hath indignation at evil deeds" (*Od.* 14.278–84). Although Odysseus is protected under the sacred guest-host friendship custom, the fact remains that Zeus does not punish Odysseus and his unruly cohorts for their insidious, Cyclopian, behavior toward the Egyptians. However, when the insolent suitors are murdered by Odysseus for violating the same sacred guest-host friendship custom, their fate is considered as having been sanctioned by Zeus (*Od.* 24.351f.; see also 1.31f.).

On the other hand, the gods themselves, and in particular Zeus, appear to openly indulge—albeit in a social group—in the most devious type of asocial behavior and, in particular, the joyous consummation of sexuality. In fact, it is quite stunning to what degree the order of events in the Trojan war is actually dictated by Aphrodite's sphere of activity (and this is also the case, as we shall see, in Hesiod's *Theogony*). Aphrodite seduces Paris, who in turn seduces Helen. Sex and intrigue, seduction and carnal pleasure, go hand in hand throughout the epic. Hera is well aware that sex, if anything, will take Zeus' eyes off the Trojan war (*Il.* 14.160f., 215f.). And the various homecomings of the heroes are no less haunted by the same phenomena: adultery, incest, and murder.[188]

In reality, neither one of the prime royal couple reflects a model of marital bliss. Hera and Zeus are more of a role model for ill-fated Agamemnon and Clytemnestra than are Odysseus and Penelope—the quintessential couple in this drama. Homer portrays both Zeus and Hera as dysfunctional to the extreme. And while we may at times sympathize with Hera's jealousy, her perverse behavior toward her unsired son Hephaestus (*Il.* 18.394–99), to say nothing of Dionysus, is no less deplorable than Zeus abusive treatment of Hera (*Il.* 1.565, 15.118f.) and of Hephaestus (*Il.* 1.586f.). This is what constitutes the other level of asocial behavior mentioned above.[189]

Whether or not the perverse behavior of the gods corresponds to the unstable aristocratic rule at the end of the dark ages[190] or, in certain instances, to a patriarchal (Cyclopian?) society in which the leader can indulge in his wildest fantasies, the fact remains that the gods, and in particular Zeus, do not always conform to a standard of right behavior. A contradiction indeed for the impartial protector of social order. This is perhaps better reflected in Hesiod, where we learn the Zeus is not just the protector but actually the creator of a code of values which is not to be infringed—albeit only after he comes to terms with the more dysfunctional side of social life.

The *Theogony* explains, to a large degree, the origin of the organizational structure and code of values of the gods (and by extension the heroes and humans) which we see in action in Homer's *Iliad* and *Odyssey*. From this perspective, Hesiod's *Theogony* is perhaps more of a basic textbook of Greek religion and mythology than Homer's epics.[191] The *Works and Days,* on the other hand, expresses the attitude of a contemporary member of the working class *dēmos* (albeit not as poor as many purport) toward the powerful and gift-devouring lords in Dark Age Greece, oblivious to the socio-political order instituted (or willed) by Zeus.

The *Theogony* provides us with an early account of how the world order in which the Greeks lived originated. It describes the origin of the world and of the gods and the events which lead to the establishment of the present order. It explains how Zeus, after a series of socio-political power struggles, defeats his enemies and distributes, as the new ruler, the *moirai* of *timai* (portions of honors) among the Immortals (*Theogony* 391f.). Hesiod's *Theogony* is thus a perfect example of a cosmogonical myth.

The gods are arranged in generations. The first generation consists of

Chaos, Gaia, Tartaros, and Eros (*Theogony* 116–22). The second generation is produced from these. Chaos gives birth to Erebos and Night (123),
who, in turn, bear Aither and Day (124). Earth (Gaia) alone spawns the
Sky (Ouranos), Mountains, and Sea (Pontos)—in sum, the physical universe as we know it (126–32). The third generation, the Titans, are the
offspring of Earth and Sky (Ouranos). They include not only Kronos and
Rheia, but also Themis (Custom) and Mnemosyne (Memory).[192] Although this third generation comes to power through a hideous deed (castration), their father, Ouranos, is no less the initiator, for he leaves his children no choice. Because of his excessive copulation with Gaia, he prevents
them from seeing the light of day (157) and thus from receiving their legit-
imate *moira* of *timai.* Since without light, the generation is stalled, Gaia
asks her children to come to her aid. Kronos, the youngest, takes up the
challenge and executes the cruel *(doliēn)* and evil trick *(kakēn tekhnēn)* de-
vised by his mother (160).[193] Kronos hides in ambush and when the oppor-
tune moment arrives (when Ouranos is engaged in sex with Gaia), he cas-
trates his father. This act represents (for the second time) the separation of
earth and sky and thus the appearance of light and the effective birth of
the Titans—and the *timai* (honors) and *gera* (privileges) associated with
victory.

Kronos and Rheia give birth to the fourth generation, the Olympians.
However, like his father Ouranos, Kronos treats his children with the same
contempt. They were given no share of honor (*moira* of *timē;* 392f., 882)
or privileges (*gera;* 393, 396).[194] Rhea, unwillingly as Gaia, gives birth to
the Olympians, but Kronos, heeding his father's threat that he would be
punished for his evil deeds (210), swallows them one after the other to
avert being usurped by one of them (462). However, he is outwitted by his
youngest son, Zeus (with the help of Gaia and Ouranos), and forced to
liberate his children (470f.). A violent battle, the famous Titanomachy,
ensues for ten years (636)[195] between two coalitions led by Kronos and
Zeus respectively, that is, until Zeus, on the advice of Gaia, retrieves the
three Hundred-Handers from the underworld where they had been rele-
gated first by Ouranos (617) and then by Kronos. With their help, the
Titans are finally defeated and dispatched to Tartarus. Following his victory, Zeus (on the advice of Gaia; 884), is unanimously declared king and
he then proceeds to distribute honors (*timai,* 885) to all those who fought
on his side in accordance with his initial oath (*horkon,* 400).[196]

In the *Theogony,* just as the world order is organized by personal and
personalized divinities, all the socio-political concepts (which must be understood in a religious context as well) are gods and goddesses.[197] In fact,

many of the most important concepts were generated prior to the Olympians: Themis and Mnemosyne are the children of Ouranos and Earth (135); Moira, Fate, Philotes, and Nemesis are the asexually generated children of Night (217–24); Metis and Eurynome are the children of Ocean and Tethys (358). It should be no surprise then that Zeus actually contracts a series of marriages following his victory with several of these concepts, beginning with Metis (Cunning Intelligence), and followed by Themis (Custom-Law), Eurynome (Good Order), and Mnemosyne (Memory). These marriages are, in fact, essential for the comprehension of Hesiod's account.

The first marriage to Metis (Cunning Intelligence) entails that the order of succession will stop with Zeus. Metis is destined to give birth to a child stronger than Zeus. But on the advice of Gaia and Ouranos, Zeus swallows Metis instead of his son, as Kronos had done, putting an end to the cycle of succession and assuring that no trick will ever surprise him (886–900). The second marriage to Themis incarnates stability, continuity, and regular order, whence the birth of the Hours (Discipline, Justice/Dike, and Peace) and the Moires (901–906), which symbolize the portion and limit attributed to each and therefore the boundary which must not be crossed. The third marriage to Eurynome bears the three Graces: Joy, Festivity, and Abundance (907–909). These are the fruits of a just and durable order, that is, any civilization worthy of the name. The fourth marriage is to Demeter (912–14). The progeny of this marriage is Persephone, who is later raped by Hades. The rape is particularly important since it symbolizes death and rebirth. Of what is there death and rebirth? Death can only be that of man. Rebirth, however, is the fruit of the first three marriages in the sense that if man dies, the Muses guarantee his survival through memory of what transpired. This explains the fifth marriage to Mnemosyne and the birth of the nine Muses (915–17). Their function is to conserve everything which characterizes the reign and will of Zeus, that is, the sacred conventions and ways of a civilized society.[198]

Hesiod's *Theogony*, therefore, explains the origin of the organizational structure and code of values of the gods and by extension, of the heroes, and of nobles of Hesiod's time. This appears clear from the prelude to the *Theogony* (100f.) where we are told that the aim of the bard is to celebrate the great deeds *(kleea)* of men of old *(proterōn anthrōpōn) and* of the inhabitants of Olympus. If such is the case, then the human kings (his contemporaries) to which he refers starting at line 80, would be the descendants of these, and "when they make judgments with correct decisions" *(diakrinonta themistas itheiēisi dikēisin, 84–85)*, these judgments are based on the *nomoi* and the *ēthē* (the sacred conventions and ways) of their human and divine ancestors (and thus the will of Zeus).

Despite the socio-political structure advocated and incorporated by Zeus in the *Theogony*, the fact remains that the description of the series of events which led to the establishment of the present order portrays the gods (on all sides) as behaving in a rather ungodly fashion. In this respect, the *Theogony* is no less reproachable in Plato's eyes than Homer's epics (Plato's demiurge, for his part, is preoccupied with goodness from the beginning to the end of the cosmogonical process). Indeed, Zeus' despicable treatment of Prometheus and the autochthonous humanity at *Theogony* 535–616, which, we must assume, comes after the new order is instituted by Zeus, only corroborates this. If anything, there is a certain inconsistency in the portrait of Zeus in Hesiod's *Theogony*, just as there is in Homer's epics.[199]

Moreover, it should be no surprise that at the end of the *Theogony*, Hesiod adds a short heroogony. After all, the heros are the offspring of Zeus and his cohorts (937f., 963f.). What is surprising, and confusing, is that Zeus must lie with mortal women and the goddesses with mortal men (963–1018). The ultimate consequence of this is that the heroic society could then be considered as coeval with, and a model of, divine society.

Of course, Plato is no less confusing in the Atlantis story. Heroes need a divine parentage. However, although Plato insists that the primeval Athenians were fashioned from the earth by Hephaestus and Athena (whose love of wisdom and its corresponding arts constitute perfect models for human behavior), he also insists that they did not, following this, procreate with them. Indeed, Plato makes a point of stating that this was precisely the beginning of the degeneration of Atlantis. The first inhabitants of Atlantis were earth-born, like the inhabitants of Attica (*Crit.* 113b–d), but their society began to slowly degenerate from the moment that Poseidon took a mortal for a wife, Cleito, daughter of Evenor and Leucippe, who, for their part, were among the original earth-born inhabitants.[200] What the primeval Athenians did receive from Athena and Hephaestus, as noted above, was a conception of how to govern society in conjunction with the true nature of mankind and its relation to that of the universe. The crucial factor was to stick to the socio-political model advocated by Athena and Hephaestus to the end. This required, of course, that the philosopher kings and the other classes would have to be educated accordingly and would have to adhere to their respective "natural" functions.

In the final analysis, Plato's cosmogonical account has a good deal in common with cosmogonical myths in general. Like the old cosmogonical myths, Plato's account expounds the conditions which would assure the socio-political organization its self-conservation. In both cases the socio-political models are "formal causes" and enjoy an extratemporal status. But whereas the cosmogonical myths refer to the actual state of society (or at least as it had initially existed), Plato refers to a society which is yet to be created. If such is the case, then primeval Athens, like the *Republic*, must be considered as the "perfect working model" for any future reform—although, well-understood, this is not what Plato wishes to convey to his audience. The performance must attempt to appear as real as possible with the hope that through constant repetition the audience will conform to the *tupoi* of their prestigious ancestors and, in doing so, become more virtuous in the new sense of the word.

As I noted at the beginning of this introduction, myth is notoriously difficult to define. Brisson's analysis of myth *(muthos)* from Plato's perspective, that is, from the perspective of the person who coined the term, goes a long way in clarifying its meaning. In his Malinowski lecture on "Theories of Myth," Percy Cohen passes in review the various approaches to (and theories of) myth and summarizes its chief characteristics as follows: "A myth is a narrative of events; the narrative has a sacred quality; the sacred communication is made in symbolic form; at least some of the events and objects which occur in the myth neither occur nor exist in the world other than that of myth itself; and the narrative refers in dramatic form to origins or transformations."[201] The reader will note that *all* of these characteristics are found in the book by Luc Brisson (and, in particular, as it pertains to Plato's famous Atlantis story). Brisson emphasizes the historical and social aspects of myth in a well-defined context, that of Athens at the end of the fifth century and the beginning of the fourth century B.C., where religion and politics entertain inextricable relations and where philosophy contests the preeminence of myth although it is also compelled to recognize its necessity. My aim here has been to give an overview of the various positions held on the subject of myth in ancient Greece and, in particular, as it pertains to the orality/literacy debate which forms the background of Brisson's book.

Notes

1. As G. S. Kirk notes in *Myth: Its Meaning and Functions in Ancient and Other Cultures* (Berkeley and Los Angeles: University of California Press, 1970), 7.

2. In his authoritative *Structure and History in Greek Mythology* (Berkeley and Los Angeles: University of California Press, 1979), Walter Burkert nowhere even mentions Plato by name.

3. According to P. Chantraine, *Dictionnaire étymologique de la langue grecque* (Paris, 1968–80),

3:718–19, the etymology of the word *muthos* is uncertain. The word *muthos* designates the content of the speech rather that the form, which is designated by *epos*. See for example, Homer *Od.* 11.561, "to hear my word and speech" *(epos kai muthon akouseis); Il.* 9.443, "to be both a speaker of words *(muthōn)* and a doer of deeds *(ergōn)*." In his recent work, *The Language of Heroes: Speech and Performance in the* Iliad (Ithaca and London: Cornell University Press, 1989), 12, Richard Martin argues that the word *muthos* must be defined as "a speech-act indicating authority, performed at length, usually in public, with a focus on full attention to every detail." *Epos,* on the other hand, must be defined as "an utterance, ideally short, accompanying a physical act, and focusing on message, as perceived by the addressee, rather than on performance as enacted by the speaker." Martin's definition of *muthos* concords rather well with the notion of oral tradition which will be discussed in some detail below. However, it may be rather forcing the issue and, further, tends to be too restrictive.

4. This meaning of *muthos* is also found in Aeschylus (*Persians* 713, frag. 139) and Sophocles (*Antigone* 11). Aeschylus employs the word *logos* in a similar sense at *Prometheus* 686–89.

5. Not the form but the content, as noted above. For examples, see LSJ: As talk in plural: *Il.* 15.393; *Od.* 1.56. As advice, *Il.* 7.358, 9.443: *muthōn . . . rhētēr* "a giver of [good] advice."

6. See also *Works and Days* 78, 789. According to Richard Martin (*Language of Heroes*, 13), Marcel Detienne, in *The Creation of Mythology* (Chicago: University of Chicago Press, 1986), 47–51, has shown that *muthos* in the sense of "tale, fiction, lie" is as ancient as Hesiodic poetry. But if this is the case, for Hesiod, could the same case not be made for Homer? Further, could not the same case be made for *logos?* Consequently, this says much, but nothing at all.

7. It is unlikely, I think, that Hesiod is employing *logos* to distinguish a true account from a false account, that is, *logos* in a "rational" sense. It seems to be employed as in the two Homeric examples cited above, although he was the first to employ *legein* as a "saying" verb (see below). It is worth noting that at *Works and Days* 10, the bard employs the verb *mutheomai* to express the truths he wants to relate to Perses *(egō de ke Persēi etētuma muthēsaimēn).* The moral of the story at the end of Aesop's (c. 600) famous fables is sometimes called a *muthos* and sometimes a *logos.* This may explain why Aesop is called both a *muthopoios* and a *logopoios.*

8. Of course, we can still clearly see the struggle for the emancipation of rational thought and language from myth in their works.

9. DK 21B1.13–14. This is in opposition to Homer and Hesiod and their rather unpious *muthoi* and *logoi* with respect to the gods.

10. DK 28B8.1–2. *Muthos* at B2.1 should also be understood in this sense.

11. DK 28B8.51–52. Although at DK 28B7.5, Parmenides explicitly states that "we must judge with reason" *(krinai de logōi)* rather than the senses *(aisthēseis),* the fact remains that *muthos* could still be substituted for *logos.*

12. DK 31B23.11. See also DK 31B17.14–15, where the plural *muthoi* is employed twice to describe his words of truth. This also appears to be the case at DK 31B24.2 and DK 31B114.1.

13. DK 31B17.26. See also DK 31B35.2. The only other occurrence of the word *muthos* in a fragment of a Presocratic is in Critias (DK 88B6.10). It is employed in the plural in the old Homeric sense of words.

14. Democritus (DK 68B297) employs the verb *muthoplastein* in a sense which is more in line with the pejorative meaning of myth (to invent fables or myths which he describes as lies, *pseudea,* to help appease their fear of death). However, there is nothing to say that he would not have substituted *logos* for *muthos* to create this verbal compound. Indeed, the word *pseudea* appears to be the determining factor here: *pseudea peri tou meta tēn teleutēn muthoplasteontes khronou,* "inventing false stories about what happens after death."

15. See 1.141, where Cyrus's tale is termed a *logos. Logos* is employed at 2.123 to signify recorded history in the context of the building of the great pyramids.

16. Burkert (*Structure and History,* 3) cites Euripides frag. 484 (*ouk emos ho muthos,* "this is not my tale") as a typical example of the opposition between *muthos* and *logos.* However, there is nothing to indicate that Euripides could not have employed *logos* in the same context. And, in any event, this *rare* example of the word *muthos* most certainly does not allow us to draw such a conclusion as if it were the norm.

17. Indeed, Anaximander's *historia* is both rational and argumentative, that is, the two prerequisites of that distinctive Greek achievement we call philosophy. On this feature of Anaximander, see Charles Kahn, *Anaximander and the Origins of Greek Cosmology* (New York, 1960) and more recently, Gerard Naddaf, "On the Origin of Anaximander's Cosmological Model," *Journal of the History of Ideas* 59 (1998): 1–28.

18. Heraclitus, if anyone, exhibits the enormous richness of the word *logos*. On the meaning of *logos* in Heraclitus in particular, and in fifth century Greece in general, see W. K. C. Guthrie, *A History of Greek Philosophy* (Cambridge: Cambridge University Press, 1962), 1:419–35. It may not be accidental that we have no occurrences of *muthos* in Heraclitus.

19. On this point, see P. Chantraine, *Dictionnaire étymologique de la langue grecque,* 3:625.

20. The first occurrence of *legein* as a "saying" verb is found in Hesiod *Theogony* 27.

21. See H. Fournier, *Les Verbes "dire" en grec ancien: Exemple de conjugaison supplétive* (Paris: Klincksieck, 1946), 53.

22. This explains why *legein* already appears in Homer in the sense of "saying, speaking" and especially "recounting." On this point, see Fournier, *Les Verbes "dire" en grec ancien,* 217.

23. Nowhere is this more evident, I believe, than in Heraclitus: where the word *logos* can designate simultaneously the intelligent speech of men and the intelligently ordered and structured speech of the universe. For an interesting analysis of the concept of *logos* in Heraclitus, see M. Fattal, "Le logos d'Héraclite: un essai de traduction," *Revue des Études Grecques* 99 (1986): 142–52.

24. See, e.g., Geneviève Calame-Griaule, "Pour une étude ethnolinguistique des littérateurs orales africaines," *Langages* 18 (1970): 22–45, at 23: "on peut définir la tradition comme l'ensemble des messages qu'un groupe social considère avoir reçu de ses ancêtres et qu'il transmet oralement d'une génération à une autre."

25. The origin of myth, strictly speaking, is extremely complex, but in conjunction with the definition of myth proposed above, it appears that myth provides both an (causal) explanation for the present social (and natural) order and a guarantee (through a sort of ritualistic/mimetic process) that the present order (social and natural) will remain as it is. This is also clearly the case with the Atlantis story, as we shall see below.

26. Ruth Finnegan, *Literacy and Orality* (Oxford: Blackwell, 1970), 108, has shown that this is not the case for Africa.

27. Plato, it is true, gives the impression that myths could also be communicated in prose, but this is in the context of literacy. I will discuss this below.

28. I will look at the notion of "contrived" in more detail below. However, it is worth noting that although there seems to be a consensus on this point, Plato, who confirms it, is never mentioned by previous scholars of oral tradition.

29. As Brisson notes (Appendix 2), if Plato systematically associates *poiētēs* (poet/maker) with *muthologos* (myth-teller) and *poiēsis* (poetry/production) with *muthologia* (myth-telling), it is because the poet is not just a "myth-teller" *(muthologos)* par excellence for Plato, but also a "myth-maker" *(muthopoios)* par excellence. Plato makes it abundantly clear that the poet or maker *(poiētēs)* is first and foremost a "maker of myths."

30. For many, this is fact. See Richard Martin, *Language of Heroes,* 8.

31. Milman Parry's influential work originated in his doctoral dissertation at the Sorbonne, *Épithète traditionelle dans Homère* (1928), in English, "The Making of Homeric Verse," in *The Collected Papers of Milman Parry,* ed. A Parry (Oxford: Clarendon Press, 1971).

32. Most obviously, the fixed name-epithet formulas such as "much-enduring Odysseus" or "swift-footed Achilles." Milman Parry defines a formula as "a group of words which is regularly employed under the same metrical conditions to express a given essential idea" (1930, 80). According to Parry (and his successor, Alfred Lord, see G. S. Kirk, *Homer and the Epic* [Cambridge: Cambridge University Press, 1965], 11f.), meter determines theme. Thus epithets changed for metrical reasons (the poet used the formula that fitted his metrical needs) and not according to the immediate needs of the narrative (it was not possible to think of theme without *writing*). This has been criticized because it leaves no room for originality or innovation. See, in particular, Rosalind Thomas, *Literacy and Orality in Ancient Greece* (Cambridge: Cambridge University Press, 1992), 31. I will discuss this below.

33. For example, keep *x* and reject *y* since *x* is more practical and aesthetically pleasing than *y*. Thus the stockpile is the result of previous rejections. For Kirk (*Homer and the Epic,* 26), improvisation has nothing to do with being "creative," since it is restricted to adding a sentence here and there. For Eric Havelock (*Preface to Plato* [Cambridge, Mass.: Harvard University Press, Belknap Press, 1963,] 93), improvisation is secondary; what is primary is the formulaic technique as a method of memorization and recall. For those who argue that literacy destroys improvisation, Rosalind Thomas has shown that improvisation was widespread in Greece well after the Homeric period (*Literacy and Orality in Ancient Greece,* 124f.). However, one important feature of improvisation from the oral perspective is that one would not be able to go back to change what was previously stated.

34. In the final analysis, only the formulae which were the most practical and aesthetically pleasing and, of course, fitted the metrical needs of the poet became part of the stockpile. The whole stockpile would be passed down from master to apprentice through a system of memory and improvisation. Havelock, as with Parry/Lord, can imagine certain Greeks getting together to "consciously" discuss which technique would be most effective for their purpose and arriving at the conclusion that "only" the formulaic technique would work.

35. Poems, of course, are songs, and the Homeric poet is an *aoidos,* or singer, one who accompanies himself on the *kitharis.* This is still clearly attested in Plato. In fact, Plato's choice of words, as Brisson notes, indicates that oral poetry and, by extension, myth is essentially "an oral performance." On the relation between the poet and the audience in Homer himself, see Charles Segal, "Bard and Audience in Homer," in *Homer's Ancient Readers,* ed. Robert Lamberton and John J. Keanly (Princeton: Princeton University Press, 1992), 3–29.

36. Plato vividly describes the power of the audience over the performer and the judge in several passages. See, in particular, *Rep.* VI 492b-c; *Laws* II 659b, III 700c–701a. However, he never looses sight of the fact that the poet equally inspires the multitude (*Ion* 535b-e; *Laws* III 701a). It is worth noting that he mentions that the "educated" listen in silence during the performances (*Laws* III 700c, 701a). Are we to infer that this is the effect of literacy? I will address the context, that is, the Panathenaia, below.

37. Although memory plays a crucial role since, the stockpile of formulae (and not just the technique) which was passed down from master to apprentice entailed memorization. Plato makes the importance of memory in an oral culture abundantly clear, as we shall see below.

38. Thus Albert Lord: "What is important is not oral performance but rather the composition *during* oral performance" (*The Singer of Tales* [Cambridge, Mass.: Harvard University Press, 1960], 5).

39. Parry and Lord turned to the surviving traditions of oral verse-making among the contemporary illiterate bards of Yugoslavia in the 1930s and 1950s for a confirmation of their thesis. The Yugoslavic oral poetry, which had a comparable formulaic system, confirmed that the oral poet does not memorize but actually composes in performance, reacting to his audience and the context. The bards could compose without writing because they could retrieve the formulae as they were needed from a vast stockpile.

40. Indeed, while most philologists agree that the basic Homeric dialect is that of Ionia in the archaic period, there are many variants foreign to that time and place, including the Greek of the Mycenean period some 500 years before. This in turn helps explain a number of historical inconsistencies. For example, why bronze is the metal of choice for weapons and armor (as it was during the Mycenean Bronze Age) rather than iron, the metal of choice during the Archaic (and Iron) Age; or, then again, why the dead are cremated (an Iron Age practice) rather than buried (a Mycenean Bronze Age practice). There even appears to be several references to the hoplite. For a detailed analysis and references, see G. S. Kirk, *The Songs of Homer* (Cambridge: Cambridge University Press, 1962).

41. M. I. Finley is a notable exception. In his influential *World of Odysseus* (New York: Viking Press, 1965), Finley argues that Homer is describing the socio-political values and general worldview of Dark-Age Greece of about 1050–900 B.C.

42. See Kurt A. Raaflaub, "Homeric Society," in Ian Morris and Barry Powell, eds., *A New Companion to Homer* (Leiden: Brill, 1997), 624–48.

43. This seems to entail, as Havelock notes (*Preface to Plato,* 89), that Homer (as well as his poetic predecessors) saw himself as a passive recorder and preserver of a tradition which, moreover, he deeply

accepts (122). I concur with much of this, for it follows, in my view, from the fact that the poets saw themselves as divinely inspired (see Marcel Detienne, *The Masters of Truth in Archaic Greece* [1967], trans. Janet Lloyd [New York: Zone Books, 1996]). However, I believe that entertainment also played a role. It is also worth noting that Greek society and thus oral tradition evolved far faster than most so-called traditional societies: something few commentators appear to mention. And most of this evolution occurred "prior" to the advent of literacy.

The audience must have thought that as long as something (even "new") conformed to tradition, it was acceptable. In fact, at *Od.* 1.352, we are told that people like what is newest: "for men praise that song the most which is newest *(neōtatē)* to their ears."

44. This is Rosalind Thomas's biggest criticism (*Literacy and Orality in Ancient Greece,* 40), although this is certainly not Lord's position. He spends a whole chapter on originality in *Serbocroatian Heroic Songs Collected by Milman Parry,* ed. Albert Lord (Cambridge, Mass., Harvard University Press, 1974), 3:13–34. Jack Goody, for his part, in *The Interface Between the Written and the Oral* (Cambridge: Cambridge University Press, 1987), sees the oral tradition as "characterized by continual creation" (85), which is something Eric Havelock (*Preface to Plato,* 124) would strongly disagree with. As Goody notes, the problem is, how do we explain how Homer is so obviously an oral poet and yet still creative (90).

45. Rosalind Thomas, *Literacy and Orality in Ancient Greece,* 29–51. Thomas finds support for her thesis in Ruth Finnegan (1988) and in Minna S. Jensen, *The Homeric Question and the Oral-Formulaic Theory* (Copenhagen, 1980). While Jensen (who supports the role of conscious composition) argues for the orality of the poems, Finnegan argues that it is virtually impossible to draw a clear distinction between orality and literacy in the context of oral tradition. Thomas also argues that literacy did not destroy the oral traditions but complemented them. In this, her position is radically different from some people of the formulaic school (e.g. Lord). It is also becoming somewhat widespread, as John Foley notes in "Oral Tradition and its Implications," in Morris and Powell, eds., *A New Companion to Homer,* 161.

46. G. S. Kirk, *Homer and the Epic,* 3. Kirk is replying essentially to Lord and Bowra. See below.

47. Gregory Nagy, "An Evolutionary Model for the Making of Homeric Poetry: Comparative Perspectives," in Jane B. Carter and Sarah P. Morris, eds., *The Ages of Homer* (Austin: University of Texas Press, 1995), 163–79. Nagy argues that although the stabilizing process began with the Panhellenic festivals, it continued until the middle of the sixth century when a definitive status was attained in the context of performance by rhapsodes at the Panathenaia. These, in turn, were finally written down in the fifth century. Nagy's position, which is developed in other works (see his bibliography), is different from that of Kirk. According to Kirk, an individual Homer created the work orally in the eighth century, and this version was passed down more or less verbatim until the sixth century, when it was written down (*Homer and the Epic,* 174 n. 131).

48. In 1965 Geoffrey Kirk wrote: "During the last ten years an old view has been regaining ground: that the *Iliad* and the *Odyssey* are so long, complex and skilful that they must have been composed with some aid from writing" (*Homer and the Epic,* 29). Fifteen years later Minna Jenson writes: "At present, the virtually unanimous general opinion about the *Iliad* and the *Odyssey* is that they were not composed orally, but by a writing poet building on an oral tradition; that the introduction of writing into Greece was in some way connected with Homer's originality" (*The Homeric Question and the Oral-Formulaic Theory,* 10). More recently, Barry Powell makes a bold assertion: "It is idle to believe that circa 700 B.C., for unknown reasons, the *mise en scène* of the poems was frozen *without the aid of writing*" ("Homer and Writing," in *A New Companion to Homer,* 3). It is worth noting that Milman Parry argued that Homer's poetic style was oral, not that Homer was necessarily an oral poet ("The Making of Homeric Verse," 321). Matthew Clark, in a conversation, has assured me that some people working in the formulaic school (that is, the Parry/Lord tradition) are now more concerned with demonstrating the feasibility of oral composition than with arguing about the role of writing in the early stages of the Homeric tradition. And he emphasized the importance of the more nuanced model proposed by Gregory Nagy. See Matthew Clark, *Out of Line: Homeric Composition Beyond the Hexameter* (Lanham, MD: Rowman & Littlefield, 1997).

49. Maurice Bowra, *Homer and His Forerunners* (Edinburgh: Nelson, 1955).

50. Albert Lord, *Singer of Tales,* 124f. This is the case for Lord even if Homer knew how to write. Of course, Lord also concurs with the linguistical and historical evidence which suggests that the Homeric epics could not have been composed later than the eighth century. Lord's thesis on dictation has been championed most recently by R. Janko, "The *Iliad* and its Editors: Dictation and Redaction," *Classical Antiquity* 9 (1990): 326–34.

51. Adam Parry, "Have we Homer's *Iliad?*" [1966], *The Language of Achilles and Other Papers* (Oxford: Clarendon, 1989), 105, n.3. His position is essentially a reaction to both Kirk and Lord. J. Griffin, in *Homer on Life and Death* (Oxford: Clarendon, 1980), xii–xiv, also argues that writing did not change the oral art.

52. Adam Parry believes that it was only later that writing initiated new ways of thought ("Have We Homer's *Iliad?*" 138). In this regard, he appears to be following Havelock (see below).

53. Ibid., 139, n. 61. For Kirk's reply to Parry and Havelock, see his *Homer and the Oral Tradition,* ch. 6.

54. Eric Havelock, *The Greek Concept of Justice* (Cambridge, Mass.: Harvard University Press, 1978), 228. In fact, Havelock thinks that Homer's composition was actually influenced by the visual examination of such writings. They are works of the "eye," not the "ear." See Havelock, *The Literate Revolution in Greece and its Cultural Consequences* (Princeton, N.J.: Princeton University Press, 1982), 181–82. Havelock seems to imply that their composition began after 650 B.C. (180).

55. Eric Havelock, *Preface to Plato,* 39.

56. Ibid., 48.

57. Although Havelock notes that it is the poet who "profoundly accepts" tradition in his "functional role of recorder and preserver" (*Preface to Plato,* 89), not everyone agrees with this assessment. Oliver Talpin sees Homer as rather critical of the milieu he is describing; see his "Homer," in John Boardman, Jasper Griffin, and Oswyn Murray, eds., *Oxford History of the Classical World* (New York: Oxford University Press, 1988) 68. See also John Halverson, "Havelock on Greek Orality and Literacy," *Journal of the History of Ideas* 53 (1992): 156.

58. Jack Goody, *Interface Between the Written and the Oral,* 107.

59. Ibid., 294. Kirk would agree with Havelock on this point.

60. Those who acknowledge their debt to Havelock are quite diversified. See, for example, Walter Ong, *Orality and Literacy* (London: Methuen, 1982); David Olson and Nancy Torrance, eds., *Literacy and Orality* (Cambridge: Cambridge University Press, 1991); Jack Goody, ed., *Literacy in Traditional Societies* (Cambridge: Cambridge University Press, 1968); Robert K. Logan, *The Alphabet Effect* (New York: Morrow, 1986); Tony M. Lentz, *Orality and Literacy in Hellenic Greece* (Carbondale, Ill.: Southern Illinois University Press, 1989).

61. This is the case even though Havelock believes that the epics are not "verbatim transcriptions" since Homer was already influenced by writing. Of course, the question naturally arises: if Homer was already influenced by writing, how can Havelock be so certain that the epics are an accurate record of orality? Havelock's response to this, I believe, is that it was because of "repetition" and "audience control" (*Preface to Plato,* 46).

62. This is the case according to Havelock because the poetic statement had to be phrased in such a way as to allow the pupil to habitually identify himself psychologically with the poetry he heard. This meant that the content could only deal with actions and events involving persons. As he notes, actions presuppose actors (*Preface to Plato,* 167). Ruth Finnegan (*Literacy and Orality,* 158) and others have shown that Havelock was wrong to exclude any other mnemonic techniques from nonliterate societies. I will examine this in the context of Solon's recital of the Atlantis story below.

63. Havelock, *Preface to Plato,* 173.

64. Havelock states: "Kantian imperatives and mathematical relationships and analytical statements of any kind are inexpressible and also unthinkable" (*Preface to Plato,* 182). See also his *Greek Concept of Justice,* 244; and "The Linguistic Task of the Presocratics," in Kevin Robb, ed., *Language and Thought in Early Greek Philosophy* (La Salle, Ill.: Hegeler Institute, 1983), 13f. Havelock has been taken to task for this. For an excellent discussion, see Arthur W. H. Adkins, "Orality and Philosophy," in Robb, ed., 207–27. On the other hand, in opposition to Adkins, Marcel Detienne seems to concur with Havelock's analysis of the influence of writing on geometric demonstration; see Detienne's Intro-

duction to *Les Savoirs de l'écriture en Grèce ancienne* (Lille: Presses Universitaires de Lille, 1988), 7–26, at 22.

65. Havelock, *The Literate Revolution in Greece,* 15–16, 180–82.

66. Ibid., 87. Writing enables cultural information to be stored more permanently and effectively and with much less mental exertion than is possible for acoustically trained memory. Havelock states that writing therefore removes "the pressure to have storage language in a memorizable form"; hence, "psychic energies hitherto channeled for this purpose were released for other purposes" (*The Muse Learns to Write* [New Haven: Yale University Press, 1986], 101. This must have occurred early on, for Havelock already sees a change with Hesiod (101–102).

67. Ibid., 112. Havelock adds: "As language became separated visually from the person who uttered it, so also the person, the source of the language, came into sharper focus and the concept of the self was born" (113). However, Havelock sees this as occurring much later; indeed, he believes the discovery of the self began with Socrates.

68. Ibid., 103. See also Havelock, *Literate Revolution in Greece,* 8.

69. Havelock, *Muse Learns to Write,* 101.

70. See Jack Goody, *Literacy in Traditional Societies,* 44; and Havelock, *Muse Learns to Write,* 112.

71. Havelock, "The Linguistic Task of the Presocratics," 21.

72. Marcel Detienne (*Les Savoirs de l'écriture,* 22f.) sees writing as developing early since he believes that writing already influenced the geometry behind Anaximander's map-making and other geometrical models.

73. Havelock, "Linguistic Task of the Presocratics," 21.

74. Of course, attributing the Greek "revolution" to the development of their alphabet is very much contested by scholars in various fields. Roy Harris, in *Signs of Writing* (London and New York: Routledge, 1995), 165, contends that it is nonsense.

75. The thesis that the addition of vowels radically transformed the writing system is endorsed by Walter Burkert, *The Orientalizing Revolution* (Cambridge, Mass.: Harvard University Press, 1992), 26. But he also adds that the "inventor" must have initially "participated in at least one school lesson" (29)—a point which did not go unnoticed by Plato.

76. Havelock, *Muse Learns to Write,* 60; see also *Literate Revolution in Greece,* 6.

77. Havelock, *Literate Revolution in Greece,* 72–73.

78. Ibid. Havelock believes that contemporary writing systems which originated in pre-Greek Semitic systems still "retain a traditional residue of ambiguity" because of this (*Muse Learns to Write,* 61). The alphabet has often been called the democratic as opposed to theocratic script. On this, see Jack Goody, *Literacy in Traditional Societies,* 38f.

79. Goody states that the Greek alphabet "makes it possible to write easily and read unambiguously about anything which society can talk about" (*Literacy in Traditional Societies,* 39, 67). See also Walter Burkert, *Orientalizing Revolution,* 28–29.

80. Havelock writes: "The Greeks did not just invent an alphabet; they invented literacy and the literate basis of modern thought" (*Literate Revolution in Greece,* 82).

81. As Goody notes (*Interface Between the Written and the Oral,* 219) — and I assume that Havelock would concur, although the passage at *The Muse Learns to Write,* 39, is somewhat vague—this does not mean that "oral man" was incapable of "logical reasoning" altogether; rather, it means that "oral man" was not capable of the kind of logical analysis associated with the syllogism and other forms of logical procedure. See also Goody, *Literacy in Traditional Societies,* 68.

82. Jean-Pierre Vernant, *The Origins of Greek Thought* ([1962] Ithaca: Cornell University Press, 1982), 49.

83. Ibid.

84. See, in particular, G.E.R. Lloyd, "Greek Science and Greek Society," *Magic, Reason and Experience* (Cambridge: Cambridge University Press., 1979), 226–67; and idem, "The Social Background of Early Greek Philosophy and Science," *Methods and Problems in Greek Science* (Cambridge: Cambridge University Press, 1991), 121–45.

85. Lloyd, "The Social Background of Early Greek Philosophy and Science," 124.

86. Oswyn Murray, *Early Greece,* 2d ed. (Cambridge, Mass.: Harvard University Press, 1993), 101, 182.

87. Ibid., 182.

88. Marcel Detienne, "L'espace de la publicié: ses opérateurs intellectuels dans la cité," *Les Savoirs de l'écriture,* 29–81.

89. According to Jack Goody (*Literacy in Traditional Societies,* 44), the capacity to identify inconsistencies between past and present is one of the essential differences between an oral society and a literate society.

90. On the evidence in general, see Charles Kahn, *Anaximander and the Origins of Greek Cosmology* ([1960] Indianapolis: Hackett, 1994). I am not aware of any scholar who has ever challenged this.

91. DK 12A6. For an interesting discussion, see Christian Jacob, "Inscrire la terre sur une tablette," in Marcel Detienne, ed., *Savoirs de l'écriture,* 273–304.

92. Marcel Detienne, "L'espace de la publicié," 81.

93. On this, see Robert Hahn, "Technology and Anaximander's Cosmological Imagination: A Case-Study for the Influence of Monumental Architecture on the Origins of Western Philosophy/Science," in Joseph C. Pitt, ed., *New Directions in the Philosophy of Technology* (Amsterdam: Kluwer, 1995), 95–138.

94. See Gerard Naddaf, "On the Origin of Anaximander's Cosmological Model." I do not contend here that Detienne is not aware of the political factors. However, he appears to give them too much prominence. In an earlier influential work, *The Masters of Truth in Archaic Greece* Detienne hardly mentions writing. The fact that Anaximander's cosmology exhibits the same solidarity between physical and political space as in the mythical cosmologies leads me to believe that writing was perhaps less important than politics, although it is difficult to say how far the Greeks would have gone without writing.

95. In this respect, it is important to note that virtually all of Anaximander's successors, including Plato, saw the universe as composed of a harmonious community of adversaries living together under the same law. Indeed, the word *kosmos,* which denotes a universal order with moral and social implications, is attested in almost all of the Presocratics, including Democritus. See Gerard Naddaf, "Plato and the *Peri Phuseōs* Tradition," in Tomas Calvo and Luc Brisson, eds., *Interpreting the Timaeus-Critias,* International Plato Studies 9 (Sankt Augustin: Academia Verlag, 1997), 30.

96. See Naddaf, "On the Origin of Anaximander's Cosmological Model."

97. This explanation became the norm among the Presocratics and had a profound impact on Plato. See Gerard Naddaf, "Mind and Progress in Plato," *Polis* 12 (1993): 122–33.

98. See Gerard Naddaf, "Mind and Progress in Plato"; "Lefkowitz and the Afrocentric Question," *Philosophy of the Social Sciences* 28 (1998), 451–70; and *L'origine et l'évolution du concept grec de* phusis (Lewiston: Mellen, 1992), 159–73. A revised English edition of the latter is in preparation for SUNY Press. I assume that the origin of the alphabet was no doubt connected with a more rational account of the origin of society. Barry Powell, "Homer and Writing," in Ian Morris and Barry Powell, eds., *A New Companion to Homer,* 25–26, reinforces my assumption that there was a Milesian interest in the origin of the alphabet around the time of Anaximander.

99. Although there is no reference to Homer and Hesiod in the doxographical tradition relative to Anaximander, there is little doubt that much of his rational *historia* is a reply to their respective positions.

100. See Oswyn Murray, *Early Greece,* 21f. Felix Jacoby calls Hecataeus "the father of Greek historiography" in *Atthis: The Local Chronicles of Ancient Athens* (Oxford: The Clarendon Press, 1949), 68. Hecataeus' *Genealogies* begins: "I write these things as they seem true to me; for the stories told by the Greeks are various and in my opinion absurd" (Felix Jacoby, *FGH,* 1, F.1). Hecataeus offers (or seems to offer) his own critical rationalization of the information he collected on the genealogies of families who claimed to descent from gods or heroes (Plato will also capitalize on this). It is interesting that Hecataeus is also a prominent statesman (Herodotus 5.36; 125) who Herodotus actually ridicules for claiming to have a god for his sixteenth generation (a naivete his predecessor and compatriot, Anaximander, would most certainly have avoided). And it is not insignificant that Hecataeus made the declaration to a high priest in Egypt, who quickly showed him the absurdity of such a claim (2.143). There is, as we shall see, an interesting parallel here with the Atlantis story. Further, we are told that Hecataeus used the information he gathered from his extensive travels (an important ingredient in adding an element of objectivity to most empirical research) to improve upon Anaximander's map. Herodotus

appears aware of the map (5.36) which he ridicules for being too geometrical, which implies (again) that Hecataeus was following Anaximander (see Strabo 1.7). Although Hecataeus seems to want to emancipate history from myth, he appears incapable of distinguishing between them, and this is why Herodotus appears more deserving of the famous title: father of history. His book, in prose, which has survived intact, is an account of the conflict between Greece and Persia based on his *historia* or investigation. It is a monument to a new race of heroes: "so that their memory will not be obliterated by time" (1.1). There are some interesting parallels here, as several have commented (see below), with the clash between Primeval Athens and Atlantis in Plato's Atlantis story. To give a proper account of the conflict, Herodotus feels compelled to explain the origin of the conflict, and the result is a history and picture of the known world (including geography, customs, beliefs, monuments, etc. of various peoples) based on his extensive travels and his collection and interpretation of available oral traditions. Although sight and hearing rather than written documents are the most important sources of Herodotus' investigations (indeed, there is little trace of the later), could he have recorded his own investigations without writing? Just as Herodotus comments on Hecataeus' gullibility, Thucydides is no less critical of Herodotus. Thucydides interestingly describes himself from his opening sentence as a writer although, as I will mention below, there is every indication that even Thucydides' work was meant to be read aloud. For the case at hand, it is important to note that his *History of the Peloponnesian War* could hardly have been composed without the aid of writing.

101. However, it is Xenophanes' pointed criticism (and skepticism) of Homer's and Hesiod's representation of the gods which merits special attention. After providing a "logical" refutation of their anthropomorphic ideas, he advances his own "rational" concept of God. The "oral tradition" from at least one perspective has a new "master of truth." No one contests that Xenophanes was not literate, and there is little doubt that he heard the poetry of Homer and Hesiod performed on numerous occasions. But could Xenophanes have composed his own arguments (and/or orally expounded them) without the aid of writing? Without the skepticism fostered by historical inquiry?

102. If the work were short and listener wealthy, there would be no reason not to purchase an account to have a closer "look."

103. Walter Burkert, *Greek Religion,* trans. John Raffan (Cambridge, Mass.: Harvard University Press, 1985), 310.

104. G.E.R. Lloyd, "The Social Background of Early Greek Philosophy and Science," 124; Jack Goody, *Literacy in Traditional Societies;* Marcel Detienne, "L'espace de la publicié"; Oswyn Murray, *Early Greece,* 98; Rosalind Thomas, *Literacy and Orality in Ancient Greece,* 8.

105. And this included classical Athens. See Rosalind Thomas, *Literacy and Orality in Ancient Greece,* 8.

106. *Crat.* 424e; 434a–b. Plato does admit that this theory does not take us very far in illuminating language.

107. However, the notion of deception does not appear in the *Cratylus.* Indeed, Plato appears to place the spoken word and the painter's picture on the same level, for he sees the painter's pigments as natural just as letters are natural (*Crat.* 424e). In both cases, they still represent something else: the spoken word "man" and the picture "man."

108. Plato seems to imply that the written word only represents one aspect of the spoken word (to wit: how it sounds), just as the painting of the bed represents only one feature of the bed.

109. *Phdr.* 275d–e. Alphabetic letters are thus a static form of representation and are incapable of apprehending the nature of the spoken word.

110. *Phdr.* 275a. I would argue that Plato makes a distinction between reading and writing. To compose a written work of philosophy would most certainly require a good deal of "dialectical discussion" with oneself. To read, without prior training, the work of another is another matter.

111. As Jack Goody maintains (*Literacy in Traditional Societies,* 50).

112. See *Phdr.* 276e–77c on the dialectical method.

113. This is also the case for written texts (verse or prose) which are recited in public. The reciter (in particular, the rhapsode), like the text, cannot be questioned, cannot be asked for explanations (*Phdr.* 277e–f). Dialectic is thus a "private affair."

114. In reality, it is paradoxical that Plato even wrote, let alone wrote one of the most famous and influential body of works ever written.

115. Ironically, direct speech was precisely the form which Plato claimed to be proper to tragedy in the *Republic*, a form of composition which he considered theatrical and dangerous. See *Republic* III 394a–c.

116. For an interesting analysis, see Mario Vegetti, "Dans l'ombre de Thoth: Dynamiques de l'écriture chez Platon," in Marcel Detienne, ed., *Savoirs de l'écriture,* 387–419.

117. See my "Mind and Progress in Plato," *Polis* 12 (1993): 122–33. At *Laws* VI 781e–82d, Plato even discusses the modifications of living organisms. For a concise summary of the Presocratic position, see *Laws* X 888d–90a.

118. This is not the flood which destroyed Atlantis. In *Critias* 111a we are told that several occurred after the one which destroyed Atlantis. For Plato there have always been floods and other natural disasters that periodically destroy humanity (*Laws* III 677a).

119. The aim of which is to discover what conditions tend to preserve or destroy a constitution. See *Laws* III 683b.

120. *Laws* III 677b. This is consistent with what we find in the *Timaeus* 23a–b and the *Critias* 109d with respect to the condition of the flood survivors.

121. *Laws* III 677d1. This is reiterated at *Laws* VI 781e–82d.

122. *Laws* III 679a. Of course, the caves provided a natural form of shelter (680b). This is not, strictly speaking, a conjecture on the part of Plato. According to him, this form of existence is/was still found in many parts of the world, including Greece.

123. Further on (682e), Plato employs the verb *muthologeō* with respect to how the events connected with the return of the Dorians unfolded according to Spartan tradition. This may be just one of several versions connected with oral tradition before they were recorded in writing. See also 685c–e.

124. Even Thucydides certainly believed in the Trojan war (1.1f.).

125. *hōste ou peri kenon ti zētēsomen [ton auton logon], alla peri gegonos te kai ekhon alētheian* (683e11–84a1; see also 683a8–b1).

126. Palamedes is also associated with showing the Greeks how to use Phoenician letters. The question is, then, did Plato believe the alphabet was invented by the Greeks or that it was the result of diffusion? Plato is working with such long time frames, either would be possible. On Palamedes, see Timothy Gantz, *Early Greek Myth* (Baltimore: Johns Hopkins University Press, 1993), 604–605.

127. The degree to which the past can be forgotten without poetry or writing is demonstrated in Solon's ignorance of Athens' glorious past. Not only were the actions of the heroes forgotten, but even most of their names. Thanks to the Egyptian priest, Solon will be able to reconstruct the past history/tradition of Athens.

128. As Plato notes (*Laws* VII 822e), all the citizens will be slaves to the laws.

129. The laws, of course, are expressions of *nous*. See *Laws* IV 713a, 714a, and X 890d.

130. This is reiterated at *Laws* IV 713c–e. Ironically, Plato's reaction to law is similar to his reaction to the written word and art: it is too rigid in a world of change, that is, it lacks the flexibility of a true statesman (*Pol.* 294d).

131. This appears to be the meaning of a passage at *Laws* VII 810b, where Plato states that there are two contemporary schools of thought with regard to educating the young in the matter of poetry: one school contends that they should listen to recitations (readings) of the great poets over and over until they are memorized; the other school argues that only the most outstanding passages should be committed to memory and learned by rote.

132. Dances and songs are so important as an instrument of education that Plato defines the educated man *(ho kalōs pepaideumenos)* as one who has learned to sing and dance well and an uneducated man as one who is *akhoreutos,* that is, untrained in choral performance (*Laws* II 654b).

133. The lyre will give the child a better sense of rhythm and harmony, but it is to be used not as a solo instrument but only as an accompaniment to words and dance. See Glenn Morrow, *Plato's Cretan City* (Princeton, N.J.: Princeton University Press, 1960), 341. See also *Laws* VII 800a, where music and dance must not be changed; we should spend our whole life at play, that is, sacrificing, dancing

and, singing (803e). *Laws* I and II give the most detailed description of the moral role of singing and dancing in the state.

134. Since the entire code of laws must be performed, even the argument for the existence of the gods in *Laws* X, the most beautiful and important preamble of all (887c1), must be put into a suitable form so that it can be memorized and performed.

135. According to Nicole Loraux, "Solon et la voix de l'écrit," in Marcel Detienne, ed., *Savoirs de l'ecriture,* 116–17, this would assure that the laws, despite their secular origin, would have a religious authority. Plutarch (Lycurgus 4.2.3) tells us that the songs which Lycurgus composed were "exhortations to obedience and concord, and the very measure and cadence of the verse, conveying impressions of order and tranquillity, had so great an influence on the minds of the listeners, that they were insensibly softened and civilized." There is thus a strong evidence that legislation was, at least initially, put into verse to make it more effective.

136. Plutarch (*Lives,* Solon), for his part, believes that Solon actually heard such a story from the Egyptian priests but abandoned writing because of his age.

137. The act of orally recuperating the story is mentioned at *Tim.* 26b, and there is no indication of reading or writing being a factor. In fact, the description would lend credence to the position advocated by Thomas, as noted below. Brisson, for his part, puts the accent on the oral transmission of the story, including where, when, and by whom. As he notes, there is always a sacredness associated with the oral transmission and this is clearly attested in the vocabulary.

138. The fact that he constantly asked his grandfather questions about the story is reminiscent of Euclides' constantly questioning Socrates about his encounter with Theaetetus in order to ensure that he got the story correct.

139. Plato also takes the time to tell us that he also recited it to Timaeus and Hermocrates the following morning so that they too would be able to verify his account.

140. On the importance of these festivals for the case at hand, see Gregory Nagy, "An Evolutionary Model for the Making of Homeric Poetry."

141. The reference is found in Diogenes Laertius 1.57.

142. *Tim.* 19b–c. See also Gerard Naddaf, "The Atlantis Myth: An Introduction to Plato's Later Philosophy of History," *Phoenix* 48 (1994): 194; and "Plato and the *Peri Phuseōs* Tradition," 32f.

143. This appears to be confirmed at *Critias* 108b.

144. At least in part, this is reminiscent of a rock concert where, if successful, there is a lively interaction between the star/hero and his audience. If the song is popular, the crowd actively participates. If the performance is sensational, then the crowd is enchanted as indeed is the performer. And the crowd continues to perform the song, with friends or in private either through recall or through the medium of the radio, television etc., often in a trace-like state.

145. Plato laments at *Rep.* X 606e2–3 that Homer is "the "educator of Greece." To what degree this is true, considering the influence of the sophists on higher education and public speaking, is open to debate. However, the influence of poetic education on the masses must have been considerable. It may not be fortuitous that the best description of the power of poetry is by one of the greatest rhetors and sophists of the fifth century, Gorgias, in the *Helen.* For a stimulating and brilliant contextual analysis, see Jacqueline de Romilly, *Magic and Rhetoric in Ancient Greece* (Cambridge, Mass: Harvard University Press, 1975), 3–22.

146. It is interesting to note here that although Protagoras states that poetry is the most important part of a man's education, he is engaged in a critical analysis of poetry rather than being carried away by its hypnotic power (*Prot.* 339a–41e, 343d–47a).

147. In conjunction with this, Plato laments in the *Republic* II 377d–78d that children are exposed to certain disturbing *muthoi* about the gods and heroes by mothers and nurses even before they attend school, that is, at an age when they are the most vulnerable of all.

148. The gods accept bribes, and the heroes themselves fear death.

149. Of course, Plato's main critique is ethical and political rather than epistemological and ontological, although the latter provide him with the necessary ammunition to explain precisely why the poets are incapable of doing otherwise. In this respect, it is worth noting that Plato returns to this point in *Rep.* X 605c–608b in his attack on poetry only after he has demonstrated, on the one hand,

that the soul is composed of three distinct elements and, on the other hand (and in conjunction with this), that there are two epistemologically and ontologically distinct worlds: the intelligible and the sensible. The poet, the lover of sights and sounds, contrary to the philosopher, only recognizes the latter.

150. This is the sine qua non of the ideal state, and it is reiterated in detail from 394e to 398b.

151. This explains why, when Adeimantus is asked to choose between three styles of expression *(lexis)*—the complex, the simple, or the combination of the two—he opts for the simple style, which represents the good man *(ton tou epieikous mimētēn akraton,* 397d4–5).

152. *Tupos* is being translated as "mold," that is, an "empty mold" as opposed to the *apotupōma* or "impression in relief." This explanation is given by A. Diès in his translation of *Theaetetus* (Paris: Societé d'edition "Les Belles Lettres"), 236. On the meaning of *tupos,* see G. Roux, "Le sens de *TUPOS,*" *Revue des études grecques* 63 (1961): 5–14.

153. It is worth noting that it is not by chance that Plato finishes up the section on *mousikē* with a discussion of harmony and rhythm (398c–400c). Harmony and rhythm along with words are the basic ingredients of song, music, and dance. Since song can only increase the effectiveness of the imitation employed in words (401c), and since different styles of music and dance are associated with different types of character, Plato wants to ensure that the music and dance in his ideal state will conform to the *tupoi* and the goodness of character which the citizens associated with them must exhibit. Much of what we find here is developed and clarified in the *Laws,* as I noted above. For an interesting discussion, see G. Morrow, *Plato's Cretan City,* 302–18.

154. Indeed, as A. J. Festugière points out in *Contemplation et vie contemplative selon Platon,* 3d ed. (Paris: J. Vrin,, 1967), 96–97, 102–103., the characteristics that Plato attributes to his gods are similar to those he attributes elsewhere to the forms, notably, simplicity, immutability, and intelligibility.

155. *Rep.* II 380c5, 7, d1, 383c7. In the *Laws,* as we saw above, the laws are to be employed as the real catechism of the state (VII 811c-d) and any other literature, prose or poetry, written or unwritten, must conform to it.

156. According to the first law, if God is absolutely good, then he cannot, contrary to popular opinion, be the cause of all things. Consequently, Homer and the other poets are wrong to represent Zeus and the other gods as allotting a mixture of both good and evil. If mortals are punished by the gods, it can only be because of justice (*Rep.* II, 379c–80c).

157. According to the second law, if God is absolutely perfect, then he could not, contrary to popular opinion, change his proper form to deceive others. Consequently, Homer and the other poets are wrong to portray the gods as being protean and deceitful in word and deed (*Rep.* II 380d–83c).

158. For the distinction between *nooumena* and *horōmena,* see *Rep.* VI 508d13–c2. C. Gill makes a similar observation in "The Genre of the Atlantis Story," *Classical Philology* 72 (1977): 290.

159. See *Rep.* VI 508d4–9, 511d6–e4.

160. Although this expression is taken from the *Theaetetus* 176b, this is precisely the model for the citizens of the ideal city.

161. To ban the poets entirely entails that the members of all three classes are obliged to follow the *tupoi* and the corresponding *muthoi.* A perfect example of this is the myth of the three metals at *Rep.* III 415a–d.

162. While it is true that poetry in general and myth in particular appeal to the emotional, that is the irrational part of the human soul, it is still the case that the philosopher's aim is to harmonize the irrational part as much as possible with the spiritual and rational parts of the human soul.

163. See Timothy Gantz, *Early Greek Myth,* 233. My reading of Felix Jacoby's *Atthis* confirms this. There is no more than a single (uncertain) exploit associated with the heroic figures mentioned below, that is, Plato's true heroes.

164. Erechtheus is mentioned twice in Homer and on both occasions in connection with Athena, his mother and protector: *Od.* 7.80–81 and, more importantly, *Il.* 2.547.

165. Walter Burkert, *Greek Religion,* 232–33.

166. *Tim.* 25c-d. On Plato and the *peri phuseōs* tradition, see Naddaf, "Plato and the *Peri Phuseōs* Tradition." I am recapitulating certain sections of that article here.

167. As Mircea Eliade points out in *Myth and Reality,* trans. Willard R. Trask (London: Allen & Unwin, 1964), 21, this is a fundamental feature of "origin" myths in general. For a succinct summary

of the relation between magic and cosmogony, see W. Burkert, *Orientalizing Revolution,* 124–27. This explains why certain schools of medicine like the "physicists" wanted to know the fundamental constituents from which man and by extension the universe were composed in the beginning (see, in particular, the Hippocratic treatise *On Fleshes* 1.2). They thought that by discovering the "original" state of things, they could penetrate the central secret of things. This was precisely the reproach that Socrates made with respect to the "physicists" in Xenophon's *Memorabilia* 1.1.11–15. Did they expect to know how to manipulate meteorological phenomena, etc., by speculating on how the universe originated?

168. Timaeus, Critias and Hermocrates, contrary to the poets and sophists, are said to be all truly immersed in both politics and philosophy (*Tim.* 19e–20a).

169. For the analogy between the tripartite structure of human soul in the *Republic* and the *Timaeus,* see in particular Tim. 69c–d and 69d–71a.

170. While it is true that the activity of the Demiurge is most often described in terms of production, the same can also be said for the legislator in the *Laws.*

171. At *Tim.* 27b we are led to believe that the Primeval Athenians were initially educated by Socrates. This gives the impression that Socrates can "manipulate" the outcome I have mentioned above in the context of myth.

172. Plato is, in fact, ambiguous on the origin of humanity. At times, he appears to agree with Anaximander and the rational/natural tradition and, at times with Hesiod and the mythical tradition. On this point, see Gerard Naddaf, "Mind and Progress in Plato."

173. Which is clearly the case with Erichthonius and his cohorts. See *Crit.* 110a.

174. It is worth pointing out that in *Critias* 110b–c both the male and female sex are included in the collectivity and capable of exercising the same functions as in the *Republic* (cf. *Tim.* 18c; *Rep.* 453e–57b).

175. The appropriate modes of behavior are not limited to the heroes, but also apply to wives, children, parents, and servants.

176. *Geras* is generally understood in the sense of "gift of honor," *Il.* 11.534, or "privilege," *Il.* 20.182. *Moira* and *geras* go hand in hand. See also Oswyn Murray, *Early Greece,* 52. This also appears to be how the gods proceed, following the victory of Zeus in the *Theogony*—that is, in conformity with Zeus' promise at *Theogony* 391f.

177. However, this is not always respected, as in the case of Zeus' confronting Poseidon, *Il.* 15.158f. It is true that Agamemnon lost his initial share through a foolish mistake: a sacrilege. For more detail see Havelock, *Preface to Plato,* 66f.

178. See Arthur W. H. Adkins, "Cosmogony and Order in Ancient Greece," in Robin W. Lovin and Frank E. Reynolds, eds., *Cosmogony and Ethical Order* (Chicago: University of Chicago Press, 1985), 59; Walter Burkert, *Greek Religion,* 248.

179. For the elders in the *boulē,* see *Il.* 19.303; for the full council in the *agora,* see *Il.* 18.497f.

180. *Anax, Il.* 3.351, or the "lord of counsel" or "all wise" (*Olumpie mētieta, Il.* 1.175; see also Hesiod, "father of gods and men" (*patēr andrōn te theōn te, Theogony* 542). Victory always entails violence and power. The gods battle one another at *Il.* 20.31f.; they are always angry with one another when one god gives the advantage to another. Hera is a prime example; for her tricking Zeus and Zeus' reaction, see *Il.* 15.1f.; feasting, *Il.* 19.165.

181. *Anax andrōn, Il.* 1.506, 9.114.

182. On the nodding of the head, see *Il.* 1.527f. On this important point and how it corresponds to how a petitioner approaches a prince, see Havelock, *Preface to Plato,* 68. See also the consequence of Hera's and her son Hephaestus' challenge to Zeus at the end of *Iliad* 1. For an excellent example of where Zeus makes it clear that he is stronger than all the other immortals combined, see *Il.* 8.17f. But he also purports to be omniscient; see Burkert, *Greek Religion,* 129.

183. During the Mycenean period, the king more closely followed the paradigm of Zeus, whereas in the Homeric period, debate among the elders—that is, the heads of noble families, *basileis* (or heroes here)—appears to be the basis of decision-making; and for the more important decisions even the *dēmos* are included. See Oswyn Murray, *Early Greece,* 56f.

184. *Il.* 2.205–206, 9.98ff. In the *Od.* 9.112f the Cyclops are considered as uncivilized because they do not assemble for council or make judgments according to custom *(themistes);* they take no heed of one another; nor are they god fearing.

185. See, for example, *Il.* 19.136f., 270f. The claim that "the god made me do it" is one that Paris uses to explain his kidnapping of Helen—he did it under the auspices of Aphrodite. This sentiment does appear to change in the *Odyssey* (e.g. 1.26f.). Although the gods, in particular, Athena, continue to intervene, the whole tenor seems somewhat different from the *Iliad:* humans appear much more responsible for the consequences of their actions. Indeed, the *Odyssey* ends with a "peaceful" conclusion thanks to Athena.

186. And fear is an effective antidote. Aristotle (*Politics* 1252b27) comments that men in the Homeric period imagined gods to have the same forms and ways of life as their own. In the *Metaphysics* (1074b1–8), he sees mythology as being introduced to persuade the multitude. Odysseus' accustomed way of asking if a people were god-fearing or not (after all, the Cyclops were not god-fearing) leads one to conclude that the fear of god is certainly associated with the beginning of morality. For an interesting discussion, see Burkert, *Greek Religion*, 247.

187. See Burkert, *Greek Religion*, 249.

188. The myth of Aegisthus, Agamemnon, Clytaemnestra, and Orestes is alluded to in *Od.* 1.29f. The events are not, of course, sanctioned by Zeus.

189. Everything is not as neat and tidy as Alasdair MacIntyre would like us to believe in his influential *After Virtue*, 2d ed. (Notre Dame, Ind.: University of Notre Dame Press, 1984).

190. As Burkert notes in *Greek Religion*, 128. The ruses and metamorphoses surrounding Zeus' adulterous affairs are more reminiscent of a hangover from a patriarchal family order where the dominant male can fulfill his most extreme fantasy.

191. See Herodotus 2.53. There can be little question that had Homer not begun his account in the middle of the Trojan war, then he would have begun with a cosmogony (alluded to on one occasion)—the necessary starting point for any oral tradition.

192. Although all the entities are personalized and reproduction occurs sexually between Gaia (Earth) and Uranos (Sky), it is only with the Titans, their offspring, that fully anthropomorphic mythical persons appear. The first two generations thus represent a cosmogony strictly speaking.

193. This is reminiscent of Clytaemnestra encouragement of Orestes to murder his father Agamemnon.

194. According to Martin West, (Hesiod, *Theogony* [Oxford: Clarendon Press, 1966], 274), *geras* and *timē* are used synonymously.

195. This may be an allusion to the Trojan War.

196. The oath was that whoever fought on his side would either retain (or be given) their honors and privileges. On the importance of taking an oath in the name of the river Styx, see *Theogony* 403. According to Burkert, the function of the oath is to guarantee that a statement is absolutely binding, whether about something past or future (*Greek Religion*, 150). In the *Theogony*, Zeus kept his promise (402–403) and because of this he has absolute power and thus commands and rules majestically. The castration of Ouranos may symbolize the consequence of failing to keep an oath (see Pausanias 5.24.9). The fact that only the fear of the gods provides a guarantee that the oath will not be broken explains the importance of honoring the gods. However, the oath as an intentionally misleading solution is employed by Hera (*Il.* 15.41); and, in matters of love, even Zeus is ready to swear falsely without hesitation (Hesiod, Frag 124). These are things which rightfully appall Plato. On the importance of oaths in Plato's *Laws,* see Burkert, *Greek Religion*, 254.

197. There are also non-social concepts such as Death, Sleep, Lies, Distress, Sarcasm, etc. These are already prominent in Homer.

198. See Havelock, *Preface to Plato,* 101f.

199. Of course, the socio-political model advocated and enforced by Zeus following his victory must have reflected some kind of historical reality in which there was a certain degree of stability. I would suggest the socio-political structure which existed in the Mycenean period. For a comparison with the *Enuma Elish* creation story, see Gerard Naddaf, "Hésiode, précurseur des cosmogonies grecques de type évolutionniste," *Revue de l'Histoire des Religions* 203 (1986): 355–80.

200. For a more detailed account of events which followed the marriage, see Gerard Naddaf, "The Atlantis Myth," 198–99.

201. Percy Cohen, "Theories of Myth," *Man,* n. s. 4 (1969): 337–53.

The translations of Plato are taken from the Princeton University Press edition of *The Collected Dialogues of Plato,* edited by E. Hamilton and H. Cairns (unless otherwise noted). In a number of cases, I revised the English translation to make it conform to Brisson's translation and interpretation. Where I may have failed, I alone am responsible.

The first part of the English translation diverges from the French second edition. It attempts to avoid the technical language at the beginning of the French edition in order to reach out to those less specialized in the area. It thus contains what is hopefully a more lucid introduction to the thesis defended in this book. The decision to do this was a joint one.

Translations always require some degree of consultation. I would like to thank, in particular, Michael Chase for his illuminating suggestions.

First Alcibiades	*Alc. I*	Meno	*Men.*
Apology	*Ap.*	Minos	*Min.*
Charmides	*Charm.*	Menexenus	*Mnx.*
Cratylus	*Crat.*	Phaedo	*Phdo.*
Critias	*Crit.*	Phaedrus	*Phdr.*
Demodocus	*Dem.*	Philebus	*Phlb.*
Epinomis	*Epin.*	Protagoras	*Prot.*
Letters VII, VIII, XII	*Epist.*	Republic	*Rep.*
Euthydemus	*Euthd.*	Sophist	*Soph.*
Euthyphro	*Euthph.*	Statesman	*Pol.*
Gorgias	*Gorg.*	Symposium	*Symp.*
Lesser Hippias	*Hipp. I*	Theaetetus	*Tht.*
Greater Hippias	*Hipp. II*	Timaeus	*Tim.*
Laches	*Lach.*		

PLATO THE MYTH MAKER

"Well, my dear Albert," said Franz, turning back toward his friend, *"what do you now think of citizen Luigi Vampa?"*

"I say he is a myth," replied Albert, *"and that he never existed."*

"What is a myth?" asked Pastrine.

"That would take too long to explain to you, dear host," replied Franz.

Alexandre Dumas, *The Count of Monte Cristo,* end of chapter 33

A fter its publication in 1982, *Platon, les mots et les mythes* was reviewed in a number of journals. Here is the list: *Rivista Storica Italiana* 94 (1982): 787, Momigliano; *Spirale* 39 (1983): 13, Hébert; *Dialogue* 22 (1983): 543–47, Lafrance; *L'Homme* 23 (1983): 78–79, Ellinger; *Journal of Hellenic Studies* 104 (1984): 207–8, Gill; *Revue Philosophique de Louvain* 82 (1984): 107–8, Reix; *Antiquité Classique* 53 (1984): 357–58, Joly; *Museum Helveticum* 41 (1984): 247, Lasserre; *Revue des Études Grecques* 101 (1985): 193–94 Vernière. From these reviews, it is possible to get a good idea of how the book was received by specialists in the field. Their reactions were generally favorable, and this explains why I did not undertake any major modifications.

Whereas the text itself has remained largely unaltered, a number of notes have been lengthened to take into consideration the most recent work in the area. I have also included a more complete and detailed bibliography. There is now an inventory of the recent works on the different myths and certain mythical figures mentioned in the Platonic corpus. I hope that these additions will make this work clearer and more useful.

I have continued my research on Plato's attitude with regard to myth, and I hope, within a reasonable time frame, to publish two works which will develop the following ideas.

I would like to show to what degree Plato is conscious of the fact that reason—at least human reason—cannot be liberated from the myth. This is the case because myth provides reason with the axioms from which it can deduce its most important propositions. A reading of the *Meno* and the *Phaedo* shows, in particular, how the doctrine of Forms, knowledge of which is reactualized by the soul, has its origin in what the priests and priestesses relate (*Meno* 81a). Their account presupposes the existence of an immortal and indestructible soul which, once separated from the body, is rewarded or punished according to how it lived during its previous exis- *3* tence. This leads to the following paradoxical hypothesis: sensible things are only images of nonsensible realities, which are the Forms and these are the true objects of the highest faculty of the soul, reason (*nous*).

I would also like to show how, starting with Aristotle, philosophers refused to be part of the community tradition transmitted through myths; how they made this tradition part of their own theories by exposing it to the hermeneutic tool called "allegory"; and how this tool enabled mythical discourse to be "translated" into a physical, ethical, political, and even metaphysical discourse.

This work is based on a lexical inquiry into the term *muthos* and its derivatives and compounds in Plato. It is also based on papers given during Pierre Vidal-Naquet's seminars at the École des Hautes Études en Sciences Sociales during the 1980–81 academic year. The subsequent discussions, notably those with Vidal-Naquet, resulted in a number of important changes.

Introduction

In French, the term "myth," and this is also the case in the other European languages, derives from a transcription of the ancient Greek *muthos*. In ancient Greece, the meaning of *muthos* was modified according to the transformations which affected the vocabulary of terms relating to "say" and "speech" during a period of historical evolution which culminates with Plato. Indeed, Plato fixes the meaning of *muthos* once and for all both in its primary sense and in its broad sense.

Muthos in the Primary Sense

When Plato uses the word *muthos* in its primary sense, he fulfills two functions: one descriptive, the other critical. With the help of the word *muthos,* he describes a discursive practice of a particular kind, a discursive practice to which the poets give a form. From this perspective, a myth is a story that a poet constructs by reorganizing the content of a message which a community wants to keep in its memory, and by giving this content a particular form. This explains why Plato sees myth as an instrument which tradition employs to convey values and inherited explanations. At the same time, however, Plato gives a negative evaluation of the status of myth, when compared to another discursive practice which is considered as superior: philosophy.

What a *Muthos* is for Plato

What does myth speak about? Myth is about a "beyond" which must be located in a distant past or a space which is different from the one in which the narrator and his public reside. In *Republic* II and III, Plato lists the five classes of entities to which myth refers: gods, daimons, heroes, the inhabitants of Hades, and men of the past. These mythical beings cannot be apprehended by any sense. In Plato's work, they fall under the jurisdiction of the soul. Since these realities cannot be apprehended by any of the senses, two questions arise. Why speak so often of such entities that cannot be the objects of any experience, and how are these imaginary beings to be described and defined?

In the context of this book, it is impossible to give a satisfactory reply to the first question. It is too vast, for it entails an enquiry into the causes of religious phenomena in their totality. Archaeological and historical evidence seem to indicate that humanity has always looked to a "beyond" considered as ontologically superior, for the explanatory principles of the origin and development of the world in which they lived. They looked to myth for the assurance that their actions would be crowned with success, and, more importantly, for the justification of their ephemeral existence. But, in order for such a maneuver to make sense, it was not a radical break between the sensible world and the beyond which was conceived, but rather a gap which could be temporarily filled by such intermediaries as seers, performers of initiation, and poets.

To give life to these imaginary beings and to summon the "beyond," the poet first produces a story which, through language, gives a picture of the beings who populate this other world. By totally identifying himself with these beings, the poet alienates his own identity. He places in his own mouth the speech which these beings should utter and the sounds which they should emit. He even physically becomes these beings and, with the help of masks, he takes on their attitudes and postures, postures which are expressed by music and given rhythm by dance. When summoning the beyond, the whole bodies of the poet and of his interpreters are mobilized in the theater and sanctuary.

The aim of the imitation employed by the poet or his interpreters is in the last analysis to rouse the public into identifying with the beings summoned before them. Now, such a will to modify mass behavior immediately poses an ethical problem. This is the real crux of the matter. Any poet, and in particular Homer, can be considered as a true educator because he wants to transform the behavior of his audience by offering them the beings he is summoning as models. In fact, the poet strongly urges his public to obey the laws of the city by giving it positive and negative examples. These laws are themselves ultimately based on myths. The poet wants to mold the souls of his public in the name of a community which seeks to assure, through persuasion, the obedience of its members to a system of values. To attain this goal, the poet employs imitation which relies on sentiment, pleasure, and especially fear. Consequently, whoever is persuaded by the myth surrenders his liberty, for he is led, without being fully aware of the fact, to modify his behavior according to a system of inherited values which, by definition, is foreign to him.

In brief, for Plato, myth in the true sense of the word is a form of discourse which transmits all information that a community conserves in memory of its distant past and passes on orally from one generation to the next. This is true whether or not the discourse has been elaborated by a specialist in the collective communication of the memorable such as the poet. However, in most cases, the community appeals to the poet, for he alone can confer stability and continuity to this discourse. At each stage of this communication process, imitation intervenes, showing itself at the levels both of the fabrication and of the interpretation of the myth. It disposes the addressees to determine or modify their physical and especially their moral behavior according to the model which is thus proposed to them, or rather imposed upon them. In such a context, the poet is the privileged intermediary between a community and the system of explanations and values to which it adheres. A community presents itself as a model to itself through the myths that it transmits. For both the community and the individual, these myths fix the reference points in every essential area of existence, and even propose explanations concerning the origin of the gods, the world, human beings, and the society in which they live. Both the community and the individual have questions for which they have no reply. Myths offer replies to these questions, but they are replies which can only be set forth, for they tolerate neither questions nor explanations. Thus, a myth is never a "myth" for the person who adheres to it. It only becomes a "myth" for those who consider it from the outside and who question its validity. Further, it is significant that when a myth is related in a Platonic dialogue, the discussion comes to an end and the only character who expresses himself is he who recounts a myth, to which he adheres.

Plato's Critique of *Muthos*

Myth suffers from a certain number of defects, which are inherent in its very nature:

1. The information transmitted by myth is unfalsifiable. The events evoked by a myth are located in a distant past or in a space—Hades, for example—which makes it impossible to verify the validity of the transmitted information. Myth, therefore, belongs in the category of the likely, and

not in the category of certitude. For these reasons, myth can impose itself only by the persuasion which it carries with it and by the fear which it arouses—rational demonstration is outside of its scope.

2. Since myth is slowly but surely transformed at each stage of its transmission, it eventually accumulates a certain number of disparate elements which seem to be so many incoherencies, whether shocking or simply ridiculous.

3. Myth remains too closely connected to the sensible world it is supposed to explain and to the society whose values it must transmit. The characters who intervene in myth—gods, daimons, heroes, inhabitants of Hades, and men of the past—have the appearance of men and behave like men. Therefore, myth can have no pretensions to universality, and myth is restricted to describing the physical appearance of individuals who belong to a well-defined community and who are not universal. Xenophanes had already insisted on this deficiency in the sixth century B.C. The gods of black people are black whereas those of the north of Greece, and in the Caucasus, are white, and even blond and blue-eyed. Furthermore, whereas gods should be morally superior to human beings, they behave, at times, worse than men: they steal, cheat, lie, rape, fight among themselves, etc. This lack of universality entails either a conflict between the various traditions, or a general doubt with regard to all of them.

4. Myth appears as an account which tells a story. It does not develop a series of arguments of the kind utilized by the deductive method. It is a discourse whose parts are not linked together by rigorous rules, which logic could enumerate. Rather, its parts are linked as a function of a particularly primitive process, in which actions and reactions follow one another. They are organized in a more general narrative framework in which a new state of equilibrium is instituted after the rupture of the old.

5. It follows, then, that myth is addressed not to the intellect but to the emotions and that it plays especially on the sensations of pleasure and pain that humans share with other animals. Myth aims to modify human behavior not through education strictly speaking but through imitation, which makes it akin to magic and incantation.

Muthos in the Broad Sense

The meaning of *muthos* combines all of the aforementioned deficiencies when the term is used derivatively, not in its primary but in its broad sense. In its broad sense, myth designates a discourse—not very rigorous in form or in the organization of its content—that transmits unfalsifiable information and that gives rise not to certainty but to belief, which nonetheless may be particularly strong. When, in the course of this book, we use "myth" in the broad sense, we shall understand thereby unjustified and unjustifiable propositions which are proposed solely to persuade; that is, which are advanced independently of any preoccupation with truth.

Definition of *Logos*

Following a long line of thinkers, Plato denounces myth's deficiences and contrasts myth with philosophical discourse or *logos*. The *logos* is a discourse which must be based solely on reason, that is, without any recourse to experience. It is a discourse which claims to attain certitude and universality. In order to attain this goal, it develops a demonstration of the same kind as that which, in Plato's time, was proposed by mathematicians, and more specifically by geometers: the *deductive method*. This was considered the paradigm of rational activity.

Plato, however, is realistic. He knows very well that philosophy is restricted to a small number of men in society and that, in man, philosophy has recourse only to reason. So, to be able to convince the majority within society and, within man, to be able to tame emotions as powerful as pleasure and fear, the philosopher has recourse to the marvellous instrument of persuasion: myth. When the deductive method reaches its limits, it abandons reason to return to myth. And, because Plato repudiates allegory, that type of interpretation which makes traditional myths conform to a philosophical doctrine, he is driven to this rather extreme solution which is also the mark of his originality. He constructs new myths which incorporate many traditional elements but which also respond to certain requirements peculiar to himself.

PART I

PLATO'S TESTIMONY

The Communication of the Memorable

The following is a brief synopsis of what to expect in the first part of this work.

Myth appears as a message (chapter 1) by means of which a given collectivity transmits that which it preserves in memory of its past from generation to generation. The identification of this message as a myth depends largely upon the nature of the signal (chapter 2) which during a long period of time has been its privileged means of transmission.

In an oral civilization, the making of a message is indissociable from its transmission, whereas in a written civilization, these two spheres are clearly distinguished. The ambiguity of the Platonic vocabulary on these points (see appendix 2) testifies to the gradual transition of ancient Greece to writing. Nevertheless, Plato often fairly clearly distinguishes the making of a myth from its transmission. This explains the amount of important information on the making of myth (chapter 3) to be found within the Platonic corpus.

The transmission of a myth (chapter 4)—as distinguished from the making of a myth—becomes the work either of professionals such as rhapsodists, actors and choral dancers, or of nonprofessionals who present two characteristics: advanced age and femininity.

The reception of myth (chapter 5) which, in an oral civilization, cannot be distinguished from its transmission and consequently from its making, is basically a matter of hearing for those to whom both professionals and nonprofessionals address themselves: children or the *hoi polloi*.

On the whole, the communication of a myth depends on mimesis (chapter 6). Even the addressee of a myth tends to identify himself, as a result of a kind of emotional fusion (chapter 7), with the realities which those who fabricate, narrate, and/or interpret a myth evoke by means of words, music, and/or dance. This merging obliterates practically all the distinctions inherent in the model on which a theoretical analysis is based.   *13*

Plato presents this emotional fusion as the result of a charm, of an incantation, or simply of persuasion, which is produced by the pleasure brought about by the communication of the myth to the lowest part of the human soul. Though Plato recognizes the effectiveness of myth, he vigorously denounces its harmful effects. Nevertheless, this does not prevent Plato from having recourse to myth, as an alternative to violence in the area of ethics and of politics.

Throughout this description, which was inspired notably by the schema proposed by Geneviève Calame-Grimaule,[1] reference will be made to the account of the war between primeval Athens and Atlantis, which Plato relates at the beginning of the *Timaeus* (17a–27c) and in the *Critias*. This story is a pastiche or, more precisely, a pseudo-historical account, in which Plato takes Herodotus as a model.[2] By presenting ironically—or, in the words of Pierre Vidal-Naquet, "with astonishing perversity"—this fictional story as true, Plato gives his readers a concrete example of the nature of fiction, which he describes from a literary perspective in the *Republic*. Yet many readers have remained insensitive to Plato's irony and have thus considered the account made by Critias the Younger a true story.[3] It is difficult not to see in this Critias—even if only in a shadowy way— Critias the tyrant, who was considered as a sophist. Plato's genius in this matter resides in demonstrating to what degree it is difficult in practice to distinguish fiction from reality, and the sophist from the historian and the philosopher.

The fact that this account is a pastiche does not, however, disqualify it as a reference text. Its artificial character brings to light a certain number of fundamental elements, which indeed occur in all the myths, but which

1. Geneviève Calame-Griaule, "Pour une étude ethnolinguistique des littérateurs orales africaines," *Langages* 18 (1970): 22–45.

2. See Pierre Vidal-Naquet, "Athènes et l'Atlantide," *Revue des études grecques* 77 (1964): 420–44, reprinted in *Le Chasseur noir* (Paris: Maspero: 1981), 335–60; idem, "Hérodote et l'Atlantide: entre les Grecs et les Juifs. Réflexions sur l'historiographie du siècle des Lumières," *Quaderni di Storia* 16 (July–December 1982): 3–76; Christopher Gill, "The Genre of the Atlantis Story," *Classical Philology* 72 (1977): 287–304; Luc Brisson, Platon, *Timée/Critias* (Paris: Flammarion, 1992); and more recently Gerard Naddaf, "The Atlantis Myth: An Introduction to Plato's Later Philosophy of History," *Phoenix* 48 (1994): 189–209. Naddaf argues that contrary to Vidal-Naquet, for whom the Atlantis story is a game, and a game that was not "serious" because for Plato history always and inevitably takes the form of a progressive degeneration, so that humanity cannot escape its destiny, the Atlantis story is to be taken quite seriously. It may be considered as a sort of preamble to the foundation of a new constitution—the one proposed for the future city of Magnesia in the *Laws*. This constitution, although "second best," if one were to compare it to the *aristē politeia* of the *Republic* (or the constitution of primeval Athens which amounts to the same thing), is nevertheless the best possible constitution when one takes into consideration the conditions of existence here on earth.

3. On the identification of that Critias, see chapter 2.

are not, at first glance, as explicit in traditional myths. This is because the making of a pastiche implies a prior analysis of the kind of discourse the imitation is concerned with. It is precisely to this kind of analysis, which in both parts of this book will deal primarily with traditional myth, that we are introduced by this philosophical myth.

ONE

INFORMATION

A myth never relates an actual or recent experience. Instead, it always evokes a recollection preserved in the memory of an entire community, which has orally transmitted it from generation to generation, over a long period of time. So, if we want to define myth, we must begin by determining the criteria a group employs in order to preserve within its memory the recollection of a specific event.

Not all events—whether real or supposed to be so—are susceptible of becoming the occasion of communication as myth. Some events are known only to a limited group of individuals. Others will be of interest to the entire community. But most of these events are quickly forgotten. There are some of them, however, which this community strives to remember.

An example of this is the war between primeval Athens and Atlantis. This is confirmed by the usage of the verbs *sōizō,* "to conserve"[1] and *diasōizō,* "to conserve faithfully."[2] It is also confirmed by the abundant vocabulary relative to memory: *mimnēiskomai,* "to remember,"[3] *anamimnēiskomai,* "to recall,"[4] *epimimnēiskomai,* "to bethink oneself of,"[5] *apomnēmoneuō,* "to recall a memory,"[6] *diamnēmoneuō,* "to remember distinctly,"[7] *ekhō mnemeion,* "to subsist as a memory, to remain in memory."[8]

The memory which matters in this case is not so much the individual memory[9] as the collective memory.[10] Of course, there cannot be a collective memory without an individual memory. But in order for the recollection of an event to be preserved over a long period of time, it must be

1. *Tim.* 22e4, 23a5; *Crit.* 109d3.
2. *Crit.* 110a7.
3. *Tim.* 21c3, 23b6, 26a2.
4. *Tim.* 26b1.
5. *Tim.* 21a1.
6. *Tim.* 20e4.
7. *Tim.* 22b3.
8. *Tim.* 26b3.
9. *Tim.* 20e4, 21a1, c3, 22b3, 26a2, b1, b3.
10. *Tim.* 22e4, 23e5, b6; *Crit.* 109d3, 110a7.

shared by a considerable number of contemporary individuals who try to transmit it to members of the following generation.[11]

These two conditions compensate for the weak temporal autonomy and the contingent character of the individual memory. This is subtly described by Critias:

> CRITIAS I have told you briefly, Socrates, what the aged Critias heard from Solon and related to us. And when you were speaking yesterday about your city and citizens, the talk which I have just been repeating to you came into my mind, and I remarked with astonishment how, by some mysterious coincidence, you agreed in almost every particular with the narrative of Solon, but I did not like to speak at the moment. For a long time had elapsed, and I had forgotten too much; I thought that I must first of all run over the narrative in my own mind, and then I would speak. And so I readily assented to your request yesterday, considering that in all such cases the chief difficulty is to find a narrative suitable to our purpose, and that with such a narrative we should be fairly well provided. And therefore, as Hermocrates has told you, on my way home yesterday I at once communicated the narrative to my companions as I remembered it, and after I left them, during the night, by thinking, I recovered nearly the whole of it. Truly, as it is often said, the lessons of our childhood make a wonderful impression on our memories, for I am not sure that I could remember all the discourse of yesterday, but I should be much surprised if I forget any of these things which I have heard very long ago. I listened at the time with childlike interest to the old man's narrative; he was very ready to teach me, and I asked him again and again to repeat his words, so that, like an indelible picture, they were branded into my mind. As soon as the day broke, I rehearsed them as he spoke them to my companions, that they, as well as myself, might have something to say.[12]

Critias the Younger's effort to remember what his grandfather related to him a long time ago constitutes an individual act. Yet this individual act is the meticulous manifestation of a vaster effort on the part of the entire community: in this case, Greece.[13]

Such an effort can only be selective. Indeed, memory is indissociable from forgetting in an oral civilization.[14] Whereas writing permits a storage

11. See Maurice Halbwachs, *La Mémoire collective,* 2d ed. revised and enlarged with a preface by Jean Duvigaud and an introduction by J. Michal Alexandre ([1950] Paris: PUF, 1968).

12. *Tim.* 25d7–26c5.

13. See *Crit.* 109d3, 110a7.

14. Jack Goody and Ian Watt, "The Consequences of Literacy," in *Literacy in Traditional Societies,* ed. Jack Goody (Cambridge: Cambridge University Press, 1968), 28–34.

of messages which is—in theory, at least—infinite, the accumulation of orally transmitted messages can only be individual, and therefore limited by the capacity of an individual memory. But what criteria does a community employ to select the events worthy of recollection? The priest of Saïs is explicit on this point:

"And whatever happened either in your country or in ours, or in any other region of which we are informed—if there were any actions noble or great or which present a difference, they have all been written down by us of old and are preserved in our temples."[15]

What about the details?

Everything which "stands out" *(tina diaphoran ekhon)* from the customary order of things is liable to become an object of collective memory. This, it must be admitted, is a class which includes a particularly large number of events.

However, the adjectives *kalos,* "noble," and *megas,* "great," when coordinated with the expression *tina diaphoran ekhon,* restrict this class remarkably. These two adjectives evoke a system which assigns values in such a way as to cause some events to stand out from others. Everything extraordinary cannot become an object of collective memory. The extraordinary event must be significant with regard to the values of the community. In other words, the community only retains the information that fits its own value system and that can be employed for its defence and glorification in either a positive (by commending loyalty to the community) or negative way (by acting as a warning).

Finally, the expression, *ē tēi de ē kai kat'allon topon,* "either here or in any other region," provides an additional stipulation. It shows that the events likely to become objects of collective memory are related not only to that community but also to others. In other words, a given community defines itself both by being attentive to the events which concern it and by considering those which happen in other communities, provided, of course, that these events are of significance to it.

To illustrate the preceding, here is an inventory of the different kinds of events mentioned in the texts of the *Timaeus* and the *Critias* which serve as a reference point in the first part of this work. These events include:

1. Events concerning the gods, considered primarily as agents of the generation, preservation, and destruction of the two communities of primeval Athens and Atlantis.

---

15. *Tim.* 23a1–5.

2. Events concerning the roles of the two communities in military and political activities.

3. Events relative to human individuals who have found themselves in exceptional situations (Phoroneus and Niobe, the first man and woman; Deucalion and Pyrrha, the only man and woman to survive the deluge), or who have performed heroic deeds (Theseus).

4. Genealogies which describe relations between gods and men on both the individual and community levels.

5. Natural catastrophes caused notably by water and fire, which originate in the sky and fall on earth.

This inventory, which is far from being exhaustive, nonetheless gives an idea of what kind of events are susceptible to becoming objects of collective memory. Furthermore, several of these events give rise to explicit value-judgments calling for praise or blame:

1. The fact that Plato insists that distribution of the whole earth by regions among the gods occurred without dispute in accordance with the allotments of justice *(dikē)*[16] indicates that the Egyptian priest rejects other versions known elsewhere, according to which the gods entered into conflict on this occasion. Whence the negative reminder of the rule: there can be no conflict between the gods.

2. Furthermore, it is said of Hephaestus and Athena that "their love of wisdom *(philosophiai)* and crafts *(philotechniai)* orients them in the same direction,"[17] and that Attica was alloted to them "since it was naturally compatible with their virtue and understanding" *(aretēi kai phronēsei).*[18]

3. Therefore, it is not surprising that the primeval Athenians, who were their descendants, constituted "the fairest and noblest race of men which ever lived" *(to kalliston kai ariston genos ep' anthrōpous).*[19]

4. Hence, it naturally follows that their city "was the best *(aristē)* in war and in every way the best-governed *(eunomōtatē),* of all cities."[20] The Egyptian priest is yet more precise: "Athens is said to have performed the noblest *(kallista)* deeds and to have had the fairest *(kallistai)* constitution of any of which tradition tells, under the face of heaven."[21]

5. Lastly, the war between primeval Athens and Atlantis is described as follows: "great and marvelous *(megala kai thaumasta)* were the actions of the Athenian city which have passed into oblivion through the lapse of

16. *Crit.* 109b–c.
17. *Crit.* 109c7–8.
18. *Crit.* 109c9–d1.

19. *Tim.* 23b7.
20. *Tim.* 23c5–6.
21. *Tim.* 23c6–d1.

time and the destruction of mankind. But one, in particular, was greater than all the rest *(pantōn de hen megiston)*."[22]

This inventory of value judgments (much of which is exaggerated) clearly shows to what extent the information reported to Solon by the Egyptian priest is indissociable from a system of values. This system gives meaning to the information, which in turn, in the case we are examining, serve to illustrate the system. To sum up, only an event which is extraordinary and which, moreover, is significant within the framework of the value-system recognized by the community in question can become an object of collective memory. This is true regardless of whether the event unfolded within this community or elsewhere. In other words, there are two types of criteria which allow the community's memory to make a selection from a set of events. The first criterion is objective. It entails singularity, and it is that which stands out from the usual order of things. The second criterion is ethical. It entails exemplarity, and it is that which can be integrated into the system of values recognized by the group.

The temporal context in which these events are situated can only be the past. For "to remember" *(mimnēiskesthai)* is "to be mindful"[23] of events which unfolded "in the past" *(palai),*[24] or of "past things" *(palaia),*[25] or of "ancient things" *(archaia).*[26] In what way, however, does the past which pertains to myth differ from the past of which history speaks? What are the limits of the mythical past? In a sense, the past in question goes back to the absolute origin, which is that of the gods, as is illustrated in Hesiod's *Theogony.* But to what extent can one go in the other direction? The events with which the myths are supposed to deal must have unfolded long enough ago that the person who relates them finds it impossible to verify their validity, either directly, by having witnessed them, or indirectly, through the mediating agency of someone who did. Here is an example. Plato often speaks of the Median and Peloponnesian Wars, which were of such decisive importance for Athens, without ever using the word *muthos* in regard to them. Yet he uses this same word or one of its compounds in book III of the *Laws,* to designate the life-style of the Cyclops,[27] the found-

22. *Tim.* 20e4–6.

23. Emile Benveniste, "Formes et sens de *mnaomai*," *Sprachgeschichte und Wortbedeutung. Festschrift Albert Debrunner* (Berne: Francke, 1954), 13–18.

24. *Tim.* 23d3; *Crit.* 110a2.

25. *Tim.* 20e5, 21a7, 22a1, b8, e5, 23a4, b3; *Crit.* 110a4, a6.

26. *Tim.* 21a6, 22a5, b7.

27. *Laws* III 680d3.

ing and fall of Troy,[28] and the founding of the Dorian cities of Argos, Messene, and Sparta.[29] However, when Plato goes on to describe the constitutions of these three Dorian states,[30] he clearly indicates that he is no longer speaking in mythical terms.

The fact that a myth evokes the recollection of events which unfolded in a past—which is an object neither of direct or indirect testimony, but of tradition—entails two consequences which establish the opposition between myth and true discourse about the past (i.e. history): the absence of any precise dating, and especially the ignorance of what really happened. Myth is distinguished from true discourse about the past by its inability to precisely state when the events which it mentions took place. In this respect, the opposition between Solon and the Egyptian priest is exemplary. Even with the help of genealogies, Solon cannot organize a chronology of the events he evokes:

> CRITIAS On one occasion, wishing to draw him [the priest of Saïs] on to speak of antiquity, Solon began to tell about the most ancient things in our part of the world. He related the myths *(muthologein)* about Phoroneus, who is called "the first man," and about Niobe, and after the Deluge, of the survival of Deucalion and Pyrrha; and he traced the genealogy of their descendants and, reckoning up the dates, tried to compute how many years ago the events of which he was speaking happened.[31]

And the Egyptian priest did not hesitate to make this judgment about his procedure: "As for those genealogies of yours which you just now recounted to us, Solon, they are no better than the myths of children."[32] Moreover, immediately after having made this statement, the priest begins his account of the war waged by primeval Athens against Atlantis, pretending that he is speaking about the Athens of 9,000 years ago whose foundation preceded that of Saïs by 1,000 years.[33] The account is preserved in writing on the walls of a temple in Saïs.

Precise dating is as essential to history as measure is to physics.[34] Myth, however, relates events whose temporal situation presents an indeterminate

---

28. *Laws* III 682a8.
29. *Laws* III 682e5, 683d3.
30. *Laws* III 683e10–684a1.
31. *Tim.* 22a4–b3.
32. *Tim.* 23b3–5.
33. *Tim.* 23d–e.
34. See I. Meyerson, "Le temps, la mémoire, l'histoire," *Journal de psychologie normale et pathologique* 53 (1956): 337. Reprinted in *Ecrits 1920–1968: Pour une psychologie historique,* introduction by Jean-Pierre Vernant (Paris: PUF, 1987), 267.

quality—indicated by the indefinite temporal adverb *pote,* "once,"[35] and by the expression *ēn pote,* "once upon a time"[36]—which one finds at the beginning of certain myths recounted by Plato. And even if numbers are mentioned in a myth, this still has nothing to do with the procedure of a historian, as Herman Fränkel explains by taking the *Odyssey* as an example: "These numbers (they are for the most part typical recurring numbers which indicate all kinds of measures) are generally fortuitous and cannot be used as a basis for calculating operations or for proving that events are contemporary. They only indicate a general order of size, and simply symbolize a long duration. Here, there is practically no interest in chronology, whether relative or absolute."[37] The Egyptian priest claims that he can precisely date the events he recounts, while Solon cannot do so. From this assertion, he argues that his account is a true discourse based on history, while Solon's is merely a myth. From this point of view, the priest's argument appears, if not convincing, at least coherent. Furthermore, time only adds to our ignorance concerning the events related by myth. As we will see in the following chapter, this effect is even more pronounced when information about these events has been transmitted only orally, and when the technique of poetry has not been used. It is this ignorance regarding the distant past which enables the narrator of a myth to utilize a certain number of manipulations which may or may not go in the direction Plato wishes:

> SOCRATES And also in the account of these myths *(en . . . tais muthologias)* of which we were just now speaking, owing to our ignorance of the truth about antiquity, we liken the false to the true as far as we may and make it useful.[38]

Ultimately, a myth is so autonomous of the reality to which it refers that it may be considered to be self-referential. This is due to the fact that in an oral civilization, the past becomes present each time it is transmitted; and since the making, transmission, and reception of a message cannot

---

35. *Rep.* II 359d1, X 614b4.
36. *Prot.* 320c8; *Phdr.* 259b6.
37. Herman Fränkel, "Die Zeitauffassung in der frügriechischen Literatur" [1931], *Wege und Formen frühgriechischen Denkens,* 2d. ed., hrsg. Franz Tietze ([1955] Munich: Beck, 1960), 2. Here is the German text: "Diese Zahlen (meist sind es typische Zahlen, die für alle möglichen Masse wiederkehren) sind im allgemeinen unverbindlich, und nicht als Grundlagen für Rechenoperationen und Synchronismen gemeint. Sie bezeichnen nur allgemein die Grössenordnung, und symbolisieren mit ihrer stilgerechten Scheinpräzision einfach eine lange Dauer. Es besteht so gut wie gar kein Interesse an Chronologie, weder an relativer noch gar an absoluter."
38. *Rep.* II 382c10–d3.

then be distinguished, the content of the transmitted message is recon-
structed each time according to the requirements of the context (religious,
political, social, economic, etc.) of its enunciation. From this viewpoint,
for the one who makes the myth or the one who relates the myth, the past
is not an object as it is for the historian; rather, it is a project that must
adapt itself to the circumstances of its realization. By objectifying the past,
writing renders this constant adaptation of the past to the present impossible. It thereby kills myth, whose relationship to reality is then denounced
as unfalsifiable.

Two

Means of Transmission

In the final analysis, a discourse concerning the same event is considered to be either a myth or a true account depending on the way the memory of it is transmitted. This is the case, for example, of the war between primeval Athens and Atlantis which is related at the beginning of the *Timaeus* and in the *Critias*. In Greece, catastrophes periodically destroy the cities, within which only a few citizens can have the leisure necessary for research into the past and for the development of writing and poetry; thus here the transmission was exclusively oral.[1] On the other hand, in Egypt—which was not as subject to natural catastrophes[2]—the memory of this heroic exploit was preserved in written form, which then became the source and instrument of control for the tradition on which Plato pretends to depend. Consequently, it is in Egypt that Solon, who until then could only relate myths on the subject, became aware of the true history of Athens from the mouth of a priest of the city of Saïs. That the story has a written origin is the case even if Plato's position on writing is ambiguous—an ambiguity typical of the historical situation in Greece in the fifth and sixth centuries B.C.

Here then, as a reference point, is a detailed account of the twofold tradition regarding the war between Athens and Atlantis. Solon was informed of the event in question when he was passing through Saïs during his trip to Egypt. The Egyptian priest who relates the story of the war tells Solon that the event occurred 9,000 years ago.[3] According to the writings to which the priest refers, Saïs was founded 8,000 years previously,[4] and Athens was 1,000 years older than Saïs.[5] Consequently, the account of the war between Athens and Atlantis, after having been transmitted orally for

---

1. *Tim.* 22b–23b.
2. *Tim.* 22d.
3. *Tim.* 23e4–6, *Crit.* 108e1–2.

4. *Tim.* 23e2–4.
5. *Tim.* 23d7–e1.

1,000 years or so, was put into writing at Saïs nearly 8,000 years in the past.[6] The priest considers this work as the source of his account. He does not read it out to Solon, however, for he does not have the time.[7] Thus Solon learns of this heroic exploit without the direct intervention of writing. The transmission of this deed will be made orally by successive generations of the same family until Plato. Indeed, even if it is impossible to exactly determine the family tie implied by the term *oikeios,* it is stated that Solon "was a relative *(oikeios,)* and dear friend of Dropides (II)."[8] Whatever the case on this precise point, here is a genealogical table which summarizes everything known about this family.[9]

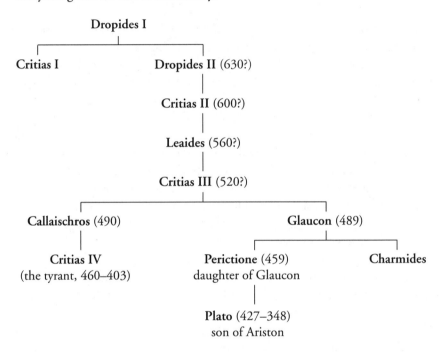

In all likelihood, the life of Solon stretches from 630 to 558 B.C. His trip to Egypt can be situated around 600, to judge by the following phrase: "by reason of the factions and troubles which he found stirring in his own

6. *Tim.* 23a1–5.

7. *Tim.* 23e6–24a2.

8. *Tim.* 20e1–2.

9. Warman Welliver, *Character, Plot and Thought in Plato's "Timaeus and Critias"* (Leiden: Brill, 1977), 51. Welliver follows J. K. Davies, *Athenian Propertied Families (600–300 B.C.)* (Oxford: Clarendon Press, 1971), 322–35. Brill, 1977), 51.

country when he came home."[10] Indeed, this must refer to the troubles which preceded his archontate of 594. If this assumption is correct, the first step in the oral transmission of the account of the war between primeval Athens and Atlantis, in the framework of Plato's family, occurs around 600, for it is during his trip to Egypt that Solon learns of this account.[11]

The second step of this oral transmission cannot be precisely dated, but we know the protagonists: they are Solon and Critias II. Critias II—who will here be referred to as Critias the Elder—must have been born in about 600. Thus, the account of the war between Athens and Atlantis would have been related to Critias the Elder by Solon between 600 and 558. Solon would have used the version which he had brought back from Saïs, given that there are four passages in the *Timaeus* which refer to this event.[12]

The third step of this transmission poses major problems regarding the identification of Critias the Younger. Until John Burnet's study,[13] it was generally thought, following Proclus,[14] that the Critias in question was Critias the tyrant (460–403), the Critias IV of Warman Welliver's table. However, this interpretation has not been unanimously accepted.[15] Alfred

10. *Tim.* 21c6–7.

11. *Tim.* 21c5–d1, 21d7–8; *Crit.* 108d5, 110b3, 113a5.

12. *Tim.* 20d8–e1, 20e3–4, 21a4–6, 25d7–e2.

13. John Burnet, *Greek Philosophy: From Thales to Plato* (London: Macmillian, [1914] 1928), 338, n. 1.

14. Proclus, *In Tim.*, vol. 1, p. 70, l. 20ff., Diehl.

15. For at least two reasons: (1) In *Timaeus* 20e1–4, Critias declares: "He [Solon] was a relative and dear friend of my great-grandfather Dropides *(hēmin Drōpidou tou propappou)* . . . and he told the story to Critias, my grandfather" *(pros de Kritian ton hēmeteron pappon)*. Now, it is impossible that Critias the tyrant had for a great-grandfather a contemporary of Solon (630?–558? B.C.). (2) In addition, the proper noun *Kritias* only appears in five dialogues in the Platonic Corpus: the *Charmides*, the *Protagoras*, the *Timaeus*, the *Critias*, and the *Eryxias*. Since the *Eryxias* is generally considered apocryphal, it can be discounted. Now in the *Charmides* (153c7, 169b5) and in the *Protagoras* (316a5), the Critias in question is clearly identified: it is the son of Callaischros *(Kritias ho Kallaischrou)*, Critias the tyrant, that is, Critias IV. The *Charmides* adds more precision to the genealogy of this Critias: he is Solon's relative and descends from a Critias, son of Dropides (157e4–5), who was praised by Solon and Anacreon and is, as Glaucon's nephew, the cousin of Charmides and Perictione (154a–b), Plato's mother.

But there are two other arguments: (1) In *Timaeus* 21b5–6, Critias says of Solon's poems that they were "new" *(nea)*, when he was himself a child. This assertion makes no sense if it is a question of Critias the tyrant (460–403 B.C.). Around 450 B.C., when this Critias would have been around ten years old, the poems which Solon wrote at the end of his life (in 560 B.C., for example) would have dated back more than a hundred and ten years. But, even if it is a question of another Critias (III), born around 520 B.C., other difficulties remain. Indeed, around 510 B.C. Solon's poems would have dated back at least fifty years. In this case the unlikeliness is less obvious, but it still exists. In fact, as I. M. Linforth (*Solon the Athenian* [Berkeley: University of California Press, 1919], 11) explains, we

E. Taylor,[16] Francis M. Cornford,[17] and especially Warman Welliver[18] followed Burnet in postulating the existence of a Critias III between Critias II and Critias IV. But things are not that simple. It was with good cause that Thomas G. Rosenmeyer[19] wrote an article in 1949 in opposition to John Burnet. Rosenmeyer returns to the traditional opinion according to which the Critias who appears at the beginning of the *Timaeus* and in the

---

must understand *Timaeus* 21b5–6 in the following way: "The explanation is to be found in the fact that these poems would have been thought of as modern in contrast with Homer and Hesiod. Plato may also have been led to speak as he does by the fact that in his own day Solon's poems were no longer recited on such occasions, having become old-fashioned in the midst of the Athenian poetry of the fifth century." (2) In *Timaeus* 26 b5–6, Critias the Younger declares: "These things which I heard very long ago . . ." *(tauta de ha pampolun khronon diakēkoa)."* The context of this phrase implies that Critias the Younger is a very old man when he relates the account of Critias the Elder to Socrates and Hermocrates. But since this is not explicitly stated, we must abstain from hasty conclusions on this point, as on the preceding one.

16. Alfred E, Taylor, *A Commentary on Plato's "Timaeus"* (Oxford: Clarendon Press, 1928).

17. Francis M. Cornford, *Plato's Cosmology* (London: Routledge & Kegan Paul, 1937).

18. Warman Welliver (cf. n. 9) devoted himself to seeking for historical references to assure the validity of this assumption. He found two of them. (1) A scholium to verse 128 of Aeschylus' *Prometheus Vinctus* relates that Anacreon (572?–488?) came to Athens, "because he fell in love with Critias" *(erōn Kritiou),* and that he was enchanted by the works of Aeschylus (525–456). (2) An ostracon, found in the agora of Athens in 1936 and published in 1949 by Eugène van der Pool ("Some ostraca from the Athenian Agora," *Commemorative Studies in the Honor of Theodore Leslie Shear,* Hesperia supplement VIII, American School of Classical Studies at Athens, 399, n. 12, fig. 5 and plate 58), indicates that a certain "Critias, son of Leaides" *(Kritias Leaido [u])* was to stand for ostracism around 480 B.C. Warman Welliver therefore assumes that these two testimonies refer to the same person, a Critias III, whose grandfather would have been Critias II and whose great-grandfather would have been Dropides II. This Critias II, in turn, would have been grandfather of Critias IV.

19. Thomas G. Rosenmeyer, "The Family of Critias," *American Journal of Philology* 70 (1949): 404–10. Rosenmeyer's arguments are essentially negative, since they oppose those of Burnet point by point. In this regard, they are somewhat disappointing. The following points are, however, worth noting: We know nothing about this Critias III, who must have been born around 520 B.C. Yet what Socrates says about Critias IV in the *Charmides* (162e1–2)—"But you [Critias], who are older, and have studied *(kai hēlikias kai epimeleias),* may well be assumed to know the meaning [of the definition of temperance]"—corresponds to the Socrates' portrait of him in the *Timaeus* (20a6–7): "And here is Critias, whom every Athenian knows to be no novice *(idiōtēn)* in the matters of which we are speaking [philosophy and politics]." Now the meeting between Socrates and Charmides is situated during the siege of Potidaea, which lasted from 432 to 429. It would, therefore, be nearly contemporary with the one related in the *Timaeus* and the *Critias,* which, as we just saw, is situated between 430 and 425. In both cases, it appears to be Critias the tyrant, whose writings have been classed among those of the Sophists (DK 88); and who would be around thirty, that is, nearly the same age as Hermocrates who plays a considerable role on the Syracusan side during the Peloponnesian war. For a complete study of this Critias, see Dorothy Stephans, "Critias: Life and Literary Remains," Ph.D. diss., University of Cincinnati, 1939 (I was not able to consult this work). In addition, Critias and Hermocrates shared a similar hostility towards democracy. At the fall of Athens in 404, Critias assumed the head of an oligarchic coup d'Etat, known as the Thirty Tyrants; less than a year later, the democratic institutions were reestablished and Critias was forced into exile. Xenophon, for his part, informs us that during his exile from Athens, Critias organized the democracy in Thessalia and armed the poor against their masters (*Hell.* 2.3.36). For a general presentation of Critias the Tyrant, see Luc Brisson, "Critias," *Dictionnaire des philosophes antiques,* ed. Richard Goulet (Paris: CNRS, 1994), 2:512–20.

Critias is the tyrant Critias IV. But what position should be taken? From a dramatic point of view, there is a lot to gain in identifying Critias the Younger with the tyrant, Critias IV; however, this identification poses unsolvable chronological problems. Only the assumption of a Critias III can reasonably account for a true continuity in the oral transmission of the account of the war between Athens and Atlantis. This ambiguity has been confronted in several ways. There has been an attempt to eliminate it with the assumption of a Critias III. It has been considered to be the result of ignorance on Plato's part, who wrote the *Timaeus* and the *Critias* nearly eighty years (between 358 and 356) after the meeting in question (between 430 and 425). And finally, there has been an attempt to show that the ambiguity is intentional. Plato inserted this ambiguity for two reasons: on the one hand, in order to push the date of his story back close to the time of his famous ancestor Solon, who "by the mid-fourth century had become the hero of the moderate partisans of the *patrios politeia*."[20] On the other hand, Plato sought to give his story an immediate relevance which could only be conferred upon it by Critias the tyrant, who took part in the Peloponnesian war and revived the civil war at Athens. The war between Athens and Atlantis is thus a paradigm of these wars.[21]

If we assume the existence of a Critias III, *Timaeus* 21a8–b1 must be interpreted as follows: "Indeed, at that time, Critias was, as he said, nearly ninety years of age, and I was about ten." Since the birth of Critias II must be placed near 600, whereas that of Critias III dates around 520, the event is situated about 510 Further, it is on the day of Coureotis, during the Apatouria, that the old man tells his story to the child.[22] The Apatouria were Athenian and Ionian festivals, which were celebrated during the month of Pyanepsion (October) and which lasted three days. On the third day, called Coureotis, young boys (three or four years old), whose hair was cut for the first time, were admitted into the phratries.[23] At Athens, the four tribes were each divided into three *trittyes*, which were also called phratries. Therefore, it is in October of 510 that Critias II would have related to Critias III the account of the war between Athens and Atlantis.

Consequently, the following may be said about the fourth stage of the oral transmission of this account. The date of the event corresponds to the date of the meeting related in the *Timaeus* and the *Critias* between Socra-

---

20. Pierre Vidal-Naquet, "Athènes et l'Atlantide," *Revue des études grecques* 77 (1964): 433; *Le Chasseur noir* (Paris: Maspero, 1981), 348.

21. Vidal-Naquet, "Athènes et l'Atlantide."

22. *Tim.* 21b1–2.

23. *Phratria* is mentioned at *Tim.* 21b7.

tes, Timaeus, Hermocrates, and Critias III or IV. Leaving aside the problem of the relation between this meeting and the one described in the *Republic,* the action must have occurred during the Panathenaia.[24] The Panathenaia, Athenian festivals in the honor of Athena, were celebrated on the 28th of Hecatombaeon (the Athenian lunar month, which began with the new moon after the summer solstice, on June 20–21), that is, in mid-July. Although it is important to distinguish between the Great Panathenaia, celebrated every four years, and the Little Panathenaia, celebrated every other year, it is impossible to know which one is referred to in the present case. We must now determine the year in which the meeting reported in the *Timaeus* and the *Critias* supposedly occurred. In all likelihood, the date is between 430 and 425. Critias III would then have been ninety or ninety-five years old, Critias IV thirty or thirty-five years old, and Socrates (470–399), forty to forty-five years old.

The important point about this date resides in the fact that it makes plausible the presence at Athens of Hermocrates, the Syracusan general of this name (died in 407). Thucydides (6.72) describes Hermocrates as a man of exceptional intelligence, remarkable courage, and extensive military experience. During the Gela congress of 424, Hermocrates (*Thcd.* 4.58) intervened to advise the cities of Sicily to reach a peace settlement and to face the danger of Athenian aggression. At this time, Hermocrates was already an important statesman, which corresponds with what Socrates says in *Timaeus* 20a7–b1: "And as to Hermocrates, I am assured by many witnesses that his genius and education qualify him to take part in any speculation of the kind." The speculation in question has to do with politics and philosophy.

Finally, it seems clear that the *Timaeus* and the *Critias* belong to Plato's last period,[25] and that they were written ten or twelve years before his death, that is, between 358 and 356. This story, then, which was obtained from an Egyptian priest and then fell into almost complete oblivion in ancient Greece, claimed to refer to events which predated it by 9,000 years. Its transmission extended over 270 years, in the course of which seven generations succeeded one another.

Now, it must be recalled that this testimony belongs to the genre of

---

24. *Tim.* 26e3, cf. 21a2.

25. Christopher Gill, "Plato and Politics: The *Critias* and the *Politicus,*" *Phronesis* 24 (1979): 148–67, is opposed to G. E. L. Owen, "The Place of the *Timaeus* in Plato's Dialogues," in R. E. Allen, ed., *Studies in Plato's Metaphysics* (London: Routledge & Kegan Paul/ New York: Humanities Press, [1953] 1965), 313–38; reprinted in Martha Nussbaum, ed., *Logic, Science and Dialectic: Collected Papers in Greek Philosophy* (Ithaca: Cornell University Press, 1986), 64–84. For a synthesis, see Luc Brisson's introduction to the *Timaeus* in Platon, *Timée/Critias* (Paris: Flammarion, 1992), 72–75.

the pastiche. Nevertheless, since it is based on a complex and meticulous analysis of the process of transmission over a long period of time, with or without the intervention of writing, it gives us a valuable and plausible description of the survival of a story which relates memorable (pseudo-) events. This example of the events of the Atlantis story raises two questions: What can we say about oral transmission as such? And what is the relation between orality and writing both in this precise case, and, more generally, in Plato?

Oral transmission can be defined most simply as a transmission from mouth to ear. This simplistic definition finds its exact counterpart in the terms: *phēmē*[26] and *akoē*,[27] which derive from the verbs *phēmi,* "to say," in the sense of "to manifest by speech," and *akouō,* "to hear." The meaning of these two words appears more precisely when we consider the totality of their occurrences in Plato's work. *Phēmē* is a "speech"-noun loaded with religious and political values. Two uses of this word can be distinguished in Plato: one, which expresses a religious value, and another, which expresses a secular value of a collective nature. When it expresses a religious value, *phēmē* signifies a "divine revelation," as in *Laws* I 624b2, II 664d4, V 738c6, VII 792d3; *Phdo.* 111b7; *Tim.* 72b3. In all these cases, the subject is the manifestation of the divine through speech, in the context of divination. When it expresses a secular value, *phēmē* essentially designates a collective "speech." A new distinction must, however, be introduced in this context; for this collective "speech" can be either that of the short term or that of the long term.

When it refers to the short term, this collective "speech" corresponds to the "reputation" of someone, or more simply, to the "rumors" which circulate about him. This is the meaning of six occurrences of *phēmē* in Plato.[28] But this collective "speech" is most pertinent when it refers to the long term. *Phēmē* in the long term designates what today we call "tradition," whether this tradition refers to a religious sphere—gods, daimons, heros, and even the world of Hades—or to a secular sphere—institutions, heroic military deeds, etc. From this perspective, *phēmē* designates collective speech which is destined to be preserved. This is the meaning of twenty-one of the occurrences of *phēmē* in Plato's work.[29] *Phēmē* remains a "speech"-noun, even when the speech is recorded by writing, as in the fol-

---

26. *Tim.* 27b4.
27. *Tim.* 21a6, 22b8, 23a2, 23d1, 25e1.
28. *Ap.* 18c1, 20c7; *Laws* IX 878a5, XI 932a6, XI 935a1; *Pol.* 309e8.
29. *Crat.* 395e5; *Laws* II 672b3, IV 704b1, 713c2, VI 771c7, VII 822c4, VIII 838c8, 838d6, IX 870a7, IX 871b4, 878a5, X 906c1, 908a7, XI 916d7, 927a5, XII 952b7, 966c5; *Phlb.* 16c8; *Rep.* III 415d6, V 463d6; *Tim.* 27b4.

lowing expression in the *Timaeus:* "the tradition of sacred writings" *(hē tōn hierōn grammatōn phēmē).*[30] This expression refers to the account of the war between primeval Athens and Atlantis, which was kept in writing in a temple in Egypt for 8,000 years.

In sum, the "speech" designated by *phēmē* is either divine or collective. In the first case, *phēmē* is equivalent to "revelation," and in the second, to "tradition." This collective "speech" can deteriorate in the short run and become equivalent to a "reputation," that is, to "rumors" which circulate about someone. This, then, is the true meaning of the message transmitted by the kind of story which we call "myth." It is a *phēmē,* which is both a divine and a collective speech. In the end, however, every divine word becomes an integral part of the collective word, which, to a large extent, deals with the sphere of religion. This is the case, for example, in nine[31] of the twenty-one occurrences enumerated above.[32] This is not surprising, since divine and human speech in the past tended to be confused because of the extreme proximity of gods and men. This is, moreover, the sense in which the following passage in the *Philebus* must be understood: "The men of old, who were better than ourselves and dwelt nearer the gods, passed on to us this tradition" *(tautēn phēmēn).*[33] Here is another example, from *Phaedrus* 273c1–3:

> SOCRATES I can tell you the tradition I have heard from our forefathers *(akoēn tōn proterōn),* but they alone know the truth of it. However, if we could discover that for ourselves, should we still be concerned with the fancies of mankind?

Thus is explained the valorization that sets the past apart and that makes it the paradigm of the present and future, the object of the collective "speech" we call tradition.

But "word" entails "listen," since communication is only possible if these two poles are in contact. This "act of listening" is designated by the word *akoē,* which also has several meanings. In the majority of cases in Plato, the word *akoē* simply signifies "hearing" as opposed to "seeing."[34] Sometimes, however, this hearing is much more specific. In this case it is a

---

30. *Tim.* 27b4.

31. *Crat.* 395e5; *Laws* II 672b3, IV 704b1, VI 771c7, VII 822c4, VIII 838c8, 838d6, X 906c1, XI 927a5.

32. See n. 29.

33. *Phlb.* 16c7–8.

34. *Charm.* 167d4, d5, 168d3, d4, e9; *Crat.* 431a2; *Lach.* 190a7, b1; *Laws* XII 961d8; *Phdo.* 65c6, 98d7, 111b3; *Phdr.* 227c3, 228b7, 235d1, 243d5; *Rep.* I 342a3, V 477c3, VI 507c3, c10; *Tht.* 142b4, 156c1, 185a2, b8, c2, 201c1, 206a6; *Tim.* 33c3, 64c6, 67b5.

"heeding" whose object is revelation or tradition, as we can see in the *Meno*[35] and the *Laws*.[36] This hearing or heeding of revelation or tradition occurs within a precise sphere: that of the Muses[37] and, in a more restricted way, of poetry.[38] This last case is extremely interesting, as it is found in the context of a definition of poetry:

> SOCRATES Does that [the mimetic art] hold only for vision, or does it apply also to hearing *(kata tēn akoēn)* and to what we call *poiēsin* [in the twofold sense of "making" and "poetry"]?
>
> GLAUCON Presumably to that also.[39]

Since myth, as the content of poetry, constitutes the element of discourse within the sphere of music, it is natural that the word *akoē* should designate that "hearing" of a story in which the myth consists.[40]

Six of these nine occurrences noted above refer to the war between Athens and Atlantis—that is, to the process of oral transmission just described. The meanings of *akoē* thus correspond point for point to those of *phēmē*. There is nothing surprising about this, if we first place ourselves in the perspective of oral transmission where the emission of a message is inseparable from its reception.

From this perspective, a message experiences a certain number of transformations each time it is transmitted, essentially due to the fact that there is no written reference point, which might allow orality to be checked. Each oral version covers and erases the preceding one.[41] When this occurs, two disruptive elements enter into the picture: pressures exerted by the public on the transmitter[42]—since production, emission and reception are indissociable—and all kinds of handicaps which can affect the transmitter—notably, ignorance.

Plato gives at least two examples of messages relating very distant events which have experienced a serious deterioration as a result of a long oral transmission devoid of research, poetry, and writing.

The first, of course, concerns the message or communication about

---

35. *Men.* 94c6.

36. *Laws* VII 798b2, VIII 839e5, X 900a2.

37. *Tim.* 47c4, d1.

38. *Rep.* III 401c8, X 603b7.

39. *Rep.* X 603b6–8.

40. *Crit.* 109e2; *Phdo.* 61d9; *Phdr.* 274d1; *Tim.* 20d1, 21a6, 22b8, 23a2, d1, 25e1.

41. Claude Lévi-Strauss gives a good example of this in a text first published in 1975, then reprinted under the title "Au-delà du Swaihwé," *La Voie des masques*, 2d ed. (Paris: Plon, 1979), 153–63. See also Jack Goody, *The Myth of the Bagre* (Oxford: Clarendon Press, 1972).

42. Jesper Svenbro, *La Parole et le Marbre* (Lund, 1976), 16–35.

the war between Athens and Atlantis. In Greece in general and at Athens in particular, this orally transmitted message did not subsist (*ou diarkō*),[43] but disappeared *(aphanizō)*,[44] that is, was forgotten *(lanthanō)*.[45] As for the cause of this oblivion, Plato mentions, on the one hand, the length of time which has passed;[46] and on the other the destruction of the human beings—in this case, the city-dwellers—who could have ensured the proper transmission of the message.[47]

However, the oblivion into which the story of the war between Athens and Atlantis had fallen was not complete. This was only the case for the acts which were accomplished *(erga)*[48] and the action itself *(praxis)*.[49] Indeed, the names *(onomata)*[50] of those who completed these actions[51] were preserved by the mountain-dwellers who willingly handed them down to their children.[52]

Another equally interesting example concerns the message relative to a set of facts connected with the reversal of the direction the sun and stars travel across the sky. Plato begins by referring to the damage caused by the "immensity" of time which has elapsed since these events occurred:

> All these stories originate from the same event in cosmic history, and so do hosts of others yet more marvelous than these. However, as this great event took place so long ago, some of them have faded from man's memory; others survive but they have become scattered and have come to be told in a way which obscures their real connection with one another.[53]

As in the case of the war between Athens and Atlantis, these events have been only partially forgotten. Some have completely "faded," but most have survived. However, the unique cause which explains them all has been forgotten. In this case, what is forgotten is less the events themselves and more the fact that they all derive from a single cause.

However, Plato does not challenge the testimony of this oral transmission, whose limits he recognizes. A little further on we read the following:

> Now it was this 'earthborn race' which at the moment of crisis began to return [following a cycle] to life out of the earth. The memory of this race has lived on, for it was handed down to us by the earliest of our forebears. These early forebears were the children of earthborn parents; they lived in

43. *Tim.* 21d6.
44. *Tim.* 20e6; *Crit.* 109d4.
45. *Tim.* 232c2.
46. *Tim.* 20e5, 21d6, 26a1; *Crit.* 109d4.
47. *Tim.* 20e6, 21d6, 23c3; *Crit* 109d3–4.
48. *Tim.* 20e5, 21a4; *Crit.* 109d3, d8, 110a7.
49. *Tim.* 21d5.
50. *Crit.* 109d3, d7, d8, 110a6.
51. *Tim.* 21d6.
52. *Crit.* 109d8–e1.
53. *Pol.* 269b5–8.

the period directly following the end of the era of the earthborn, at the close of the former period of cosmic rotation and the beginning of the present one. These ancestors of ours passed on to us these stories of the earthborn, and it is an unsound judgment to disbelieve them as so many do nowadays.[54]

To be sure, an oral transmission which is so rudimentary—i.e. which develops without poetry as a technique of communication, implies a serious degradation of the message to be transmitted. However, the continuity of the generations between those who have witnessed these events and those who now relate them gives some credibility to the bits of memory that were thus preserved.

We cannot expect more from rustic transmission. Only urban life can improve quantitatively and qualitatively the transmission of messages about a very distant past.

With the appearance of the city, the past, which the collective memory preserves, becomes the subject of research.[55] Such activity is impossible for mountain people, who are too busy procuring the necessities of life. Instead, it is carried out by city-dwellers, who enjoy the leisure brought about by the satisfaction of their elementary needs. They are thus able to retrace the deeds accomplished by men of the past, whereas all the mountain people know about them is their names.

But, once this past is completely restored, it must be transmitted with minimum degradation. Two solutions are possible. This past is either recorded in writing, or else it is the object of oral transmission—not in a rudimentary way, as was the case with the mountain people—but only after it has been worked on by a poet.

This last remark is based on observations taken from the *Timaeus* and the *Critias*. The mountain-dwellers are there presented as illiterate *(agrammatous)*,[56] that is, ignorant of writing; and unfamiliar with the Muses (ἀμούσους),[57] that is, ignorant of poetry. In addition, it is said that "mythtelling *(muthologia)* and the inquiry into ancient things both visit cities in the train of leisure."[58] Now, it is important to note that in Plato,[59] the term *muthologia*, which is connected at least once with the term *poiēsis*, "poetry," designates not only "myth-telling" but also "myth-making."

But let us leave aside for the moment the intervention of the poet as a "mythmaker" and focus specifically on the way in which writing intervenes

---

54. *Pol.* 271a5–b3.
55. *Anazētēsis tōn palaiōn. Crit.* 110a3–4.
56. *Tim.* 23a8; cf. *Crit.* 109d6.

57. *Tim.* 23b1.
58. *Crit.* 110a3–4.
59. See appendix 2.

in the transmission of the memorable, using the example of the story told to Solon by the priest of Saïs. This story—which is based on the written version of the facts—is presented as true discourse in contrast to the oral version of the same facts, which is likened to a myth. There are three things to note concerning this story: (1) the written version on which it is based is itself dependent upon a thousand-year-old oral tradition; (2) the Egyptian priest refers to this written version, but he does not read it to Solon, since he knows it by heart; (3) finally, the priest's story gives rise to an oral version, transmitted in ancient Greece from Solon to Plato over a period of nearly 270 years.

When writing plays a role in the transmission of the memorable, it always occurs after the fact. It is restricted to recording, with physical signs on a material medium, the latest version of the tradition on the subject. It is in this sense that the expression *hē tōn hierōn grammaton phēmē,* "the tradition of the sacred writings," must be understood; that is, if it is paraphrased as "the tradition recorded by writing in a Saïs temple." This is the case because writing is only a representation of the word.

One thing is surprising in the description of Solon's discussion with a priest of Saïs by Critias the Younger. Although the account of the war between Athens and Atlantis had been recorded in writing, the Egyptian priest is never described in the act of reading. He relates[60] and Solon listens.[61] The reason for this is simply that the priest has not had the time to resort "to the writings themselves" *(auta ta grammata).*[62] The priest, therefore, knows the story he tells to Solon by heart. Thus, even in Egypt, writing appears as only an instrument of recollection. True memory is found in the soul and in the word through which the soul directly expresses itself.

Finally, when Solon returns from Egypt, where he has been informed of the war between Athens and Atlantis, the story he relates is transmitted orally at Athens for nearly 270 years. This is the case even though written notes on the names of the kings of Atlantis both exist and are mentioned by Critias II and Critias III or IV. Of course, it is comprehensible that Solon did not find the time on his return from Egypt to compose poems on the subject—poems which certainly would have been put into writing. It is, however, surprising that following this, nobody at Athens made the effort to fix this story, in a time and place where writing was playing an increasingly important role.

In the specific case of the war waged by primeval Athens against Atlan-

---

60. *Tim.* 21d7–8, 23d1–4.
61. *Tim.* 21d7–8, 23d1–4.
62. *Tim.* 24a1.

tis, writing plays the following role. It allows for the constitution of a reference-version, by contact with which a particularly defective oral tradition is regenerated and the regularized. This makes possible the control—in the etymological sense of the word (*contre-rôle:* to check accounts by comparison with a duplicate register)—of an oral tradition; however, it never replaces it.

Everything said so far is consistent with Plato's position on writing. As we shall see, for Plato, writing is a part of the wider sphere of imitation, because it is only a copy.[63] It is a copy of the word of the soul which is silent in the case of thought and vocal when the voice is used as a medium. In this case, as in all others, imitation tends to transgress its limits by presenting its copy as a complete reality. Thus Plato often goes to great lengths not to discredit writing completely—which would be a paradoxical attitude on the part of someone who makes such an important and remarkable use of it—but to remind us of its ambiguity.

This is the purpose of the myth related by Socrates in the *Phaedrus* on the invention of writing by Theuth. By means of this myth, Socrates gives a precise definition of the usefulness of writing, the special relationship of which to Egypt is once again emphasized:

> SOCRATES I can tell you the tradition that has come down from our forefathers; but they alone know the truth of it. However, if we could discover that for ourselves, should we still be concerned with the fancies of mankind?
>
> PHAEDRUS What a ridiculous question! But tell me the tradition you speak of.
>
> SOCRATES Very well. The story is that in the region of Naucratis in Egypt there dwelt one of the old gods of the country, the god to whom the bird called Ibis is sacred, his own name being Theuth. He it was that invented number and calculation, geometry and astronomy, not to speak of draughts and dice, and above all writing. Now the king of the whole country at that time was Thamus, who dwelt in the great city of Upper Egypt which the Greeks call Egyptian Thebes, while Thamus they call Ammon. To him came Theuth, and revealed his arts, saying that they ought to be passed on to the Egyptians in general. Thamus asked what was the use of them all, and when Theuth explained, he condemned what he thought the bad points and praised what he thought the good. On each art, we are told, Thamus had plenty of views both for and against; it would take too long to give them in detail. But, when it came to writing, Theuth said, "Here, O king, is a branch of learning that will

63. See chapter 6.

make the people of Egypt wiser and improve their memories; my discovery provides a recipe for memory and wisdom." But the king answered and said, "O man full of arts, to one it is given to create the things of art, and to another to judge what measure of harm and of profit they have for those that shall employ them. And, so it is that you, by reason of your tender regard for the writing that is your offspring, have declared the very opposite of its true effect. If men learn this technique, it will implant forgetfulness in their souls; they will cease to exercise memory because they rely on that which is written, calling things to remembrance no longer from within themselves, but by means of external marks. What you have discovered is a recipe not for memory, but for reminder. And, it is no true wisdom that you offer your disciples, but only its semblance, for by telling them of many things without teaching them you will make them seem to know much, while for the most part they know nothing, and as men filled, not with wisdom but with conceit of wisdom, they will be a burden to their fellows."[64]

So ends the myth. Socrates is then forced to defend its plausibility against Phaedrus' irony.

Having done so, Socrates then comments on this myth and insists upon two major points: first, writing cannot be substituted for memory because writing is limited to activating memory and reassuring it runs smoothly; second, writing is only an image of knowledge and must not therefore be considered as knowledge itself. In other words, by presenting to the soul the image of knowledge, writing allows the soul to rediscover this knowledge within itself. Such a position is based in particular on the fact that, in ancient Greek, *graphein* signifies at the same time "to write," "to draw," and "to paint."

Moreover, this ambivalent feeling with respect to writing—of which Plato is the spokesperson—reflects a precise historical situation in ancient Greece. The oral civilization of which the Homeric epic constitutes the model was not submerged by some civilization of writing, which was introduced in the eighth century B.C. In fact, an important part of Greek culture remained oral up until—and even beyond—the end of the fifth century.[65]

Plato's testimony on myth is thus balanced on a razor's edge. At the

64. *Phdr.* 274c1–275b2.

65. As E. A. Havelock tries to show in his *Preface to Plato* (Oxford: Clarendon Press; Cambridge Mass.: Harvard University Press, Belknap Press, 1963). For an assessment, see Alfred Burns, "Athenian Literacy in the Fifth Century B.C.," *Journal of the History of Ideas* 42 (1981): 371–87. On the history of literacy in ancient Greece, see the bibliography by Giorgio Camassa and Stella Georgoudi, "Traces bibliographiques," in Marcel Detienne, ed., *Les savoirs de l'écriture en Grèce ancienne,* Cahiers de Philologie 14 (Lille: Presses Universitaires de Lille, 1988), 525–38. On the history of reading, see Jesper Svenbro, *Phrasikleia: Anthropologie de la lecture en Grèce ancienne* (Paris: La Découverte, 1988).

turning point between two civilizations, one founded on orality and the other on writing, Plato in fact describes the twilight of myths. In other words, Plato describes that moment when, in ancient Greece in general and at Athens in particular, memory changes; if not in its nature, then at least in its means of functioning. A memory shared by all the members of a community is now opposed by a memory which is the privilege of a more limited number of people: those for whom the use of writing is a matter of everyday habit. A memory condemned to transforming what it repeats is challenged by a mnemonic activity which consists in storing and faithfully reproducing a specific passage. A memory for which all repetition is equal to a re-creation is confronted with a memory for which the past—objectified by writing—constitutes a given fact.[66]

A clear distinction of the past from the present was made possible by such an objectification, and, beginning in the sixth century, this favored "philosophical and historical" investigations. As a backlash, these investigations initiated a general skepticism concerning the past and the worldview which it conveyed. It is in reaction to this skepticism, largely responsible for the crisis which shook the Athens of his time, that Plato integrates into his own discourse a discourse which he condemns as unfalsifiable and nonargumentative.[67]

These few remarks were intended to "contextualize" the testimony of Plato—the first Greek philosopher whose entire written production has come down to us—about an oral civilization whose downfall he, by describing and criticizing it, contributed to ensure. But this is an excellent occasion to remember Hegel's famous words: "It is only at the beginning of the twilight that the owl of Minerva takes flight."[68]

66. Jack Goody, "Mémoire et apprentissage dans les sociétés avec et sans écriture: la transmission du Bagre," *L'Homme,* 1977, no. 1, 29–52.

67. Jack Goody and Ian Watt, "The Consequences of Literacy," in Jack Goody, ed., *Literacy in Traditional Societies* (Cambridge: Cambridge University Press, 1968), 27–60.

68. ". . . die Eule der Minerva beginnt erst mit der einbrechenden Dämmerung ihren Flug." *Hegels sämtliche Werke,* hrsg. von Georg Lassen, Band 6: *Grundlinien der Philosophie des Rechts* ([1911] Leipzig: Meiner, 1921), 2:17.

THREE

FABRICATION

Insofar as a message is the object solely of oral transmission, its fabrication is as indissociable from its emission as its emission is from its reception. When writing intervenes, however, the fabrication, emission, and reception of the same message can be clearly distinguished. Plato's terminology relative to myth maintains the trace of the passage from orality to literacy, which occurred in Greece between the eighth and sixth centuries B.C.

Plato likens the work of the poet in the literary realm to that of the demiurge in the cosmic realm. This explains why the poet is characterized as "father" *(patēr)*[1] and especially as "maker" *(poiētēs)*[2] of myths, following the example of the demiurge who, in the *Timaeus,* is presented as "the father and maker of this whole" *(ton poiētēn kai patera toude tou pantos),*[3] that is, the world. Further, Homer,[4] Hesiod,[5] and Aesop[6] are specifically presented as mythmakers in Plato. Finally, it is worth noting that in the *Phaedo,* the "mythmaker" *(poiētēs)* is contrasted with the "philosopher" *(philosophos),*[7] and in the *Republic,* with the "founder of the city" *(oikistēs).*[8]

The parallel between the creator of the universe and the creator of myths extends to the verbs which designate their action. The action of the maker of the world is described with the help of the verbs *plattō,*[9] *poieō,*[10]

---

1. *Tht.* 164e2.
2. *Phdo.* 61b3, 4; *Rep.* II 379a1.
3. *Tim.* 28c3–4.
4. *Rep.* II 377d4.
5. *Rep.* II 377d4.
6. *Phdo.* 60c1, 61b6.
7. *Phdo.* 60b–61c.
8. *Rep.* II 378e7–379a4.
9. *Tim.* 42d6, 73c8, 74a2, 78c3.
10. *Tim.* 31b2, b8, c3, 34b3, 35b1, 36c4, 37d5, d6, 38c7, 45b7, 71d7, 76c6, 91a4.

and *suntithēmi*.[11] It is also the verbs *plattō*,[12] *poieō*,[13] and *suntithēmi*[14] which describe the action of the mythmaker. The use of the verb *plattō* to designate the action of "making" a myth goes back at least to Xenophanes, who characterizes the battles of the titans, giants, and centaurs as "moldings of the ancients" *(plasmata tōn proterōn)*.[15] When the verb *plattō*[16] designates the action of "fabricating" a myth, it is used in a derivative sense. In its primary sense, *plattō* designates the act of fashioning, modeling, or giving a form to malleable materials such as gold, wax, clay, etc. In order to preserve this meaning as it is transposed into the level of discourse, *plattō* must be translated as "to form."

Sun-tithēmi, for its part, is a verbal compound which is easy to analyze. It is the result of joining the verb *tithēmi,* "to place," with the verbal prefix *sun-,* "together." In its primary sense, this compound refers to the action of assembling something out of its component parts. When transferred to the level of discourse, this verb means "to compose."

The most important verb in this series is *poieō*.[17] In general, this lexeme means "to make" or "to do." In this respect, it is akin to *prattō* and to *draō*. However, whereas *prattō* implies effort toward an accomplishment and presents a subjective orientation, *draō*, which is close to *prattō*, expresses the idea of acting. In Homer, *draō* has the more specific meaning of "doing someone a favor," while in Attic Greek it connotes a responsibility one undertakes rather than an action which is accomplished. *Draō* is also used for the performance of rituals. Thus, *poieō* is distinguished from *prattō* and *draō* because of its implicit objective orientation. Indeed, the primary meaning of *poieō* is that of a "physical making" which takes into consideration neither the subjective element of the action nor the responsibility connected to it.

We now come to the most important element of this semantic analy-

11. *Tim.* 30d2, 69d6, 72c5.

12. *Rep.* II 377b6; *Tim.* 26e4.

13. *Phdo.* 61b4; *Rep.* II 377c1, 379a3–4.

14. *Phdo.* 60c2; *Rep.* II 377d6.

15. DK 21B1.22.

16. My source of information with respect to the etymology and morphology found in this chapter is Pierre Chantraine, *Dictionnaire étymologique de la langue grecque* (Paris: Klincksieck, 1968–80); *La Formation des noms en grec ancien* (Paris: Champion, 1933). On the vocabulary relative to the "fabrication" of speech and the universe, see Luc Brisson, "Le discours comme univers et l'univers comme discours: Platon et ses interprètes néoplatoniciens," *Le texte et ses représentations,* Études de littérature ancienne 3 (Paris: Presses de l'Ecole Normale Supérieure, 1987), 121–28.

17. On this verb and its derivatives, see Paul Vicaire, *Recherches sur les mots désignant la poésie et le poète dans l'oeuvre de Platon* (Paris: PUF, 1964).

sis. The verb *poieō* maintains its objective orientation with respect to the sensible even when it is used in a cosmological or literary context.[18]

The action of the demiurge is very limited in the cosmological realm. It must take the intelligible forms as its model and make do with the medium of space. Thus, it can only exert itself "as far as possible."[19]

The same restrictions are found in the literary sphere. For Plato, as we shall see, the function of the poet is to take an element of that which is orally transmitted in a particular community, reorganize its content, and give it a particular form.

The action undertaken in the case of the demiurge is similar to that of the poet. It is therefore natural that the maker of the world and the maker of myths should be designated by the substantive *poiētēs,* the nominal derivative of *poieō,* with the suffix *-tēs* indicating the agent. This substantive, which designates the "maker" in general,[20] can also designate any kind of particular maker, in a primary or derivative sense. *Poiētēs* can be used of the maker of diverse implements;[21] or of god, the "maker" of the "real" bed;[22] whereas the artist is the maker only of an image of this bed;[23] or the imitator, the maker of images (whose action will be described in chapter 6 on imitation);[24] or even Socrates who is accused of being a "maker" of divinities.[25] The polysemy of *poiētēs* thus covers that of *poieō,* which is only natural, since the former is a derivative of the latter. Although the word *poiētēs* is most often employed by Plato in the proper sense of "poet," this is only one of the numerous meanings of *poiētēs*—all of which are, moreover, connected to the general meaning of "maker."

The same holds true for the substantive *poiēsis,* another nominal derivative from *poieō,* with the suffix *-sis* indicating the action. This term, like *poiētēs,* manifests a polysemy which covers that of *poieō.* The substantive *poiēsis* thus designates either "fabrication" in general[26] or else "fabrication" in a particular area. In the latter case, there is fabrication in the literary

18. Bruno Snell, "Das Bewusstsein von eigenen Entscheidungen im frühen Griechentum," *Philologus* 39 (1930): 141–58.

19. Luc Brisson, *Le Même et l'Autre dans la structure ontologique du "Timée" de Platon* (1974; new ed. with corrections, Sankt Augustin: Academia Verlag, 1994), ch. 1, esp. 31, 35–50.

20. *Rep.* X 596d4.

21. *Rep.* X 601d9, e7.

22. *Rep.* X 597d2.

23. *Rep.* X 597d11.

24. *Rep.* X 601b9.

25. *Euthph.* 3b2.

26. *Charm.* 163b9, c4, d3, e1; *Rep.* 603b7; *Soph.* 234a1, 265b1, 266c5, 268d1; *Symp.* 196e5.

realm,[27] and still more particularly, the fabrication of melodies[28] and trage-dies.[29] In the *Statesman*,[30] there is even an allusion to the fabrication of clothing. In this area, as in many others, Plato himself offers a theoretical analysis of the semantic facts which were just mentioned:

> DIOTIMA You'll agree that there is more than one kind of "fabrication" *(poiēsis)* in the true sense of the word—that is to say, calling something into existence that was not there before is "fabrication" *(poiēsis)*, so that the practices *(ergasiai)* connected with the arts are "fabrications" *(poiēseis)* and all "craftsmen" *(dēmiourgoi)* in these are "producers" *(poiētai)*.
>
> SOCRATES True.
>
> DIOTIMA But all the same, as she said, we don't call them all "poets" *(poiē-tai)*, but they have other names. But, from fabrication *(poiēseōs)* in its totality, only a small part has been separated, the part that deals with music and meter and it is this part that is called the name of the whole. And, that is the only art that we call "poetry" *(poiēsis)*, while those who practice this part of "fabrication" *(poiēseōs)* are known as "poets" *(poiētai)*.
>
> SOCRATES Quite.[31]

This passage from the *Symposium* clearly explains how the term *poiēsis*, which designates the action of producing in general, comes to designate the particular fabrication of discourse in the realm of music.

We must still specify in what this particular type of discourse consists. Socrates provides the expected clarification in the *Gorgias:*

> SOCRATES Well now, if you should strip from all "poetry" its melody *(melos)*, rhythm *(rhuthmon)*, and meter *(metron)*, the residue would be nothing else but speeches *(logoi)?*
>
> CALLICLES That must be so.[32]

It is not necessary to clarify the meaning of the terms *melos, rhuthmos,* and *metron* to understand what Socrates means. Poetry implies a discourse—in verse in most cases—which is recited or sung, is accompanied by music, and which sometimes includes elements of the dance.

But let us for a moment leave aside song, musical accompaniment, and dance, which belong to the realm of interpretation, and restrict our-selves, within the domain of fabrication, to discourse considered from the point of view of its form and its content. The most clarifying passage in

27. *Mnx.* 239c6; *Phdr.* 267c2; *Laws* II 656c4.

28. *Gorg.* 449d4.

29. *Phdr.* 268d1.

30. *Pol.* 282a7.

31. *Symp.* 205b8–c10.

32. *Gorg.* 502c5–7.

this respect is surely the following from the *Phaedo,* which is worth quoting in full:

PHAEDO   Socrates sat up on the bed and drew up his leg and massaged it, saying as he did so, what a queer thing it is, my friends, this sensation which is popularly called pleasure! It is remarkable how closely it is connected with its conventional opposite, pain. They will never come to mean both at once, but if you pursue one of them and catch it, you are nearly always compelled to have the other as well; they are like two bodies attached to the same head. I am sure that if Aesop had thought of it he would have made up a myth *(muthos an suntheinai),* something like this—God wanted to stop their continual quarrelling, and when he found that it was impossible, he fastened their heads together; so whenever one of them appears, the other is sure to follow after. That is exactly what seems to be happening to me. I had a pain in my leg from the fetter, and now I feel the pleasure coming that follows it.

Here Cebes broke in and said, Oh yes, Socrates, I am glad you reminded me. Evenus asked me a day or two ago, as others have done before, about the poems which you have been composing *(tōn poiēmatōn hōn pepoiēkas)* lately by adapting Aesop's stories *(tous tou Aisōpou logous)* and 'The Prelude' to Apollo to verse *(enteinas).* He wanted to know what induced you to produce these poems *(epoiēsas auta)* now after you had gone to prison, when you had never done *(poiēsas)* anything of the kind before. If you would like me to be able to answer Evenus when he asks me again—as I am sure he will—tell me what I am to say.

Tell him the truth, said Socrates, that I did not produce these poems *(epoiēsas tauta)* to rival either him or his poems *(tois poiēmasin)*—which I knew would not be easy. I did it in the attempt to discover the meaning of certain dreams, and to clear my conscience, in case this was the art which I had been told to practice. It is like this, you see. In the course of my life I have often had the same dream, appearing in different forms at different times, but always saying the same thing: make this music *(mousikēn poiei kai ergazou).* In the past, I used to think that it was impelling and exhorting me to do what I was actually doing; I mean that the dream, like a spectator encouraging a runner in a race, was urging me on to do what I was doing always, that is, producing music *(mousikēn poiein),* because philosophy is the greatest music, and I was practicing it. But ever since my trial, while the festival of the god has been delaying my execution, I have felt that perhaps it might be this popular form of music that the dream intended me to produce *(tautēn tēn dēmōdē mousikēn poiein),* in which case I ought to produce *(poiein)* it and not disobey. I thought it would be safer not to take my departure before I had cleared my conscience by producing poems *(poiēsanta poiēmata)* and so obeying the dream. I began by producing a poem *(epoiēsa)* in honour of the god whose festival it was. When I finished my hymn, I reflected that a poet, if he is to be worthy of the name, ought to produce myths, not argumentative speeches *(ennoēsas hoti ton poiētēn deoi, eiper melloi poiētēs einai, poiein muthous all'ou logous)*, and I was not good at telling myths *(kai autos ouk ē muthologikos)*. So I availed myself of some of Aesop's myths *(muthous)* which were ready to hand and familiar to me, and I produced into poems *(epoiēsa)* the first of them that suggested themselves.[33]

This passage, which was recently discussed by D. Sabbatucci,[34] conceals a good deal of important information.

First, poetry is presented here as an element of the realm of music which also includes harmony and rhythm. Furthermore, it shows that the process of poetic fabrication has two distinct moments: a fabrication which focuses on the content of a discourse, as in the case of Aesop; and a fabrication which focuses on the form of the same discourse, as in the case of Socrates. Finally, Plato illuminates the connections which exist between music and a certain kind of inspiration.

Let us go back to what is most important in this passage, that is, poetic fabrication. The first process of this action focuses on the content of poetry. This content is necessarily a discourse which Socrates calls "myth" and which he contrasts with the type of discourse that the philosopher must fabricate, that is, an "argumentative discourse" designated here by the word *logos*. The poet makes this "myth," not by creating something from nothing, but by taking up one or more element(s) of a specific tradition—whether or not they have already undergone poetic elaboration—in the manner of a story. This is done to either preserve or to recall the memory of these elements, in accordance with a specific context. According to Critias the Elder, this is how Solon proceeded with the story that the priest of Saïs told him:

> Yes, Amynander, if Solon had only, like other poets, made poetry the business of his life and had completed the story which he brought with him from Egypt, and had not been compelled, by reason of the factions and troubles which he found stirring in his own country when he came home, to attend to other matters, in my opinion he would have been as famous as Homer or Hesiod, or any poet.[35]

33. *Phdo.* 60b1–61b7.

34. Dario Sabbatucci, "Aspetti del rapporto *mythos-logos* nella cultura greca," in Bruno Gentili and Giuseppe Paione, eds., *Il mito greco.* Atti del Convegno internazionale (Urbino 7–12 maggio 1973), Quaderni Urbinati di cultura classica, Centro internazionale di semiotica & linguistica, Istituto di filologia classica (Rome, 1977), 57–62.

35. *Tim.* 21c4–d3.

This practice would not have been fundamentally different from that of poets like Homer and Hesiod. In fact, both the *Odyssey*[36] and the catalogue of Ships in the *Iliad*[37] begin with an invocation to the Muses, daughters of Zeus and Mnemosyne ("Memory"),[38] as does Hesiod's *Theogony.*[39]

The following point should also be noted: when, in the dialogue which bears his name, Critias—following in Solon's footsteps—tells the story of the war waged by primeval Athens against Atlantis, he begins, in poetic fashion, with an invocation to the Muses and to Apollo.[40]

> HERMOCRATES . . . So you must launch out into your narrative like a man, calling Paean and the Muses to aid you in displaying and lauding the worth of your fellow Athenians of ancient days.
>
> CRITIAS . . . Meanwhile I must, at any rate, follow your encouraging advice and invoke the gods at large, including those you have mentioned, but above all Memory. She is the power on whom the whole fortune of my discourse most depends. If I can only sufficiently recall and repeat the story as it was once told by the priests and brought home to this country by Solon, I am confident that my present audience[41] will pronounce me to have discharged my task with reasonable credit.[42]

Critias the Younger appears here "to understand the Muse as a kind of religious representation of social control."[43] We must, however, remember that Plato insists more on the religious dimension of this matter than on the social dimension. By invoking the Muses and especially their mother Mnemosyne at the beginning of his work, the poet indicates what his function is. Like the seer,[44] to whom Plato likens him on many points, the poet "is the one who knows, because he, among men, remembers and witnesses the past."[45] Having short-circuited his rational activity, the poet becomes the interpreter of the divinity which manifests itself through him.[46] In the

---

36. *Od.* 1.1–10.

37. *Il.* 2.484–93.

38. On this subject, see E. A. Havelock, *Preface to Plato* (Oxford: Blackwell, and Cambridge, Mass.: Belknap Press, Harvard University Press, 1963), 97–14; and Marcel Detienne, *Les Maîtres de vérité dans la Grèce archaïque* ([1967] Paris: Maspero, 1973), 9–27.

39. *Theogony* 1–2, 22–23, 36–55.

40. For an explicit link between these divinities, see *The Homeric Hymn to the Muses.*

41. Cf. *Crit.* 108b3–7.

42. *Crit.* 108c2–d7.

43. Jesper Svenbro, *La Parole et le Marbre* (Lund, 1976), 32.

44. Luc Brisson, "Du bon usage du dérèglement," *Divination et Rationalité* (Paris: Seuil, 1974), 220–48.

45. Pierre Vidal-Naquet, Préface à Homère, *Iliade* (Paris: Gallimard, 1975,) 19, and "'Iliade' sans travesti," *La Démocratie vue d'ailleurs: Essai d'historiographie ancienne et moderne* (Paris: Flammarion, 1990), 41.

46. *Ion* 533c–534b.

last analysis, myth may be truly considered as the "divine word." For Plato, however, things are far from being so simple because mimesis, to which the poet has recourse "to fabricate" a myth, is full of ambiguities.[47]

The work of the poet focuses as much on the form as on the content of the myth. In the *Phaedo,* Socrates explains that he put into verse the myths made by Aesop. Since these myths are presented as being those made by Aesop,[48] Socrates also employs the verb *poieō* to designate this action without any risk of confusion. Furthermore, Socrates had already explicitly stated that he had put the myths of Aesop into verse.[49]

The use of the verb *enteinō* to designate this operation is surprising. This verbal compound, made up of the verbal prefix *en-,* "in," and the verb *teinō,* "to stretch," signifies in general "to stretch, to maintain, or to subject to." Consequently, it is completely exceptional that in *Phaedo* 60d1 it signifies "to put into verse," that is, "to subject to a meter." More commonly, it is the expression *en metrōi* which evokes this operation.[50] The word *metron* designates the "measure," that is, in poetry, a group of syllables; by extension, it designates first the nature of the verse as determined by the number and value of the syllables which compose it, and then the verse itself. And to *en metrōi,* "in verse," is quite obviously contrasted *aneu metrou,* "not in verse."

The last mentioned opposition leads to the following one: *poiētēs,* "poet," versus *idiōtēs,* "prose-writer." *Idiōtēs* is formed from the adjective *idios,* "simple," and from the suffix *-tēs,* which indicates the agent. It designates the one who fabricates a simple discourse in contrast to the one who fabricates a discourse subject to a particular form. In the *Phaedrus,* Socrates is absolutely explicit on this point:

> SOCRATES   Then what is the nature of good writing and bad? Is it incumbent on us, Phaedrus, to examine Lysias on this point, and all such as have written or mean to write anything at all, whether in the field of public affairs or private, whether in verse, like a poet, or without verse, like a prose-writer *(en metrōi, hōs poiētēs, ē aneu metrou, hōs idiōtēs)?*[51]

This opposition is also found in *Laws* X 890a4. It is therefore clear that the poet, in contrast to the prose-writer, appears as a specialist, whose activity consists, among others, in giving a particular form to the story which he fabricates, by submitting it to a definite meter.

47. See ch. 6.
48. *Phdo.* 61b5 sq.
49. *Phdo.* 60d1.
50. *Rep.* II 380c1; *Phdr.* 258d10, 267a5, 277e7.
51. *Phdr.* 258d7–11.

The poet completes his work on content through his work on form. As a specialist in the collective communication of what is memorable, he reorganizes an oral tradition in order to fabricate a story which adapts to the context of its enunciation. At the level of the story's form, moreover, the poet can call upon such mnemo-technical procedures as metric, formulary recurrence, etc. This makes its effectiveness even more powerful.

N A R R A T I O N

To describe how a myth is related, we must answer the following three questions: (1) Who relates a myth? (2) What verbs designate this action? (3) How is a myth related?

Those who relate a myth can be either professionals or nonprofessionals. Among the professionals are the mythmakers themselves: the poets,[1] and their subordinates: the rhapsodists,[2] actors, and choral dancers.[3] Although there are no texts in Plato in which these professionals are described in the process of relating a myth, nevertheless, each time they are mentioned we may attribute this activity to them without the slightest doubt.

If we were to believe Ion, who speaks as a rhapsodist, rhapsodists are only the interpreters of the interpreters of the divine, that is, the poets. Thus the rhapsodists, like Ion, are divinely possessed.[4] Rhapsodists appear above all at religious festivals, and particularly in the context of contests. This is clear from the words of Critias the Younger at the beginning of the *Timaeus:*

> Now the day was the day of the Apaturia which is called the *Coureōtis* [Registration of Youth], at which, according to custom, our parents gave prizes

---

1. *Rep.* II 377d4–6.

2. On the rhapsodists, see in particular Raphaël Sealey, "From Phemios to Ion," *Revue des études grecques* 70 (1957): 312–55; and more generally, Milman Parry, *L'Épithète traditionnelle dans Homère* (Paris: Les Belles Lettres, 1928); *Les Formules et la Métrique d'Homère* (Paris: Les Belles Lettres, 1928); *The Collected Papers of Milman Parry*, ed. Adam Parry (Oxford: Clarendon Press, 1971); Jesper Svenbro, *La Parole et le Marbre* (Lund, 1976). For a more detailed and updated account, see Monique Canto's introduction to Plato's *Ion* (Paris: Flammarion, 1989).

3. *Rep.* II 373b6–8. On this subject in particular, see Arthur Pickard-Cambridge, *The Dramatic Festivals of Athens,* 2d ed. rev. with supplements and corrections by J. Gould and D. M. Lewis (Oxford: Clarendon Press, 1988), and H. C. Baldry, *The Greek Tragic Theatre* (London: Chatto & Windus, 1971).

4. *Ion* 533c–34d.

for recitations, and the poems of several poets were recited by us boys, and many of us sang the poems of Solon, which at the time were new.[5]

Although Critias the Elder is not referring to real rhapsodists but to children who behave as rhapsodists on the day of the Registration of Youth during the Apaturia, there can be little doubt that what we have here is an allusion to the rhapsodes' competition that took place during the Greater Panathenaia.[6]

The Panathenaia commemorated the birth of Erichthonios. Athena had gone to pay a visit to her half-brother, Hephaestus, another child of her father Zeus, to order weapons from him. Hephaestus wanted to rape her. The goddess fled, but he caught her. During the struggle, semen was spilled on the leg of the goddess. Athena wiped it off with wool and threw it on the ground. Gaia (Earth) was thus fecundated and gave birth to a son, Erichthonios, the common ancestor of the Athenians and the warrant of their autochthony.[7] This is why the Panathenaia can be considered as the "national festival" of the Athenian people. The colonies and tributaries of Athens also participated; they acknowledged their dependency by sending sheep and cattle to be sacrificed. In fact, it was also during this festival that the allies found out the amount of their tribute for the coming four years.

The Greater Panathenaia was celebrated on the 28 Hecatombaeon (mid-July), once every four years. The Lesser Panathenaia, in contrast, was an annual festival held on the same date. The following description of the organization and development of the Greater Pananthenaea summarizes its religious, political, and competitive features.

The organization of the festival was entrusted to several ordinary magistrates: the eponymous archon (the one who "gives his name to the year"), the chief archon, and the Boulē (the Council). However, it was the special magistrates, the athlothetes (those who "preside over the games") and the hieropes (those who "preside over the religious ceremonies") who played the most important roles.

The culmination consisted in offering a garment called the *peplos* to the "old statue" of the goddess. The preparation of this garment had begun nine months earlier, on the day of the Chalkeia Festival, in honor of Athena and Hephaestus. At daybreak, on 28 Hecatombaeon, a procession left the Ceramic, a suburb of Athens, and ascended to the Acropolis. Two

---

5. *Tim.* 21b1–7.
6. J. A. Davison, "Notes on the Panathenaea," *Journal of Hellenic Studies* 78 (1958): 23–42.
7. *Tim.* 23e1–2.

sacrifices were there offered to the goddess. The lesser sacrifice consisted in a hierarchical distribution of portions of meat. The second was the great hecatomb (sacrifice of "100 oxen"), in which the meat was distributed pell-mell to the Athenian people. The offering of the new peplos to the "old statue" of the goddess then took place. This statue had first stood in the "Old Temple" of Athena, which was destroyed by the Persians in 480. After 421, it resided in the Erechtheion.

These religious ceremonies were preceded by contests, which were held over several days just prior to the ceremonies. There were three major contests: a musical competition, an equestrian competition, and a gymnastic competition. There were also several minor competitions: a pyrrhic dance competition, a torch race, and a regatta. The torch race took place on the evening of 27 Hecatombaeon, before the sacred vigil, which was held on the night of the 27th to 28th.

We do know that only Homer's poems were recited, although we do not know precisely at what moment and for how long the rhapsodic competition lasted. In the dialogue named after him, Ion came to Athens to participate in this competition.[8] He arrived from Epidaurus, where he had participated in another competition during the festival of Asclepius, which was also celebrated once every four years. The information provided in this dialogue gives us an idea of the rhapsodist's behavior. The rhapsodist was dressed in a ceremonial costume and his head encircled with a golden crown.[9] He recited, from the top of a platform,[10] poems, especially those of Homer,[11] without any musical accompaniment[12]—this is true even though Phemios is later characterized as a rhapsode (*Ion* 523c1)—but with mimic gestures proper to an actor.[13] The rhapsodists, who had a rigorous training, were subject to the authority of the Homerides.[14]

Socrates refers to the tragic poetry competition—which took place at Athens during the Dionysia—when he likens Timaeus, Critias, and Hermocrates to the three poets chosen by the eponymous archon to participate in this competition.[15] The religious and political features of these competitions are also obvious.

---

8. *Ion* 532a–b.

9. *Ion* 530b6–8, 535d2–3.

10. *Ion* 535e2.

11. *Ion* 531a1–3.

12. *Ion* 533c1.

13. *Ion* 532d6, 536a1; cf. *Rep.* III 395a8.

14. *Ion* 530d7; cf. *Rep.* X 599e6, *Phdr.* 252b4. According to Diogenes Laertius (1.57), the rhapsodic competitions that took place during the Panathenaia were codified by Solon.

15. *Crit.* 108b3–7; cf. d3–6.

Three festivals of Dionysus were celebrated at Athens.[16] The oldest were the Anthesteriae, celebrated on 11, 12, and 13 Anthesterion (end of February); they maintained no link with the theater. During the Lenaea, which took place during the month of Gamelion (end of January), dramatic competitions were organized for tragedy (starting around 442) and comedy (starting around 432). Yet the Dionysian festival in which dramatic competitions played the most important role was unquestionably the Dionysia. There were two types of Dionysia: the rural and the urban. The rural Dionysia took place during the month of Poseidon (December). The central element of this festival was a *kōmos,* or procession of drunken people who sang and danced while carrying an enormous *phallos* through the streets. At some point in time, dramatic representations were introduced, but the date of this innovation is not known. The urban Dionysia, called the Greater Dionysia or more simply Dionysia, took place during the month of Elaphebolion (end of March). The eponymous archon was in charge of its organization.

This festival had been instituted in the honor of Dionysus Eleuthereus, whose statue was supposed to have been brought to Athens from Eleutherae, on the border between Attica and Boetia. The statue was kept in the old temple of Dionysus, located within the enclosure of the theater. To reenact this arrival, the statue was transported outside the city to a temple which was located on the road to Eleutherae, not far from the Academy. It was then brought back under torchlight and placed in the theater. This festival was important not only because of the competitions which took place there—both dramatic poetry (tragedy, comedy, satyr plays) and lyric poetry (dithyrambs) were represented—but also because it was open to every Greek. Finally, it was the occasion for a number of important political events for Athens, whose citizens were on holiday.

We know less about the dithyrambic competition than we do about the tragic and comic competitions. The first step in the preparation of these competitions consisted in choosing a choregus for each of the ten tribes, five of which provided the choruses of men, and five the choruses of boys. The choregus then found a poet and a flute player, and finally formed a chorus of fifty members belonging to his tribe. The winning choregus, as the representative of his tribe, received a tripod on which an inscription was engraved and which was erected on a monument at his expense.

For the tragic and comic competitions, the poets asked the eponymous

16. Pickard-Cambridge, *Dramatic Festivals of Athens,* 1–125.

archon for a chorus. The eponymous archon chose three tragic poets and five comic poets. The tragic poets had to present four plays: three tragedies and one satyr play, whereas the comic poets had only to prepare one comedy.

For each author, the eponymous archon found a choregus who undertook to recruit a chorus of fifteen members, a flute player, and, toward the end of the fifth century, a professional chorus master. Finally, each play required three actors: a protagonist, a deuteragonist, and a tritagonist. At first, the poets performed in their plays. Near the middle of the fifth century, however, the eponymous magistrate intervened by choosing the protagonists for the tragic competition and by assigning them, through lots, to each of the three poets. Little is known about comedy.

Another preliminary formality was made necessary by the fact that these were contests. All sorts of precautions were taken to avoid corruption. The Boulē drew up a list of names taken from each of the ten tribes. We do not know the criteria behind this choice. The chosen names were placed in ten urns, one for each tribe, and these urns were sealed by the president of the Boulē and by the choregoi. They were then left in the Treasury of the Acropolis, where they remained until the time of the competition.

Finally, a day or two before the beginning of the festivities, an official ceremony, the *proagōn,* "prelude to the competition," was held to inform the city of all these preparations. Poets, choregoi, actors, musicians, and members of the chorus came to the Odeon, which was right next to the theater. It seems that each poet, accompanied by his unmasked and uncostumed actors, came upon the scene to announce the title of the play and perhaps also to give a summary of it.

On the first day of the Dionysia, the ceremony began in the morning with a procession accompanied by dances and songs. During the procession, enormous *phalloi* were carried up to the theater, where there was a sacrifice in honor of Dionysus. Then, the dithyrambic competition began, followed in the evening by a *kōmos.*

The following day, the dramatic competition was opened with a complex ritual. A piglet was sacrificed to purify the theater and libations were poured. Since this was the time of year that the allies brought to Athens their tribute—whose amount had been fixed for four years during the last Greater Panathenaia—young Athenians paraded before the public carrying a talent of silver in a jar to show the surplus of the tribute over the expenditures of the preceding year. The honors conferred on citizens and foreigners who had rendered important services to the city were also proclaimed. The sons of those who died on the battlefield for Athens paraded in armor that was offered to them by the city, and they listened to a short exhortation before taking up their reserved places. Finally, the definitive election of the judges took place. The ten urns, brought from the Acropolis, were opened and the eponymous archon drew a name from each of them. The ten chosen citizens then swore to render an impartial verdict.

A trumpet then sounded and the first play began. In time of peace, the presentations lasted four days. One day was reserved for the five comedies and, during each of the other three, three tragedies and one satyr play were presented. During the Peloponnesian war, the festival was reduced to three days and the number of comedies to three. In the morning, three tragedies and a satyr play were performed, and in the afternoon, one comedy.

The verdict came at the end of the competition. Each of the ten judges indicated his choice by order of preference on a tablet. The tablets were placed in an urn. The eponymous archon took out five of them, from which the results were proclaimed. The names of the winning poet and choregos were announced, and the eponymous archon crowned them with ivy. A ceremony in honor of the winners followed. The choregos had an inscription engraved commemorating his success, and the protagonist dedicated his mask to Dionysus.

The event which closed the Dionysia was more a matter of politics than of theater. Two days after the end of the presentations, the citizens were gathered together in the theater, to examine during an extraordinary session of the *Ekklēsia* (the Assembly) how the festivities had gone. The discussion focused especially on the management of the eponymous archon and his subordinates who, on this occasion, could receive either praise or blame.

From this brief description of the progression of the Dionysia at Athens, a certain number of essential elements can be drawn to determine the circumstances in which myths were related by professionals at Athens.

Tragedy is indissociable from myth in a more obvious way than are comedy and satyr plays. Indeed, tragedy originates, as Wilhelm Nestle has shown, when myth begins to be perceived from the citizen's point of view.[17] The tragic poet once again takes up the great myths that Homer, Hesiod, and the authors of the epic cycles had "fabricated" and integrates them into a particular literary form according to the ideals of the city. The tragic heroes are all mythical characters, "and it may be said that when Agathon,

---

17. Wilhelm Nestle, *Vom Mythos zum Logos,* 2d ed. (Stuttgart: Kröner Verlag, 1942).

the young contemporary of Euripides, who represents Tragedy in Plato's *Symposium,* wrote for the first time a tragedy whose characters were of his invention, classical tragedy died, although that did not prevent it from persisting as a literary form."[18] In each tragedy, well-known myths are taken up and retold according to the preoccupations of the city of the time. Their context was marked by the following religious, political, and competitive aspects.

The Dionysia—like the Lenaea, where dramatic competitions also oc-curred—was above all a religious festival in honor of Dionysus, during which a certain number of rituals (processions, sacrifices, etc.) were per-formed. However, the Dionysia was not only a religious festival; it also constituted a political event of primary importance. Indeed, the impor-tance of the role played by the Dionysia in internal Athenian politics is reflected in the intervention of the eponymous archon, the number of acts of political significance (honors conferred on citizens and deserving for-eigners, homage paid to the sons of soldiers killed in battle, etc.), and the reunion of the *Ekklēsia* after the festivals. Moreover, since it was at this time of year that Athens' allies paid the tribute which had been fixed for them for the next four years at the Greater Panathenaia, the Dionysia also played an important role in Athenian external affairs.

Finally, the tragedies, satyr plays, and comedies were performed in the context of a competition *(agōn).*[19] The origin of this institution goes back to the practices of military life, whose model is found in the *Iliad* and the *Odyssey.* Indeed, the events organized during the funeral games of Pa-trocles[20] and Achilles[21] were performed during an *agōn* or "meeting." Only after a number of successive modifications, the word *agōn* came to desig-nate the games themselves and, in particular, the competitions they in-volved. However, there is an obvious continuity between the warrior as-sembly, the citizen assembly of the oligarchic state, and the democratic *Ekklēsia* which assembled in the agora, for political debate constitutes a codified struggle akin to the one which took place during the funeral games. The different competitions organized by the city were versions of these. One could even say that these competitions are integrated into the political life of the city as paradigms.

It is obvious that everything previously stated about the religious, po-

18. Pierre Vidal-Naquet, Preface to Sophocles, *Tragédies* (Paris: Gallimard, 1973), 13.

19. Jean-Pierre Vernant, *The Origins of Greek Thought* (Ithaca: Cornell University Press, 1982), 41–42; Marcel Detienne, *Les Maîtres de vérité dans la Grèce archaïque,* 82–84.

20. *Il.* 23.507, 685, 710, 799.

21. *Od.* 24.80–89.

litical, and competitive aspects of the Dionysia apply, *mutatis mutandis,* to the Greater Panathenaia. So much, then, for the two Athenian festivals at which the most important competitions in rhapsody, dithyramb, tragedy, satyr plays, and comedies were held. They all provided opportunities for the recitation of myths by such professionals as rhapsodes, actors, and choral dancers.[22] However, in everyday circumstances, the majority of those who related myths were necessarily nonprofessionals. In Plato, these nonprofessionals are characterized by advanced age and femininity.

Let us look at old age in the context of the story of the war between primeval Athens and Atlantis. According to Critias the Younger, at Saïs, it is a "very old" priest who transmits this story to Solon.[23] Afterwards, it is at the age of ninety that Critias the Elder relays this story to Critias the Younger.[24]

Elsewhere, Protagoras announces the following principle: it is older people who relate myths to the younger.[25] But why is old age so important in this context? Two answers to this question may be given. The first falls within the sphere of information, and the other within the sphere of communication. In a written civilization, the accumulation of messages is independent of individuals. It is the equivalent to the conservation of physical traces on material media. On the other hand, in an oral civilization, any accumulation of messages is limited to an individual, and the same holds true of the transmission of messages. From this perspective, old age is the necessary if not sufficient condition for the depth of a given individual's knowledge.

While this first answer is based upon the concept of information, another response can also be formulated, this time involving communication in the strict sense of the term. The old age of the narrator reduces to a minimum the degradation which affects any message orally transmitted over a long period of time. Degradation results from the transformation any story undergoes during each stage of its oral transmission. When the story is transmitted directly from grandparents to grandchildren, by contrast, one stage of the degradation process can be skipped.

The second characteristic of those who most often relate myths is femininity. According to Plato, myths are also related by a mother *(mētēr),*[26] a

22. See *Laws* VIII 834e2–835a1.
23. *Tim.* 22b4.
24. *Tim.* 21a8–b1.
25. *Prot.* 320c2–4.
26. *Rep.* II 377c2–4, 381e1–6; *Laws* 887d2–3.

nurse *(trophos)*,[27] or an old woman *(graus)*.[28] In the latter we see the combination of the two features we have emphasized: advanced age and femininity. But how do we account for this second characteristic? If it is primarily women who relate myths, this is quite simply because of their privileged relation with children—the primary addressees of myth, as we shall see further on. Moreover, according to Plato, for mothers and nurses, relating myths is part of the first aid they must be able to dispense to child: "And the myths on the accepted list we will induce nurses and mothers to tell to the children and so shape their souls by these myths far rather than their bodies by their hands."[29]

This remark is an important source of information on the role of myth in the education of ancient Greece.

The primary verb that Plato employs to describe the act of recounting a myth is *legō*, and there is a long list of examples in which this meaning is manifest.[30] According to this usage, *legō* exhibits the distributive value of the root **leg-* "to go over in order, according to a plan," while at the same time in ordinary usage the word appears as the present tense of the couple *eipein-erein*, "to say, to speak." Moreover, the place of *legō* is sometimes taken by *phtheggomai*, "to cause one's voice or a sound to be heard."[31] This verb occurs only once in relation with *muthos* (*Laws* II 664a5–7), but it indicates that myth-telling is, above all, an oral performance. Finally, the verbs *diēgeomai*, "to set out in detail,"[32] and *dierkhomai*, "to go through to the end,"[33] include, thanks to their second elements, respectively *hēgeomai*, "to go before, lead the way," and *erkhomai*, "to go," the idea of movement which *legō* conveys in its meaning of "telling." The verbal prefix *dia-* further indicates the completeness of the movement in question. The importance of this will be seen later on.

It is difficult to determine how nonprofessionals related a myth. But everything leads us to believe that they tried to imitate professionals. As far as we know, professionals proceeded in the following way.

---

27. *Rep.* II 377c2–4; *Laws* 887d2–3.

28. *Gorg.* 527a5–6; *Rep.* I 350e2–4.

29. *Rep.* II 377c2–4.

30. *Gorg.* 523a3, 527a5; *Phdo.* 110b1; *Laws* III 683d2, IV 712a4, 719c2, VII 790c3, VIII 840c1, 841c6–7, IX 865d5–6, 872e2, XI 913c2; *Phdr.* 237a10; *Pol.* 272c6–7; *Prot.* 320c3, c7, 324d7, 328c3–4; *Rep.* I 330d7, 350e3, II 377a4–6, c3, d4–5, 381e3, III 386b9, 398b8, VIII 565d6–7; *Tim.* 22c7.

31. *Laws* II 664a5–7.

32. *Soph.* 242c8–9.

33. *Soph.* 242d6; *Tim.* 23b4.

Myths could be communicated in prose, but most were in verse, which allowed them to be spoken—or, more often, to be sung—with musical accompaniment or even with accompanying dance-steps. Plato carefully distinguished these linguistic, musical, and choreographical techniques that professionals like poets, rhapsodists, actors, and choral dancers employed to communicate a myth.[34] As we have seen, the rhapsode restricted himself to declaiming poetry—especially that of Homer—from the heights of the stage. Crowned in gold and richly costumed, he used mimic gestures but no musical accompaniment. Actors and choral dancers by contrast utilized song and dance in their performance.

Actors wore masks of cloth, bark, or wood, spectacular costumes, and soft boots with soft soles. In fact they were not unlike opera singers. The text that they had to communicate could be sung or recited with the accompaniment of a musical instrument, generally a flute but sometimes a lyre. The actors therefore carefully trained their voice to increase its power, clarity, expressivity, and musicality. Further, they needed a musical training since they recited their declamations in various rhythms. They also had to sing lyric solos or to reply to the chorus at moments of great emotion. The actors performed some gestures and movements to illustrate what they were saying; at times, they even danced.

In the second half of the fifth century, the chorus of tragedies and perhaps of satiric dramas and comedies was composed of fifteen costumed and masked members. They were arranged in a rectangle comprising three rows of five choral singers. Thus they were distinguished from the dithyrambic chorus, which included fifty unmasked members arranged in a circle. After an introductory speech, the chorus made its entrance preceded by its accompanist, a flute player, who left by the same way. We know very little about what he did in between. It seems that during certain recitals by an actor, the chorus danced to the sound of the flute which accompanied the actor. Further, the chorus sang in unison both the *parodos* or "entrance song" and the *stasima,* that is, the choral odes performed after the chorus had reached its place *(stasis)* in the *orkhēstra* and was carrying out a dance step.[35]

One rule governs the recitation of any myth, whether performed by professionals or nonprofessionals. This rule is evoked by two types of expressions, both of which are later found as proverbs in Byzantine collec-

34. See *Rep.* III 398c11–d10, 399a5–c4; *Laws* VII 814d7–815d3. These passages will be commented upon in chapter 6.

35. Pickard-Cambridge, *Dramatic Festivals of Athens,* 126–52.

tions. The first of these expressions consists of a prescription, the most explicit formulation of which is found in the *Gorgias* where Socrates, trying to persuade Callicles not to abandon the current discussion, says: "Well, they say it is not right to leave even myths unfinished, but we should fit a head on them, that they may not go about headless. Give us the rest of the answers then, that our discussions may acquire a head."[36] Again, in the *Timaeus,* and more precisely in the introduction to the third and last part of the dialogue, Timaeus says:

> Seeing, then, we have now prepared for our use the various classes of causes which are the material out of which the remainder of our discourse must be woven, just as wood is the material of the carpenter, let us revert in a few words to our beginning, and hasten back to the point from which we set out on our road hither. We may then endeavour to give a head to our myth *(tōi muthōi)* with a suitable conclusion.[37]

There is also another relevant passage found in book VI of the *Laws.* The myth which the Athenian Stranger wants to narrate until its end is the description he is giving of the city which the Cretans wish to found: "And, to be sure, since I am telling a myth *(muthon),* I should not like to leave it without its head; it would look monstrously ugly if it roamed at large in that condition."[38]

These three passages concur on the following point: when a myth is being related, it must be told to the end, the end being likened to a head. The expression *ou themis esti,* "it is not permitted," indicates that this prescription is of a religious nature.

Such a prescription applies in fact to all discourses if we leave aside the religious element which is absolutely essential to any myth. This is clear from the following passage in the *Phaedrus:*

> SOCRATES Well there is one point at least which I think you will admit, namely that any discourse ought to be constructed like a living creature, with its own body, as it were; it must not lack either head or feet; it must have a middle and extremities so composed as to suit each other and the whole work.[39]

The comparison between a discourse and a living being generates a number of other metaphorical relations. The beginning of a discourse corresponds to its feet, and the end to its head; the same discourse has a middle which could very well be its trunk. All these parts must, as in a living

36. *Gorg.* 505c10–d3.
37. *Tim.* 69a6–b2.

38. *Laws* VI 752a2–4.
39. *Phdr.* 264c2–5.

being, be organized in such a way as to maintain harmonious relations between them.

The Eleatic Stranger must also be thinking of this prescription when he declares, at the end of the myth which he recounts in the *Statesman:* "Here let our work of relating myth come to an end."[40] Then, criticizing what was just done: "We did not give the myth an ending *(telos)* after all."[41] The same thing occurs in book VII of the *Laws,* where the Athenian Stranger employs *muthos* in a derivative sense: "And with this myth *(muthos)* what I have to say about reading and writing must come to an end."[42] In these three passages, the substantive *telos,* "end,"[43] and the verb *teleutaō,* "to have an end, to come to an end,"[44] express the same idea as the expression "to have a head."

As E. R. Dodds pointed out in his commentary at *Gorgias* 505c10,[45] it is necessary to relate the expression *akephalos muthos,* which prescribes not to leave a myth without a head, and the expression *ho muthos sōizetai,* which closes the narration of a myth. This relation is only possible insofar as it is understood that Plato is playing on the double meaning of the passive *sōizetai,*[46] which means not only "to be saved," that is, "not to have perished" *(ouk apollutai),* but also "to have arrived safe and sound."[47] In other words, the telling of a myth is likened to a dangerous trip, from which one is saved when one reaches port safe and sound.

There are four passages in the Platonic corpus in which this expression is found. At the end of the myth of Er, Socrates declares: "And so, Glaucon, the myth was saved, as the saying is, and was not lost and it can save us, if we believe in it."[48] The expression is found again in *Theaetetus* 164d8–10: "And so no one was left to tell Protagoras' myth, or yours either, about knowledge and perception being the same thing"; in *Philebus* 14a3–5: "Thereby bringing our discussion to an end like a myth that is told, while we ourselves escaped from the wreck on a quibble"; and in *Laws* I 645b1–2: "In this way our moral myth of the human puppets will find its fulfillment." The similarities in these four passages indicate that this must

40. *Pol.* 274e1.
41. *Pol.* 277b7.
42. *Laws* VII 812a1–3.
43. *Pol.* 274e1, 277b7.
44. *Laws* VII 812a2.
45. E. R. Dodds, *Gorgias* (Oxford: Clarendon Press, 1959).
46. For an example of this, see *Gorgias* 515c–e.
47. See Herodotus 4.97, 5.98, 9.104; Aeschylus *Persians* 737; Euripides *The Phoenicians* 725; Sophocles *Trachineans* 611; Xenophon *Anabasis* 6.5, 20.
48. *Rep.* X 621b8–c1.

be a familiar expression, which Plato adopts with as little modification as possible. Indeed, in all these cases, we find the words *kai houtō* followed by the verbs *sōizetai* and/or *apollutai*. In *Republic* X 621b8–c1 and in *Philebus* 14a3–5 the two verbs appear together, whereas in *Theaetetus* 164d8–10 only *apollutai* is present and in *Laws* I 645b1–2, only *sōizetai*.

This hypothesis is confirmed by the fact that the expression in question is recorded in a Byzantine collection of proverbs, where it appears under the form *ho muthos apōleto*,[49] "the myth has perished," and is explained as follows: "[proverb] relative to those who do not lead their account *(diēgēsin)* to its end." A note to this proverb indicates that *ho muthos esōthē* expresses the opposite idea,[50] in spite of the scholium which gives another interpretation to *Republic* X 621b8. It is also in the same sense that the expression *akephalos muthos*,[51] "a myth without a head," is glossed: "[proverb] relative to those whose story does not have an end."

In these popular expressions, the myth, like any other discourse, is likened to a living being. So a myth must not wander without a head; and it must, without perishing, arrive safely at a friendly port. Moreover, if Plato had suspended the account of the war between primeval Athens and Atlantis at the point where it stops in the manuscripts that we still have of the *Critias*,[52] then he himself would have violated the religious prescription according to which the relating of a myth cannot be interrupted before it has reached its end.

This likening of myth to a living being explains, in all probability, the two following formulas: "The reason for which we have rewoken the myth *(ton muthon ēgeiramen)* must be told *(lekteon)*" at *Statesman* 272d5; and: "With this myth we have no further concern" *(to men oun tou muthou khairetō)* at *Laws* I 636d4–5. A myth is awakened when it is related and dismissed on the pretext that it is immortal.

49. See Herbert Jennings Rose, "A Colloquialism in Plato, *Rep* 621b8," *Harvard Theological Review* 31 (1938): 91–92, on this proverb, which is found in *Paroemiographi graeci*, 2 vols., ed. E. L. Leutsch and F. G. Schneidewin (Göttingen: Vandenhoeck und Ruprechts, 1839, 1851). See *ho muthos apōleto* in the indexes. See also François Chatelain, "Le récit est terminé, Platon, *République* 621b," *Revue de Philosophie Ancienne* 5 (1987): 95–98.

50. CGL 2.91.

51. *Paroemiographi graeci*, vols. 1 and 2. See *akephalos muthos* in the indices.

52. See Christopher Gill, "The Genre of the Atlantis Story," *Classical Philology* 72 (1977): 304, n. 74.

RECEPTION

W ho are the addressees of myth and what words are used to describe their attention? The addressees of myth vary according to the nature of those who relate the myth. If the latter are professional poets, rhapsodists, actors, or choral dancers, then their public, which assembles on the occasion of competitions during religious festivals, is very diverse. For the dramatic competitions of the Dionysia, for example, the public included all the family members of both rich and poor Athenian citizens as well as non-Athenians. It is possible that even slaves were in attendance.[1] On the other hand, if those who relate a myth are nonprofessionals, then their public is more restricted and relates to their own characteristics of advanced age and/or femininity. Indeed, a myth is necessarily told by someone older to someone younger.[2] Moreover, it is to the child of whom they are in charge that women who relate myths, whether young or old, address themselves. From this perspective, it is easy to understand why Plato designates as the privileged subjects of the reception of myth the child *(pais)* or the grandson *(paidion)*.[3] Plato even goes so far as to specify young children who are still breast feeding[4] and who do not yet attend the gymnasium.[5] In sum, these subjects are children who can grasp what they are told but who have not yet reached the age of seven or eight—the age one generally began to attend the gymnasium in ancient Greece.[6]

We have already seen why the age of the narrator played such an important role in the oral transmission of a story. On the other hand, in an

---

1. On this point, see Arthur Pickard-Cambridge, *The Dramatic Festivals of Athens* (Oxford: Clarendon Press, 1988), ch. 6, "The Audience," 263–78.

2. *Prot.* 320c3; *Rep.* III 392a1.

3. The suffix *-ion* is used, among other things, to form diminutives in ancient Greek. See *Rep.* II 377a4, a6, 377c3; *Pol.* 265e5; *Soph.* 242c8; *Tim.* 23b5; *Laws* VIII 840c1, 887d2–3.

4. *Laws* X 887d2–3.

5. *Rep.* II 377a6–7.

6. Henri-Irénée Marrou, *A History of Education in Antiquity* (London: Sheed & Ward, 1956), 182.

oral civilization, old age is a condition for the accumulation of messages. Further, old age allows for considerable savings in the sphere of communication as long as the old age of the narrator is confronted with the extreme youth of the listener, for then communication between the two can skip a generation. More importantly, youth is characterized by its great receptivity to information. This is confirmed by Critias the Younger: "Truly, as it is often said, the lessons of our childhood make a wonderful impression on our memories, for I am not sure that I could remember all the discourse of yesterday, but I should be much surprised if I forgot any of these things which I have heard very long ago."[7]

In sum, the reasons evoked to explain the old age of the narrator and the youth of the listener in the oral transmission of a myth correspond to one another, at the levels both of information and of communication. Otherwise, the following observation would be difficult to understand:

> Nor again must the mothers under the influence of such poets terrify their children with harmful myths, how there are certain gods whose apparitions haunt the night in the likeness of many strangers from all manner of lands, lest while they speak evil of the gods they at the same time make cowards of the children.[8]

In this passage, Plato seems to be referring to characters similar to that of the bogeyman who is evoked to frighten children and make them obey. In ancient Greece these characters had names like Empousa, Gelo, Lamia, Mormo, and Mormolyce. Empousa is a ghost who is part of the company of Hecate. She belongs to the underworld and spreads terror at night. She can take on different forms and appears especially to women and children to frighten them. Gelo is the grieving soul of a girl from Lesbos who, having died young, returns to steal children. Lamia is a female monster who has the reputation of stealing and devouring children. Many adventures are attributed to her. Mormo is also a female monster, accused of biting children and making them lame. At times, she is identified with Gelo or Lamia. Mormolyce, that is, Mormo the she-wolf, is another female monster who is used to threaten children. She is supposed to be the nurse of the Acheron and therefore related to the world of the dead and of ghosts. It is in this context that Socrates evokes Mormolyce at *Phaedo* 77e7.

Everything that has been said until now holds true for the reign of Zeus, under which we now live. Indeed, whereas the communication of a

---

7. *Tim.* 26b2–7. The same idea is found at *Rep.* II 378d7–e1.
8. *Rep.* II 381e1–6.

myth is now proper only to humans, under the reign of Kronos, humans could tell myths even to animals.[9] The intimate relation between humans and animals was then akin to the close relation between humans and gods.[10] However, the same verb is employed to designate the reception of the myth, namely, *akouō*, "to hear, to listen."[11] Whether the action takes place under the reign of Kronos or that of Zeus, this verb refers to the oral transmission of that kind of discourse which is called myth.

It may be worth recalling this picturesque remark by Plato at the end of book I of the *Republic*. Socrates has just forced Thrasymachus to admit that justice is virtue and wisdom, whereas injustice is vice and ignorance. Thrasymachus reluctantly agrees. When Socrates wishes to continue with an examination of another point, that injustice has force on its side, Thrasymachus, at the end of his patience, tries to define the attitude he must take during this trial: "Either then allow me to speak at such length as I desire, or, if you prefer to ask questions, go on questioning and I, as we do for old wives telling their myths, will say, 'very good', and will nod assent and dissent."[12] It seems then that it is the listener who signals to the myth-teller when to begin his or her story, and the same listener is then content to express his assent or refusal with a nod of the head when he is addressed by the teller of the myth in question.

This attitude is considerably different from the much more active one of Critias the Younger when his grandfather, Critias the Elder, tells him the story of the war between primeval Athens and Atlantis: "I listened at the same time with childlike interest to the old man's narrative; he was very ready to teach me, and I asked him again and again to repeat his words, so that, like an indelible picture, they were branded into my mind."[13] Here, it is no longer the narrator who questions the listener, but the reverse. Plato also informs us that the public loudly expresses its emotions and appreciation at the theater.[14]

Whether it is done by professionals or nonprofessionals, the telling of a myth always takes the form of a live interaction between human beings. This state of affairs conveys the influence that the addressee of a myth exerts over one who makes and/or interprets the myth. In an oral civiliza-

---

9. *Pol.* 272c5–d1.
10. *Phlb.* 16c7–8.
11. *Gorg.* 523a1; *Phdo.* 110b1, b4; *Rep.* III 415a1; *Laws* VII 804e4, X 887d3.
12. *Rep.* I 350e1–4.
13. *Tim.* 26b7–c3.
14. *Rep.* VII 492b–c; *Laws* III 700c–701a. See Pickard-Cambridge, *Dramatic Festivals of Athens,* 272–78.

tion where the spheres of fabrication, emission, and reception of a message are inseparable, for any myth to be heard, it must be accepted by the audience to whom it is intended. This "prior restraint," which takes the form of a noisy refusal to listen, is replaced in a society where writing is established by the "horizon of expectation"[15] of the audience to whom the poet addresses himself when he "fabricates" a myth, either directly, or indirectly by means of his subordinates: rhapsodists, actors, and choral dancers.

15. See Hans Robert Jauss, *Pour une Esthétique de la réception* (Paris: Gallimard, 1978).

SIX

IMITATION

According to Plato, the activity which functions in communication of a myth is always an affair of *mimēsis,* "imitation."[1] Imitation manifests itself first and foremost in discourse in general, as is explained by Critias the Younger in the preface to the *Critias:*

> CRITIAS What man in his sound senses, indeed, could venture to dispute the excellence of your exposition? What I must try to show, as I can, is that the theme still to be expounded is more difficult to handle and consequently calls for yet more generous allowances. In fact, Timaeus, upon an audience of human beings it is easier to produce the impression of adequate treatment in speaking of gods than in discoursing of mortals like ourselves. The combination of unfamiliarity and sheer ignorance in an audience with respect to a subject they can never know for certain makes the task of the would-be speaker extremely easy. And we know how the case stands when it comes to our knowledge of the gods. But to make my meaning still clearer, kindly follow an illustration. All statements made by any of us are, of course, bound to be an affair of imitation *(mimēsin)* and representation *(apeikasian).* Now suppose we consider the relative degree of severity with which an artist's formation of images *(eidōlopoiian)* divine and human, respectively, produces the impression of satisfactory reproduction on the spectator. We shall observe that in the case of earth, mountains, rivers, woodland, the sky as a whole, and the several revolving bodies located in it, for one thing, the artist is always well content if he can represent *(apomimeisthai)* them with some faint degree of resemblance *(pros homoiotēta),* and, for another, that since our knowledge of such a subject is never exact, we must submit his design to no criticism or scrutiny, but acquiesce, in these cases, in a dim and deceptive outline. But when it is our human form that the artist undertakes to

1. See J.-P. Vernant, "Image et apparence dans la théorie platonicienne de la mimēsis," *Journal de psychologie normale et pathologique* 2 (1975): 133–60; reprinted under the title "Naissance d'images," in *Religions, histoires, raisons* (Paris: Maspero, 1979), 105–37.

copy *(apeikazein),* daily familiar observation makes us quick to detect shortcomings and we show ourselves severe critics of one who does not present us with full and perfect resemblances *(homoiotētas).* Well, we should recognize that the same is true of discourses. Where the subjects of them are celestial and divine, we are satisfied by more faint likenesses *(eikota);* where mortal and human, we are exacting critics. So with our present unrehearsed narrative; if we do not succeed in reproducing the proper touches perfectly, allowances should be made. In fact, we must understand that it is not easy to undertake a satisfactory copy *(apeikazein)* of mortal things which are a question of opinion *(pros doxan).*[2]

Discourse constitutes only an imitation or copy of the reality to which it refers. In this respect, it is akin to painting. Language, with the help of sounds, like painting,[3] with the help of shapes and colors, makes reality appear, albeit in another mode: that of the presence of absence. The problem becomes more complicated if we consider the nature of imitated realities. In the case of sensible things, the imitation used is the equivalent to a representation. There are, however, some realities which, while they are not part of the sensible world, are nevertheless not intelligible forms either: the divine, for example, the immortal part of human soul, and the whole past insofar as it is nothing other than the object of tradition. In the case of these entities, imitation becomes evocation, because it makes entities which are in fact of another order appear in the sensible world, as if they were sensible entities. However, Plato does not understand matters in this way because of a truth to which he believes he has special access. Before recalling Plato's critique in this regard, we must trace every manifestation of imitation at work in the communication of a myth.

The poet's basic material is discourse, the imitative character which Plato has just described. This imitative nature is still more important in the case of written discourse, since writing is only a copy of the word. It is precisely this actual absence, attached to all representations of reality by means of discourse, whether oral or—especially—written, that the poet tries to eliminate by procedures which also fall under the category of imitation:

SOCRATES Does that [the art of imitation *(hē mimētikē tekhnē)*] hold only for vision or does it apply also to hearing and to what we call *poiēsis* [in the double sense of "fabrication" and "poetry"]?

GLAUCON: Presumably, to that also.[4]

2. *Crit.* 107a4–e3. For a detailed discussion of this passage with respect to the dating of the *Critias,* see Luc Brisson, Platon, *Timée/Critias* (Paris: Flammarion, 1992), 335–41.

3. See Eva C. Keuls, *Plato and Greek Painting* (Leiden: Brill, 1978).

4. *Rep.* X 603b6–8.

Defining poetry as an imitative art which addresses itself to hearing does not at first appear to be relevant, because it only seems to reiterate what was already stated about discourse in general. But this is not the case. In the area of discourse (and more precisely at the level of its content), two things must be distinguished: what is expressed, that is the *logos,* and the way of expressing it, that is, the *lexis.* This distinction is based on morphology.[5]

But how does this distinction apply to the realm of poetry? With regard to *logos,* "what is expressed in [poetic] discourse," we can abide by what was already said. With regard to *lexis,* however, or "the way of expressing the content of this discourse," another type of imitation must be brought into the picture:

SOCRATES So this concludes the topic of discourses *(logōn).* That of style *(lexeōs),* I take it, is to be considered next. So we shall have completely examined both the matter and the manner of speech.

ADEIMANTUS I don't understand what you mean by this.

SOCRATES Well we must have you understand. Perhaps you will be more likely to apprehend it thus. Is everything that is said by myth-tellers or poets *(hupo muthologōn ē poiētōn)* a narration *(diēgēsis)* of past, present, or future things?[6]

ADEIMANTUS What else could it be?

SOCRATES Do they [the myth-tellers or the poets] proceed either by pure narration or by a narrative that is effected through imitation *(haplēi diēgēsei ē dia mimēseōs gignomenēi),* or by a mixture of both?

ADEIMANTUS It is still not clear to me what you mean.

SOCRATES . . . Now, it is narration *(diēgēsis),* is it not, both when he [the myth-teller or the poet] presents the speeches *(rhēseis)* and what occurs between the speeches?

ADEIMANTUS Of course.

SOCRATES But when he delivers a speech *(rhēsin)* as if he were someone else, shall we not say that he then assimilates thereby his own diction *(homoioun . . . tēn hautou lexin)* as far as possible to that of the person whom he announces as about to speak?

5. *Logos* is a thematic derivative from the root **leg-* at the level *o,* as is generally the case for roots where all the vocalic levels are allowed. It can designate the action indicated by the verb it is derived from, but it usually designates the result. *Lexis* is also based on the root **leg-* but at the level *e* from the suffix *-sis,* which specifically indicates the action and therefore the way this action is executed. See Guy Richard Vowles, "Studies in Greek Noun-Formation. Dental Terminations V. Words in *-sis* and *-tis,*" *Classical Philology* 23 (1928): 34–59, esp. 53–55. See also Pierre Chantraine, *La Formation des noms en grec ancien* (Paris: Champion, 1933), 281.

6. See Hesiod, *Theogony* 38.

ADEIMANTUS Obviously.

SOCRATES And is not likening oneself to another in speech or bodily bearing
an imitation of him to whom one likens oneself *(Oukoun to ge homoioun
heauton allōi ē kata phōnēn ē kata skhēma mimeisthai estin ekeinon hōi an
tis homoioi)?*

ADEIMANTUS Of course.[7]

Such, then, is the imitation used by the "myth-tellers" in their way of expressing the content of their discourse.

Whereas the imitation which occurs at the level of *logos,* that is, "what
is expressed in the discourse," implies a relation between an object-copy
and an object-model, the imitation which occurs at the level of *lexis,* that
is, "the way of expressing the content of this discourse," concerns the relation which the subject (in this case, the poet) entertains with the object of
which he makes the copy. This is how the opposition between exposition
and imitation is defined in terms of utterance. Wherever an utterance reveals its author, there is exposition. Where, by contrast, the author gives
up his "I" in favor of another utterance, upon which he confers reality and
behind which he disappears, there is imitation.[8]

Based on this opposition, Plato establishes a topology of genres belonging to poetry and mythical narrations:

SOCRATES You have conceived me most rightly, and now I think I can make
plain to you what I was unable to before, that there is one kind of poetry
and myth-telling *(poiēseōs te kai muthologias)* which works wholly
through imitation *(dia mimēseōs),* as you remarked, tragedy and comedy,
and another which employs the recital of the poet himself *(di'apaggelias
autou tou poiētou),* best exemplified, I presume, in the dithyramb, and
there is again that which employs both, in epic poetry and in many other
places, if you apprehend me.[9]

This topology is of interest in the context of this work only insofar as it
confirms and clarifies what was already stated on imitation in the realm
of *lexis.*

By means of this artifice, the myth-tellers and the poets try to make
their audience forget the real absence of the god or hero for whom they

7. *Rep.* III 392c6–93c7.

8. On this point, see R. Dupont-Roc, "Mimesis et énonciation," *Ecriture et théorie poétiques* (Paris:
Presses de l'Ecole Normale Supérieure, 1976), 6–14; Jacques Brunschwig, "*Diēgēsis* et *mimēsis* dans
l'oeuvre de Platon," summary of a paper given March 4, 1974, in *Revue des études grecques* 77 (1974):
xvii–xix.

9. *Rep.* III 394b8–c5.

give up their own identities; not only in word, but also in deed, since they sometimes take on the attitudes which correspond to the words they relate. This type of expression is intolerable for Plato because, at the level of the subject, it is a generator of illusion through the confusion it causes between reality and discourse, sameness and otherness. Plato's exasperation grows when he reminds us that through this expression, we can imitate not only the discourse of evil or inferior men, but also animal cries and sounds of nature.[10] This explains why the poets are necessarily followed not only by those who relate the myths that they make, but also, and especially, by those who are the addressees of these myths. Indeed, the myth-tellers, whether they be professionals like the rhapsodists, actors, and choral dancers, or nonprofessionals, model themselves on the poet who makes the myths that they tell. There is still much to say on this point. The discourse called myth can be made in prose or verse. When myth is related, it can be recited, with or without musical accompaniment, or sung; and during this interpretation, a choreographical arrangement can enter into the picture.

In ancient Greece, the works of a poet could be sung, as in the case of the works of Solon.[11] Here is an example of Plato's analysis of an interpretation of this kind:

> SOCRATES You certainly, I presume, have a sufficient understanding of this—that the melody *(melos)* is composed of three things, discourse *(logou)*, harmony *(harmonias)*, and rhythm *(rhuthmou)*?
>
> GLAUCON Yes, I agree to that.
>
> SOCRATES And so far as it is discourse, it [melody] surely in no manner differs from discourse not sung *(mē aidomenou)* in the requirement of conformity to the patterns and manner that we have prescribed?
>
> GLAUCON Obviously.
>
> SOCRATES And again, harmony and rhythm must follow discourse.
>
> GLAUCON Certainly.[12]

Three things follow from this analysis. (1) Melody consists of three elements: discourse, harmony, and rhythm. (2) Harmony and rhythm are deprived of autonomy. They are determined as a function of the discourse to which they are attached[13] (this thesis will be forcefully reaffirmed a little

10. *Rep.* III 395b–97e.
11. *Tim.* 21b6–7.
12. *Rep.* III 398c11–d10.
13. Richard Lewis Nettleship, *Lectures on the "Republic" of Plato* (1897; London: Macmillan; New York: St. Martin's Press, 1964), 118–23.

further on).[14] (3) It follows that the imitation at work in harmony and rhythm must have the aim of perfecting the imitation already manifest in the content of the discourse, and in the manner of expressing this content.

In ancient Greek, *harmonia,* "harmony," designates not the simultaneous perception of two or more tones of different pitch, but more generally, a scale or succession of tones of different pitch. This is how imitation manifests itself in this area:

> SOCRATES I don't know about harmony, but leave us that harmony that would fittingly imitate *(mimēsaito)* the utterances and the accents *(phthoggous te kai prosōidias)* of a brave man who is engaged in warfare or in any enforced business, and who, when he has failed, either meeting wounds or death or having fallen into some other mishap, in all these conditions confronts fortune with steadfast endurance and repels her strokes. And another [that would imitate utterances and accents] for such a man engaged in words of peace, not enforced but voluntary, either trying to persuade somebody of something and imploring him— whether it be a god, through prayer, or a man by teaching and admonition—contrariwise yielding himself to another who is petitioning or teaching him or trying to change his opinions, and in consequence faring according to his wish, and not bearing himself arrogantly, but in all this acting modestly and moderately and acquiescing in the outcome. Leave us these two harmonies—the enforced and the voluntary—that will best imitate the utterances *(phthoggous mimēsontai kallista)* of men failing or succeeding, the temperate, the brave—leave us these.[15]

There can be no doubt on this point: harmony must imitate discourse. From this perspective, all music does is to take up, in its own field, that imitation which is at work in the discourse which it illustrates, thereby increasing the effectiveness of the imitation. This occurs both at the level of content and on that of expression. And this is also the case for rhythm.

In ancient Greek, *rhuthmos* is linked etymologically to terms related to movement.[16] The typical form of a rhythmic movement is dance. The

14. *Rep.* III 398c11–d10.

15. *Rep.* III 399a5–c4.

16. In an article entitled "La Notion de 'rythme' dans son expression linguistique," *Journal de psychologie normale et pathologique* 43 (1950–51): 401–10, Emile Benveniste tries to determine the relation of *rhuthmos* to *rheō,* the verb from which it is derived by means of the suffix *-(th)mos.* To do this, Benveniste insists on the fact that this suffix indicates "not the accomplishment of the notion, but the particular modality of its accomplishment as it is perceived through the eyes" (407). Whence the sense of *rhuthmos* as "form," that is, "the particular way of flowing." E. Benveniste completes his article by examining the transformation that Plato imposes on the meaning of *rhuthmos.* After quoting *Phlb.* 17d, *Symp.* 187b and *Laws* 665a, he concludes: "Plato employs *rhuthmos* in the sense of 'distinctive form, disposition, proportion.' Plato innovates by applying it to the *form of the movement* that the human body accomplishes in dance, and to the disposition of figures in which this movement is re-

essence of rhythm is the fact that a given series of sounds or of movements is measured according to time, into portions which are repeated according to a determinate principle. When applied to bodily movement, rhythm constitutes dance. When applied to sounds, in the realm of discourse, it defines meter, and in the realm of music, "rhythm" in the strict sense of the term. It is when rhythm is applied to bodily movements in the dances, however, that it introduces a new kind of imitation:

ATHENIAN So much, then, at present for what we have to say of the value of wrestling. As for other movements of the body as a whole—in the main it may properly be called dancing—we must bear in mind that it has two varieties, one imitating *(mimoumenēn)* motions of comely bodies with a dignified effect, the other [imitating] those of uncomely bodies with a ludicrous, and that, further, the comic and the serious kinds have each two subspecies. One variety of the serious sort represents the movements of the comely body and its valiant soul in battle and in the toils of enforced endurance, the other the bearing of the continent soul in a state of prosperity and duly measured pleasure; an appropriate name for this latter would be the *dance of peace.* The war dance has a different character, and may properly be called the *Pyrrhic;* it imitates *(mimoumenēn)* the motions of eluding blows and shots of every kind by various devices of swerving, yielding ground, leaping from the ground or crouching, as well as the contrary motions which lead to a posture of attack, and aim at the imitation *(mimeisthai)* of the shooting of arrows, casting of darts, and dealing of all kinds of blows. In these dances the upright, well-braced posture which imitates *(mimēma)* the good body and good mind, and in which all the bodily members are in the main kept straight, is the kind of attitude we pronounce right, that which depicts their contrary, wrong.[17]

---

solved. The decisive circumstance is there, in the notion of a bodily *rhuthmos* associated with *metron* and subject to the law of numbers: this 'form' is henceforth determined by a 'measure' and subjected to an order. This is the new meaning of *rhuthmos:* 'disposition' (the proper sense of the word) in Plato is constituted by an ordered series of fast and slow movements just as 'harmony' results from the alternation of sharp and grave. And it is the order in movement, the whole process of the harmonious arrangement of bodily attitudes combined with a meter that is henceforth called *rhuthmos.* We can now speak of the 'rhythm' of a dance, a step, a song, a speech, a work, of anything that entails a continuous activity broken up by metrical alternate times. The notion of rhythm is fixed. From *rhuthmos* as a spatial configuration defined by the distinctive order and proportion of elements, we get 'rhythm' as the configuration of ordered movements in duration: *pas rhuthmos hōrismenēi metreitai kinēsei,* 'all rhythm is measured by a defined movement' (Aristotle, *Probl.,* 882b2)" (409). Reprinted in *Problèmes de linguistique générale* (Paris: Gallimard, 1966), 1:364–65; and reprinted again in *Tel* n. 7, (Paris: Gallimard, 1979), 334–35.

17. *Laws* VII 814d7–815b3.

This passage on dancing corresponds precisely to what we read on harmony in book III of the *Republic* (399a5–c4). Of course, there is nothing surprising here since dance must adjust itself to the music to which it moves. So much, then, for *mimēsis* or imitation, with regard to the narration of myth—or rather the interpretation of myth when music and dance are involved.

Music and dance which accord with one another must, moreover "become akin to," that is, "imitate" the discourse they illustrate. The imitation that each one employs is therefore an imitation of an imitation. In this case, discourse already reveals itself as imitation of reality, both at the level of its content and at the level of the expression of this content. Using the metrical structure of discourse as a support, music and dance extend spoken imitation into an acted imitation, with dance as its culmination.

Even more radically than that imitation which affects the type of discourse called myth, the imitation at work in the music and dance which can accompany the interpretation of a myth causes the absence inherent in the appearance of the evoked reality to be forgotten, in order to produce the illusion of its actual presence. This is more important than what affects myth as a type of speech. The interpretation of a myth is thus only the extension of its fabrication, in that it tries to produce the same effect by means of imitation.

In Plato's writing we feel a gradual and almost imperceptible shift from the link between the imitated reality and the imitator, whether the latter makes a myth or limits himself to telling it, to the link between the imitator and the addressee, the listener and/or spectator. The imitator brings into play a spoken and/or acted imitation in order to provoke a precise reaction from the addressee. This reaction is of the same order as the action which brings it about. It, too, is an imitation:

SOCRATES If, then, we are to maintain our original principle [*Rep* II 374a–d], that our guardians, released from all other crafts *(tōn allōn pasōn dēmiourgiōn)*, are to be expert craftsmen *(dēmiourgous)* of civic liberty, and pursue nothing else that does not conduce to this, it would not be fitting for these to do nor yet to imitate anything else *(oude mimeisthai)*. But if they imitate *(mimōntai)* they should imitate *(mimeisthai)* from childhood up what is appropriate to them—men, that is, who are brave, sober, pious, free, and all things of that kind—but things unbecoming the free man they should neither do nor be clever at imitating *(mimēsasthai)*, nor yet any other shameful thing, lest from the imitation *(ek tēs mimēseōs)* they imbibe the reality. Or have you not observed that imitations *(mimē-*

seis), if continued from youth far into life, settle down into habits and second nature in the body, the speech, and the thought *(kata sōma kai phōnas kai kata tēn dianoian)?*[18]

There is no doubt that the imitation in this passage is the one practiced by those to whom the poets and their subordinates address themselves. This is the case because the focus of the debate is ethics and not narration or fabrication.

The imitative process implemented in myth, as a type of communication, leads to this end. It is no longer a question of fabricating a discourse which imitates reality nor of actually imitating this reality, within the framework of a narration or an interpretation, by means of such discourse accompanied by music and/or dance. From the transmitter, whatever technique he employs, we move to the receiver. The imitation utilized by the transmitter affects the receiver, who tries genuinely to assimilate himself to the reality referred to by the discourse to which he is listening. This is why a problem of an ethical nature arises at this point.

Through the process of communication, the reality which is the object of the transmitted message becomes present to the receiver in a manner so intense that its actual absence is forgotten, and consequently it begins an identification process which modifies the physical and moral behavior of the receiver in question.

In the final analysis, then, the characters and beings who intervene in myth are not analogous to any reality accessible to the intellect or the senses. They are specific entities, endowed with ontological solidity (e.g., Zeus is as real for an ancient Greek as a rock or tree that can be touched). It is precisely this illusory character that Plato denounces by tracking down the imitation at work in each phase of the communication of a myth. Plato's conclusions are all the more severe in that for him, the sensible reality is already only a copy of a true being. However, the illusory character associated with myth does not prevent it from being endowed with a formidable efficacy.

18. *Rep.* III 395b8–d3.

SEVEN

PERSUASION

Although myth is illusory, it is also formidably effective. This ambivalence leads Plato to describe myth both as a game and as a serious activity by likening it to a charm or an incantation. Myth—whose communication arouses pleasure—is addressed to children and to the majority of adults in whom reason has not yet attained, or will never attain, the ultimate stage of its development. This stage is reached only by a minority of adults: philosophers. In the majority, it is the appetitive part of the soul that dominates, that is, the part which is sensitive to only pleasure and pain. For this reason, Plato describes appetitive soul as an untamed animal. One could say that myth is that discourse which alone has an effective influence on what is untamed or wild in mankind—wildness being not ethical but psychological.

In book X of the *Republic,* Plato likens the imitation employed by an imitator like the poet to a game, that is, to a non-serious activity:

> SOCRATES . . . the imitator knows nothing worth mentioning of the things
> he imitates, but that imitation is a form of play, not to be taken seriously
> *(paidian tina kai ou spoudēn tēn mimēsin).*[1]

In the Platonic corpus, there are fifteen other examples of the dichotomy game *(paidia)* / serious activity *(spoudē).*[2] The particular interest of the passage just quoted resides in the fact that it places this opposition on two levels at the same time: that of discourse and that of action. Indeed, what is serious in the sphere of action corresponds to what is falsifiable in the sphere of discourse. A falsifiable speech is one which has its goal outside itself, in the reality its serves to describe or explain and, *mutatis mutandis,*

1. *Rep.* X 602b7–8.
2. *Laws* I 647d6, II 659e4, V 732d6, VII 795d2, VII 796d4, 798b6, 803c7, d2, d5, X 887d4, 942a8; *Phlb.* 30e7, *Rep.* X 602b8; *Soph.* 237b10; *Symp.* 197e7.

a serious activity is one that has its goal outside itself, in the reality it serves to transform. The game, for its part, even if it takes place within the real, has its end in itself and does not seek to transform the real. Similarly, imitation seeks not to describe or explain the real but to cause the actual absence of the imitated reality to be forgotten, in order to give the resulting appearance, thus produced, the status of a complete reality. This bracketing of the real characterizes among other things the activity of the child, as is shown by etymology.[3] In its most direct sense, *paidia* (from *pais*, "child") means "(a child's) game." Plato, however, gives this term a much larger meaning by likening to a game anything derived from imitation in the strict sense of the word.

Plato understands by games not only the *lexis* utilized in poetry,[4] but also instrumental music[5] and especially choral art, that is, the interpretation of songs by a group that also executes dance steps to musical accompaniment.[6] In this context, Plato reminds us that the Curetes in Crete, the Dioscuri in Lacedaemonia, and Athena at Athens, were also devoted to the game of dance.[7] This was stated in order to justify the function of choral art during religious festivals[8] in conjunction with sacrifice.[9] The relation Plato establishes between games and initiations *(teletē)*[10] can also be understood, at least in part, in this context. During these initiations, dances were performed which were supposed to mime the life and death of Dionysus. Now, it was a child that the Titans killed, after having attracted him with the help of toys. This explains the overdetermination of the game as theme and representation.

From the relation between imitation and games, Plato naturally moves to the relation between communication of myth and games. Such a relation is explicitly established by the Eleatic Stranger in the *Statesman*,[11] that is, if one accepts Campbell's conjecture on the accentuation of *paidiá* at 268e5. In any case, the same relation is found in the *Phaedrus*:

> PHAEDRUS And what an excellent game *(paidian)* it is, Socrates! How far
> superior to the other game is the recreation that a man finds in words,

---

3. *Paidiá* is derived from *pais*, "child," constructed with the help of the suffix *-ia* with the accent on the final vowel—a particularity with remains inexplicable.

4. *Rep.* III 396e2.

5. *Lach.* 188d4.

6. *Laws* II 656c3, 657c4, d3, 673d4, VI 764e4, 771e6, VII 803e1.

7. *Laws* VII 796b-c.

8. *Laws* VII 796c-d.

9. *Laws* VIII 829b7.

10. *Euthd.* 277d9; *Laws* II 666b5; *Rep.* II 365a1; *Soph.* 235a6.

11. *Pol.* 268d8, e5.

when telling myths *(muthologounta)* about justice and the other topics you speak of.[12]

Whatever the interpretation given to this phrase, it is difficult to miss the close relation between "playing" and "telling myths," and therefore, between a "game" and the "communication of myth."

The same idea is found in the following passage from book X of the *Laws:*

ATHENIAN Come then, how shall we plead for the existence of gods dispassionately? To be sure, no man can help feeling some resentment and disgust with the parties who now, as in the past, impose the burden of the argument on us by their want of faith in the myths heard so often in earliest infancy, while still at the breast, from their mothers and nurses— myths you may say, crooned over them, in play and in seriousness, like charms *(hoion en epōidais meta te paidias kai meta spoudēs legomenōn).*[13]

This passage is clarified by the following, from book II of the *Laws:*

ATHENIAN That is why we have what we call songs *(ōidas),* which are really charms *(epōidai)* for the soul. These are in fact deadly serious devices for producing this concord *(sumphōnian)* we are talking about;[14] but the souls of the young cannot bear to be serious, so we use the terms game and song *(paidiai te kai ōidai)* for the charms, and practice them as such.[15]

In these two last passages, the communication of a myth appears paradoxically both as a game and as a serious activity in so far as it is likened to an incantation.[16] Plato recalls this relation again a little further on:

ATHENIAN And now, I take it, we have had quite enough of controversy with him who is prone to charge the gods with negligence.

CLINIAS Yes.

---

12. *Phdr.* 276e1–3.

13. *Laws* X 887c7–d5. With England, I consider *hoion . . . legomenōn* as an absolute genitive that Plato employs in place of the more normal construction of *hous ēkouon legoumenous,* following the example of *thuontōn* at d7.

14. Cf. *Laws* II 653b–c.

15. *Laws* II 659e1–5.

16. The book by Pierre Boyancé, *Le Culte des Muses chez les philosophes grecs* ([1936] Paris: Boccard, 1972) is a good general introduction to the problem of enchantment in ancient Greece, although his approach lacks rigor. On enchantment, see Elizabeth Stafford Belfiore, "Elenchus, *epode,* and magic: Socrates as Silenus," *Phoenix* 34 (1980): 128–37; and on possession, see Roberto Velardi, *Enthousiasmòs: Possessione rituale e teoria della comunicazione poetica in Platone,* Filologia e Critica 62 (Rome: dell'Ateneo, 1989).

ATHENIAN I mean so far as our argument has forced him to see his error. But, I still believe that we have to find a form of myth to charm him into agreement *(epōidōn . . . muthōn eti tinōn).*

CLINIAS What do you suggest, my friend?[17]

Since the Athenian evokes several mythical elements[18] in response to Clinias' last question, we can conclude that these elements function as incantations, employed to modify the opinion of a person who does not believe in divine providence.

In the *Phaedo,* Socrates wishes to free himself not from impiety but from the fear of death, by defending the validity of the eschatological myth that he relates at the end of the dialogue:[19]

SOCRATES Of course, no reasonable man *(noun ekhonti andri)* ought to insist that the facts are exactly as I have described them. But, that either this or something very like it is a true account of our souls and their future habitations—since we have clear evidence that the soul is immortal—this, I think, is both a reasonable contention and a belief worth risking, for the risk is a noble one. We should use such accounts as if we were charming ourselves *(hōsper epaidein heautōi),* and that is why I have already drawn out my myth *(muthon)* so long.[20]

These incantations are those already mentioned by Socrates in reply to Cebes and Simmias at the beginning of the *Phaedo:*

SOCRATES But, in spite of this I believe that you Cebes and Simmias would like to spin out the discussion still more. You are afraid, as children are, that when the soul emerges from the body the wind may already puff it away and scatter it, especially when a person does not die on a calm day but with a gale blowing.

CEBES (laughing) Suppose that we are afraid, Socrates, and try to convince us. Or rather, do not suppose that it is we who are afraid. Probably even in us there is a little boy who has these childish terrors. Try to persuade him not to be afraid of death as though it were a bogy.

SOCRATES What you should do is to say a magic spell over him *(epaidein autōi)* every day until you have charmed his fears away *(heōs an exepaisēte).*

SIMMIAS But Socrates, where shall we find a magician who understands these charms *(tōn toioutōn agathon epōidon)* now that you . . . are leaving us?[21]

---

17. *Laws* X 903a7–b3.
18. *Laws* X 903c–905b.
19. *Phdo.* 108d–114c.

20. *Phdo.* 114d1–7.
21. *Phdo.* 77d5–78a2.

By describing the destiny of the soul after death, the myth related by Socrates at the end of the *Phaedo* helps, if not to heal, at least to alleviate the fear of death brought on by the possibility of the disappearance of the soul as a result of the destruction of the body.

In fact, the curative function of myth, as it is described in the previous four passages, corresponds perfectly to the one assigned to incantations from the *Charmides,* which I quote *in extenso* because of its importance for the definition of incantation:

> SOCRATES Such is the nature of charm *(kai to tautēs tēs epōidēs),* which I learned when serving with the army from one of the physicians of the Thracian king Zalmoxis, who are said to be able even to give immortality. This Thracian told me that in these notions of theirs, which I was just now mentioning, the Greek physicians are quite right as far as they go, but Zalmoxis, he added, our king, who is also a god, says further, "that as you ought not to attempt to cure the eyes without the head, or the head without the body, so neither ought you to attempt to cure the body without the soul. And this," he said, "is the reason why the cure of many diseases is unknown to the physicians of Hellas, because they disregard the whole, which ought to be studied also, for the part can never be well unless the whole is well." For all good and evil, whether in the body or the whole man, originates, as he declared, in the soul, and overflows from thence, as if from the head into the eyes. And therefore, if the head and the body are to be well, you must begin by curing the soul—that is the first and essential thing. And, the cure of the soul *(therapeuesthai de tēn psuchēn),* my dear youth, has to be effected by the use of certain charms *(epōidais tisin),* and these charms are fair words *(tas d'epōidas tautas tous logous einai tous kalous),* and by them moderation *(sōphrosunēn)* is implanted in the soul, and where temperance comes and stays, there health is speedily imparted, not only to the head, but to the whole body. And when he taught me the cure and the charm *(to te pharmakon kai tas epōidas)* he added, "With this cure *(tōi pharmakōi toutōi),* let no one persuade you to cure his head, until he has first given you his soul to be cured by the charm *(tēi epōidēi).* For this," he said, "is the great error of our day in the treatment of human beings, that men must try to be physicians of health and temperance *(sōphrosunēs te kai hugieias)* separately." And he strictly enjoined me not to let anyone, however rich or noble or fair, persuade me to give him the cure, without the charm. Now I have sworn, and I must keep my oath, and therefore if you will allow me to apply the Thracian charm first to your soul *(epaisai tais tou Thraikos epōidais),* as the stranger directed, I will afterward proceed to apply the cure to your head *(prosoisō to pharmakon tēi kephalēi).* But if not, I do not know what I am to do with you, my dear Charmides.[22]

22. *Chrm.* 156d3–157c6.

This text can only be fully appreciated when situated in its general context. Charmides, the cousin of Critias IV,[23] was an adolescent when he met Socrates in the palaestra of Taureas in Athens. Like the many others who are in love with Charmides, Socrates is astonished at his beauty. Charmides complains of a headache and asks Socrates if he knows of a cure. Socrates has just returned from Potidaea, a city in Thrace on the isthmus of Chalcidice, where he served in the army during the siege of 431 to 429 to which Athens submitted the city for wishing to break away from its yoke. This is why he speaks to Charmides of the cure and incantation that he brought back from there. This causes him to speak of Zalmoxis. Zalmoxis, a Thracian god and legislator, was thought to have had a human existence during which he was either the master or disciple of Pythagoras when the latter still lived on the island of Samos.[24] It is said that he made a man immortal every five years, and this explains his association to medicine.

The interest of this text resides in the opposition Socrates establishes between the medicine *(pharmakon)*, which must assure the health *(hugieia)* of the body, and the incantation *(epōidē)*, which must cause moderation *(sōphrosunē)* to be born in the soul. This dichotomy, relative to the specific function and object of medicine and incantation, is replaced by another dichotomy, relative to their proper nature. The medicine is a material substance, whereas the incantation is a verbal practice intended to act on the disposition of the soul and, in particular, to cause moderation to be born in it. The same idea is taken up and developed in the *Euthydemus:*

> SOCRATES For indeed these men, the speechmakers *(hoi logopoioi)*, when I meet them, do seem to me to be superwise, Clinias, and their very art seems to be something divine and lofty. However, that is nothing to wonder at, for it is a portion of the art of enchanters *(esti gar tēs tōn epōidōn tekhnēs morion)*, but falls short a little. For the enchanter's art *(ē men gar tōn epōidōn)* is the charm *(kēlēsis)* of adders and tarantulas and scorpions and other vermin and pests, whereas the other [the art of the speechmakers] is really the charm *(kēlēsis)* and persuasion *(paramuthia)* of juries and parliaments and any sort of crowds.[25]

Socrates thus presents the art of speechmaking as a part of the art of incantation, which is defined as the art of charming wild beasts *(thēriōn)* and diseases *(nosōn)*. This reference to wild beasts constitutes a new element of

---

23. See the genealogical table in chapter 2.

24. On Zalmoxis, see François Hartog, "Salmoxis: le Pythagore des Gètes ou l'autre de Pythagore?" *Annali della Scuola normale superiore di Pisa, Classe di Lettere e Filosofia,* series 3, vol. 8, no. 1 (1978): 15–42; *Le Miroir d'Hérodote* (Paris: Gallimard, 1980), 102–27.

25. *Euthd.* 289e1–290a4.

special importance since it recalls, in this context, the following passage of the *Timaeus*,[26] in which the appetive part of the human soul is described as a wild beast attached to its manger in the region between the midriff and the navel:

> TIMAEUS The part of the soul which desires food and drink and the other things of which it has need by reason of the bodily nature, they [the helpers of the demiurge] placed between the midriff and the boundary of the navel, contriving in all this region a sort of manger for the nourishment of the body, and there they bound it like a wild animal *(thremma agrion)* which was chained up with man, and must be nourished if man was to exist.[27]

Timaeus goes on to explain why the appetitive part of the human soul was assigned a residence in this part of the human body. It must be located as far as possible from the immortal part of the human soul—reason—which thus runs the least risk of being disturbed by the disorder of the irrational. Moreover, the liver is found in front of the appetitive part of the human soul. The liver is a kind of screen, on which the divinity, after having blocked the normal use of reason, causes images to appear which are intended to frighten or to pacify that which, within the human soul, offers the most resistance to reason.

This incantation produced by myth is a charm, intended to modify the behavior of the appetitive part of the human soul. As we have seen, this part is the furthest removed from reason, and it is fascinated by the images which the divinity projects upon the liver for its benefit. This charm and this fascination are thus closely related. Indeed, the aim of both charm and fascination is to cure the human soul of the disease of madness.[28] The essential function of the incantation produced by myth is thus to restore reason's control over the appetitive part of the soul. This is, moreover, what Socrates indicates in the *Charmides*, when he presents incantation as a drug destined to make wisdom appear in the human soul.

Since the enchanter's art is defined as the art of charming in the passage from the *Euthydemus* just cited, it is not surprising that Plato has established an explicit relation between the communication of myth and the art of charming in the following passage concerning sexual temperance in book VIII of the *Laws:*

---

26. *Tim.* 70d7–72b5. For an analysis of the whole of this passage, see Luc Brisson, "Du bon usage du dérèglement," *Divination et Rationalité* (Paris: Seuil, 1974), 220–48, esp. 235–42.

27. *Tim.* 70d7–e5.

28. *Tim.* 86b2–4.

ATHENIAN Why then, they made no hardship of denying themselves this "heaven of bliss," as the vulgar account it, for the sake of winning a victory in the ring, or the racecourse or the like. But there's a far nobler victory to be won and I hope that our pupils are not going to fail in endurance—one whose supreme nobility we shall extol in their hearing, from their earliest years, by myths, maxims, and songs so that they will be charmed into believing that this victory will be the noblest of all *(legontes en muthois te kai en rhēmasin kai en melesin aidontes hōs eikos, kēlēsomen)?*[29]

What are the consequences of all this? In the four cases we have just examined,[30] the action that the communication of a myth exerts on the human soul is presented in a context where the effects produced are spectacular. Indeed, Plato likens this action to that exerted by the art of charming *(kēlēsis)* and incantation *(epōidē),* practices which enable those who use them to modify in an unusual way, by means of sound, the physical or moral behavior of wild animals or human beings. But this striking side of the effect produced by myth on its addressee must not deceive us. Normally, Plato simply uses the verb *peithō*, "to persuade,"[31] to designate this effect.[32] This is the same effect the following two paraphrases describe in a more expanded way: "children listen and take [these myths] into their minds";[33] and: "Listen closely to my myth as a child would."[34] It is worth noting that in both cases the addressees of the myth are, or ought to be, children. The reason for this is obvious. Childhood and youth constitute the wild side of human life.[35] During childhood or youth, the appetitive part of the soul dominates.[36] Under these conditions, the game called myth appears as the only recourse to hold it in check:

> SOCRATES And the myths on the accepted list we will induce nurses and mothers to tell to the children and so shape their souls, far rather than their bodies by their hands.[37]

We can now see why Plato in the *Laws* introduces games as the first step in education[38] and resorts to the play on words between *paidia,* "game,"

---

29. *Laws* VIII 840b5–c3.
30. That is, *Laws* X 887c7–d5, 903a7–b3; *Phdo.* 114d1–7; *Laws* VIII 840b5–c3.
31. On the word *peithō,* see Marcel Detienne, *Les Maîtres de vérité dans la Grèce archaïque,* 51–80, esp. 62–68.
32. See *Rep.* III 415c7, X 621c1; *Phdr.* 265b8; *Laws* VII 804e5, X 887d2, XI 913c1–2, 927c7–8.
33. *Rep.* II 377b6–7.
34. *Pol.* 268e4–5.
35. *Laws* VIII 808c7–809a6.
36. *Tim.* 43a6–44d2.
37. *Rep.* II 377c2–4.
38. *Laws* VII 796e–798d.

and *paideia,* "education."[39] Just like *paidia, paideia* is derived from *pais,* but with the help of the suffix *-eia,* which developed parallel to the suffix *peuō,* which is used to construct verbal derivatives like *paideuō,* "to educate."

Myth is only a game, since imitation occurs at each phase of its communication. Yet, this is a serious game because it has a powerful effect on the soul of the addressee. The game is all the more serious, in fact, in that it is addressed to every citizen from his earliest years and therefore constitutes the first stage of his education. That is why a philosopher like Plato, whose principal project is to reform the city in which he lives, insists on regulating the fabrication and the distribution of myth with the greatest severity.

But why is the imitation which occurs during the communication of myth so effective? The reply to this question is relatively simple. The communication of myth provides a pleasure of the kind provided by the practice of any game:

> CRITIAS I listened at the time with much childlike pleasure *(meta pollēs hēdonēs kai paidias)* to the old man's narrative; he was very ready to teach me, and I asked him again and again to repeat his words, so that like an indelible picture, they were branded into my mind.[40]

Critias the Younger goes so far as to consider the pleasure that the communication of a myth provides as a precious aid to memory.

This dual relation is not thematized anywhere else in the Platonic corpus. There are, however, two other passages that allude to the pleasure provided by listening to a myth. The first is found at the end of the *Phaedo:*

> SOCRATES If this is the right moment *(kalon)* to tell a myth *(muthon)* Simmias, it will be worth your while to hear what it is really like upon the earth which lies beneath the heavens.
>
> SIMMIAS Yes, indeed, Socrates, it would be with pleasure *(hēdeōs)* to us, at any rate, to hear this myth *(tou muthou).*[41]

In this passage, the adverb *hēdeōs,* "with pleasure," corresponds to the syntagma *meta hēdonēs* found in the passage from the *Timaeus* cited above. The testimony of Protagoras is more explicit than that of Simmias on this precise point:

---

39. See *Laws* II 656c2, VII 803d5, VIII 832d5.
40. *Tim.* 26b7–c3.
41. *Phdo.* 110b1–4.

SOCRATES If then you can demonstrate more plainly to us that virtue is something that can be taught, please don't hoard your wisdom but explain.

PROTAGORAS I shall not be a miser, Socrates. Now shall I, as an old man speaking to his juniors, put my explanation in the form of a myth, or give it as a reasoned argument *(alla poteron humin ōs presbuteros neōterois, muthon legōn epideixō ē logōi diexelthōn)?*
(Many of the audience answered that he should relate it in whichever form he pleased.)

PROTAGORAS Then I think, it will be pleasanter *(khariesteron)* to tell you a myth.[42]

Indeed, contrary to Simmias, Protagoras is not content to affirm that listening to a myth provides pleasure. He goes as far as to put this pleasure in a context in which several oppositions come to light, which either have been explained or soon will be.

But, in the end, from whence does the pleasure provided by the communication of a myth derive? First, there is an aesthetic pleasure, that is, the pleasure which arises from a lively story, lovely song, pleasant music, or fascinating dance. Much could be said about this aesthetic pleasure, but there is also the pleasure associated with play. Indeed, play has two essential characteristics. It allows an unrivaled amount of liberty in the sense that it is an activity which is deployed in the real, although it deliberately ignores its constraints, and it does not seek to transform it in a useful direction. Further, a game constitutes, within the limits it has fixed for itself and with regard to the rules it has adopted, a limited totality where every activity can reach its limits and always find its meaning in a finite and closed universe. Is this not another motive for justifying the obligation imposed upon the narrator of a myth to go to the very end of his story?[43] These last two characteristics, proper to play, confer on myth an added attraction, which intensifies the aesthetic pleasure provided by its communication.[44]

Finally, we must recall that such play always takes place—albeit to

---

42. *Prot.* 320b8–c7.

43. See the end of chapter four.

44. This reflection can be extended by reading Paul Veyne, *Did the Greeks Believe in Their Myths? An Essay on the Constitutive Imagination,* trans. Paula Wissing (Chicago: University of Chicago Press, 1988).

varying degrees—within a religious context, in which the interpreter and/ or maker of myth and its addressee enjoy a single emotional fusion. Together, they rediscover a past which lacks any precise boundaries between the human world, that which lies beyond it (the world of the gods), and that which lies beneath it (the animal kingdom).

PART II

PLATO'S CRITIQUE
The Discourse *of* and *for* the Other

Wovon man nicht sprechen kann, darüber muß man schweigen.
L. WITTGENSTEIN, *Tractatus Logico-philosophicus,* prop. 7

In the first part of this book, I described Plato's testimony on myth considered as an act of communication. Myth there appeared as the discourse by means of which all information about the distant past is communicated. Stored in the memory of a given community, this discourse is transmitted orally from one generation to the next, whether or not it has been elaborated by such technicians in communication as poets. Imitation occurs throughout this communication process. It appears both during the fabrication and during the interpretation of myth, by means of both speech and gesture; and it prepares its addressees to determine or modify their physical and especially moral behavior in accordance with the model which is thus proposed to them.

If Plato is so interested in myth, it is because he wants to break its monopoly and impose a type of discourse he intends to develop: philosophical discourse, which he recognizes as having a superior status.

In order to set up this opposition and fix the meaning of its terms, Plato is obliged to reorganize the vocabulary of "the word" in ancient Greece. For, if *muthos* can be likened to *logos* understood as "discourse" in general, it must nevertheless be contrasted with *logos* in the senses of "falsifiable discourse" and of "argumentative discourse." Despite this double critique, Plato concedes that myth has a certain usefulness, independently of any allegorical interpretation. Further, if we consider the derivative use that Plato makes of the term *muthos,* we can see that he goes as far as to admit that in certain areas his own discourse has characteristics similar to those of myth.

In contrast to the discourse of the philosopher, myth appears as the discourse *of* the other and *for* the other. But, in Plato, this opposition does not imply the exclusion of myth even from a theoretical point of view. The myth-teller is not asked to remain silent. His discourse must, at its own level, take over from that of the philosopher and legislator.

In Wittgenstein, philosophical discourse ends with the silence of faith, whereas in Plato, it is still abuzz with that word which comes from the gods and is shared by all the citizens. It is nevertheless true that Wittgenstein is a distant cousin of Plato; he expresses, in an extreme form, a position that originates with his ancestor.

EIGHT

MYTH AS DISCOURSE

If *logos* is understood in its broad sense as "discourse," and if, consequently, it simply designates the fact of making one's thought manifest, that is, "one's thought *(dianoian)* by means of vocal sound *(dia phōnēs)* with verbs and names *(meta rhēmatōn te kai onomatōn),*"[1] then any myth can be considered as a *logos*. This is just what Plato does, particularly in the following passage taken from book II of the *Republic:*

> SOCRATES And shall we not begin education in music earlier than gymnastics?
>
> ADEIMANTUS Of course.
>
> SOCRATES And under music you include stories *(logous)*, do you not?
>
> ADEIMANTUS I do.
>
> SOCRATES And stories are of two kinds, the one true and the other false?
>
> ADEIMANTUS Yes.
>
> SOCRATES And education must make use of both, but first of the false?
>
> ADEIMANTUS I don't understand your meaning.
>
> SOCRATES Don't you understand that we begin by telling children myths *(muthous)*, and the myth is, taken as a whole, false, but there is truth in it also? And we make use of myth with children before gymnastics.
>
> ADEIMANTUS That is so.[2]

This passage will be analyzed in detail in section 3 of chapter 9, which focuses on the problem of the value of truth and/or falsity in myth. For the moment, we will note only the following point. Myth is situated in the field of music, that is, according to its etymology, in the domain of what is proper to the Muses and of everything which—together with gymnas-

1. *Tht.* 206d1–2.
2. *Rep.* II 376e6–77a8.

tics—constitutes the essential element of the traditional education in ancient Greece which Plato wants to reform so that it will be suitable to the Guardians of the city described in the *Republic*. In this domain, myth corresponds to the element "discourse," since music also includes, as we saw in chapter 6, the elements of rhythm and harmony. There is therefore an assimilation—although not an identification—between *muthos* and *logos* in the sense of "discourse" in general.

To explain this fact, the words *muthos* and *logos* must be resituated within the totality to which they naturally belong, that is, the vocabulary of "saying" and "speech" in ancient Greek. This totality must be considered not only from a synchronic point of view—as the state of a system to which Plato refers—but also from a diachronic point of view. After all, this state is the result of a process of semantic transformation which has affected a certain number of words that show an important interdependence.[3]

The meaning of *muthos,* whose etymology is unknown, was profoundly transformed between Homer and Plato. This occurred as *logos* became more and more important in the vocabulary of "speech." One might say that *logos* was the heir of *epos* and of *muthos.* This explains why Plato can assimilate *muthos* to *logos* in the sense of "discourse" in general. Not only did the values attached to the root **leg-,* as well as the semantic evolution of *logos,* render impossible any identification of *muthos* with *logos,* but these phenomena also gave rise to a number of oppositions. Of these, the two principal ones were *muthos* as a nonfalsifiable speech vs. *logos* as a falsifiable speech, and *muthos* as story vs. *logos* as argumentative discourse. These will be clarified in the chapters to follow.

In sum, when Plato assimilates *muthos* to *logos,* he reactivates its ancient meaning: that of "discourse" as "thought expressing itself" or "opinion." This meaning which is found notably in Homer, will be taken up again by *logos.* But, by contrasting *muthos* to *logos* as nonfalsifiable discourse to falsifiable discourse and as story to argumentative discourse, Plato reorganizes, in an original and decisive way, the vocabulary of "speech" in ancient Greek, in accordance with his principal objective: that of making the philosopher's discourse the measure by which the validity of all the other discourses, including and especially that of the poet, can be determined.

3. This short chapter reproduces for the most part the conclusions of H. Fournier, *Les Verbes "dire" en grec ancien: Exemple de conjugaison supplétive* (Paris: Klincksieck, 1946).

NINE

THE OPPOSITION BETWEEN
MYTH AND FALSIFIABLE DISCOURSE

In Plato, *logos* not only designates language as performance, that is, discourse in general, but above all, falsifiable discourse.[1] It is quite obvious that the relations that *muthos* has with *logos* understood in this sense are very different from those described in the preceding chapter.

In the *Sophist* Plato defines *logos* in the sense of "falsifiable discourse."[2] The analysis employed to this effect will therefore serve as a model for a definition of myth as unfalsifiable discourse. This implies, in accordance with the accepted model, the examination of the following three questions. What classes of subjects and verbs appear in the type of discourse called myth? What are its referents? What value of truth and/or falsity can one assign to it?

The *Sophist* opens with a prologue. Theaetetus and Theodorus come to the appointment that Socrates had given to them the day before, that is, at the end of the *Theaetetus.*[3] Theaetetus is accompanied by a companion, the young Socrates, who remains silent in the *Sophist;* yet since the *Theaetetus* (147d1) his appearance as an interlocutor (*Pol.* 257c7–8; *The Philosopher*) has been carefully prepared. This time, however, Theodorus brings along a Stranger whom he presents as a philosopher from Elea and who is a disciple of Parmenides and Zeno.[4] Socrates then speaks up and

---

1. "Falsification" is here understood in the sense of "confrontation with the facts." A falsifiable discourse may be confronted with facts, which will either corroborate it or invalidate it. If a discourse cannot be declared either true or false, it is therefore unfalsifiable, and this is the case with myth. Especially in the philosophy of science, the term "falsifiable" has, following Popper, gained popularity. A discourse is true if and only if it is corroborated by the facts, but if one single fact should invalidate it, it is declared "false." To say that a discourse is unfalsifiable is the same as to say that the relation between this discourse and the facts is impossible to determine. This is the case with myth.

2. *Soph.* 259d–64 b.

3. *Tht.* 210d3–4.

4. *Soph.* 216a1–4.

asks how one defines a philosopher and how he is distinguished from the sophist and statesman.

After the usual apologies for conducting such a new and difficult inquiry, the Stranger from Elea tries to define a sophist; which is, of course, the object of the *Sophist*. Then, in the *Statesman,* he tries to give a definition of the statesman. Finally, in the *Philosopher,* a dialogue which appears not to have been written,[5] he would have defined the philosopher.

Following this prologue,[6] the Stranger from Elea develops a long inquiry intended to give a definition of a sophist. Here is an outline of the inquiry:

1. The method employed (218b–21c)
2. Application of the method (221c–22a)

    Definition 1 (222b–23b)

    Definition 2 (223b–24d)

    Definition 3 (224d–e)

    Definition 4 (224e–26a)

    Definition 5 (226a–31c)

    A. Recapitulation (231c–33a)

    B. Problems occasioned by definition 5 (233a–37a)

      (1) The reality of Not-being (237a–59d)

        (a) Error and the problem of Not-being (237a–42b)

        (b) Criticism of theories of Being (242b–50e)

        (c) The problem of predication and the problem of the community of Kinds (251a–254b)

        (d) The reality and nature of Not-being (254b–59d)

      (2) The possibility of error in discourse and opinion (259d–64b)

    Definition 6 (264b–68d)

The core of this long development deals with the fifth definition of the sophist. In this definition, the sophist appears as a charlatan of the word: he turns what is false into truth and what is not into being. This explains

5. On the presumed existence, object, and structure of this dialogue, see F. M. Cornford, *Plato's Theory of Knowledge* ([1935], London: Routledge & Kegan Paul, 1964), 165–70; E. A. Wyller, "The *Parmenides* is the *Philosopher:* A thesis concerning the inner relatedness of the late Platonic dialogues," *Classica & Mediaevalia* 29 (1968): 27–39; S. Panagiotou, "The *Parmenides* is the *Philosopher:* A reply," *Classica & Mediaevalia* 30 (1969): 187–210; F. Sontag, "Plato's Unwritten Dialogue: The *Philosopher,*" *Congrès international de philosophie* 12 (1960): 159–67; M. W. Haslam, "A Note on Plato's Unfinished Dialogues," *American Journal of Philology* 97 (1976): 336–39.

6. *Soph.* 216a–18b.

the necessity of demonstrating, against Parmenides in particular, that there is not-being as much in reality as in opinion *(doxa)* and discourse *(logos)*,[7] where it is equivalent to error.

According to the Stranger from Elea, the most basic definition of discourse is comprised of three elements, the third element being the equivalent of the relation between the first two: (1) a statement is a weaving together of names and verbs; (2) it always applies to something; and (3) consequently, it must be true or false.

A statement is composed fundamentally of names and verbs.[8] A verb *(rhēma)* is defined as "an expression which is applied to actions";[9] and the name *(onoma)* is defined as "the spoken sign applied to what performs these actions."[10] But a succession of verbs ("walks," "runs," "sleeps") or of names ("lion," "stag," "horse") strung together will never make a discourse. To have discourse, there must be weaving together of name(s) and verb(s):

STRANGER When one says 'A man understands', do you agree that this is a statement of the simplest and shortest kind?

THEAETETUS Yes.

STRANGER Because now it gives information about facts or events in the present or past or future: it does not merely name something but gets you somewhere by weaving together verbs with names. Hence we say it 'states' something, not merely 'names' something, and in fact it is this complex that we mean by the word 'statement.'

THEAETETUS True.[11]

As a result of this weaving together of names and verbs, a statement or discourse is made whose nature is to refer to an extralinguistic reality which

7. *Soph.* 259d–64b. This passage has been the subject of a number of interpretations. Here is a brief bibliography on the subject: J. L. Ackrill, *"Sumplokē eidōn,"* in R. E. Allen, ed., *Studies in Plato's Metaphysics* (London: Routledge & Kegan Paul/New York: Humanities Press, 1965), 199–206; J. L. Ackrill, "Plato and the Copula: *Sophist* 251–259," *Studies in Plato's Metaphysics,* 207–18; D. Keyt, "Plato on Falsity: *Sophist* 263b," *Exegesis and Argument: Studies in Greek Philosophy presented to G. Vlastos,* ed. E. N. Lee, A. P. D. Mourelatos, and R. M. Rorty, *Phronesis* supp. vol. 1 (Assen: Van Gorcum, 1973), 285–305; J. M. E. Moravcsik, "*Sumplokē eidōn* and the Genesis of *logos,*" *Archiv für Geschichte der Philosophie* 42 (1960): 117–29; and A. L. Peck, "Plato's *Sophist:* The *sumplokē tōn eidōn,*" *Phronesis* 7 (1962): 46–66. For more information on this passage, see the bibliography by Luc Brisson [with the contribution of H. Ioannidi], "Platon 1975–1980," *Lustrum* 25 (1983); *Lustrum* 30 (1988); *Lustrum* 35 (1993 [1994]).
8. *Soph.* 262a1.
9. *Soph.* 262a3–4.
10. *Soph.* 262a6–7.
11. *Soph.* 262c9–d7.

is situated in the present, past, or future—with the present being able to indicate atemporality as well.[12]

Here, then, the second element in the definition of a discourse is evoked: "Whenever there is a statement, it must be about something; it cannot be about nothing."[13] The third element in the definition of the discourse corresponds to the relation between this second element and the first, that is, its truth value.

This is the culminating point in the demonstration:

> STRANGER And, moreover we agree that any statement ("Theaetetus sits";[14] "Theaetetus [whom I am talking to at this moment] flies")[15] must have a certain character.
>
> THEAETETUS Yes.
>
> STRANGER Then what sort of character can be assigned to each of these?
>
> THEAETETUS One is false, the other true.
>
> STRANGER And the true one states about you the things that are.
>
> THEAETETUS Certainly.
>
> STRANGER Whereas the false statement states about you things different from the things that are.
>
> THEAETETUS Yes.[16]

In other words, any weaving of name(s) and verb(s) is true, if its relation to that upon which it bears is adequate; any weaving together of name(s) and verb(s) is false, if its relation with that upon which it bears is not adequate. In the latter case, the statement refers not to nothing, but to something other than what it states.

Finally, it is important to note that for Plato, the domains of discourse and of thought are homogeneous: "Well, thinking *(dianoia)* and discourse *(logos)* are the same thing, except that what we call thinking is, precisely, the inward dialogue carried by the mind with itself without spoken sound."[17] Consequently, whatever has been stated about discourse also applies to thought.

This analysis of *Sophist* 259d–264b is, of course, superficial in that it only retains what is essential. Moreover, within these limits, a number of problems are not dealt with. Plato defines discourse at the level of its basic constituents without distinguishing between grammar and logic. By defining the sentence as the fitting together of name(s) and verb(s), Plato is

12. Cf. *Tim.* 37c–38c.
13. *Soph.* 262e5–6.
14. *Soph.* 263a2.

15. *Soph.* 263a8.
16. *Soph.* 263b2–8.
17. *Soph.* 263e3–5.

also defining the proposition as the attribution of one or more predicate(s) to one (or more) subject(s). Further, Plato deals too vaguely and too briefly with what we call today a "referent." This is a very difficult subject on which there is still no consensus, because of the complex logical and onto-logical difficulties that it raises.[18] Finally, the question of the truth or falsity of discourse presents a degree of difficulty which is incommensurable with what we have said about it here.

Nonetheless, the consequence of this long development is clear. The definition of a falsifiable discourse—which limits the meaning of the term *logos,* at the same time as it specializes it—allows us to distinguish between the sophist and the philosopher. The sophist is characterized by false discourse. False discourse bears upon something other than what it states. False discourse gives an unfaithful image of the reality which it claims to depict. And since this falsity is voluntary for the sophist, he is defined at the end of the dialogue as a human illusion-maker in the realm of discourse.[19] On the other hand, the philosopher is characterized by true discourse. However, there is still the need, within the framework of Platonic doctrine, to distinguish between discourse bearing upon the intelligible forms and that which deals with sensible things. One of the most explicit texts in this regard is found in the *Timaeus:*

> TIMAEUS   And in speaking of the copy and the original we may assume that discourses are akin to the matter which they describe; when they relate to the lasting and permanent and intelligible, they ought to be lasting and unalterable, and, as far as their nature allows, irrefutable and invincible—nothing less. But when they express only the copy or likeness and not the eternal things themselves, they need only be likely and analogous to the former discourses. As being is to becoming, so truth is to belief.[20]

This passage is supplemented with another[21] in which the intellect, whose objects are the intelligible forms, is contrasted with true opinion, whose objects are the sensible things perceived by the body. This epistemological opposition is in turn replaced by this sociological one: "every man may be said to share in true opinion, but mind is the attribute of the gods and of very few men."[22] This very small class of men is obviously that of the philosophers.

18. Leonard Linsky, *Referring* (London: Routledge & Kegan Paul/New York: Humanities Press, 1967).
19. *Soph.* 268c–d.
20. *Tim.* 29b3–c3.
21. *Tim.* 51d3–e6.
22. *Tim.* 51e5–6.

Plato thus specifies the meaning of the word *logos*. From discourse in a broad sense, *logos* as it is defined in the *Sophist* comes to mean a falsifiable discourse, that is, a discourse susceptible of being declared true or false. The philosopher alone can conduct a true discourse because he contemplates the world of intelligible forms, whose stability is absolute. On the other hand, the sophist, who is a semblance-maker, can only produce a false discourse, because of the very definition of semblance.[23] Finally, all men, including philosophers, have an experience of sensible things apprehended by the senses, and maintain with respect to sensible things a discourse which resembles the discourse relative to the intelligible forms, of which sensible things are copies. Such a discourse is therefore unstable because of the becoming proper to sensible things. The same statement therefore can be true one moment and false the next, as is the case for example with "it is raining."

There are a certain number of problems associated with this clarification of the term *logos*. The following seems to be the most important. If the term *logos* designates only the type of discourse defined in the *Sophist*, that is, falsifiable discourse which is susceptible to being declared true or false, whether it bears upon the world of forms or upon sensible things, how can we speak of realities which we certainly must suppose to exist but about which we cannot hold a falsifiable discourse? To reply to this question, a definition of the meaning of *muthos* must be proposed, which will be modeled on the meaning of *logos* given in *Sophist* 259d–264b.

1. Composition (names and verbs)

In the *Sophist*, discourse in general is thus defined at the level of its basic component as an interweaving of verb(s) and name(s), verbs designating actions, and names the subjects of these actions.[24] On this level, what can we say about the type of discourse to which *muthos* refers, when Plato makes his own use of this term on sixty-one occasions?[25]

At the level of its basic component, myth is also an interweaving of verb(s) and name(s).

In books II and III of the *Republic*, which focus on the role of music in the education of the Guardians, Plato gives a list—in the section devoted to the type of discourse proper to music—of the five classes of names into which the subjects of mythical discourse are divided. In order to make

---

23. *Soph.* 266d9–e1.
24. *Soph.* 261e–62d.

25. See Appendix 1.

what follows comprehensible, here is a brief outline of the development of books II and III of the *Republic:*

Music (376e–403e)
   I. Introduction (376e)
  II. Development (376e–400e)
     A. Discourse (376e–98b)
       1. Content (376e–92c)
         a) Gods (and daimons) (376e–83c)
           (1) Critique of the past (376e–78e)
           (2) Suggested principle of control: to represent a god (or a daimon) as he is (378e–379a)
             (a) God is the cause only of good (379b–80c)
             (b) God does not change (380d–82c)
         b) Hades (383a–87c)
         c) Heroes (387d–92a)
         d) Men (392a–c)
       2. Form (392c–98b)
     B. Melody (398c–99e)
     C. Rhythm (399e–400e)
  III. Conclusion (401a–403c)

Consequently, according to Plato's inventory, the names of the subjects of mythical discourse are those of gods, daimons, heroes, inhabitants of Hades, and men.

This whole development is summarized in the following passage, where all five classes are listed:

> SOCRATES What type of discourse remains to be discussed for our content? We have declared the right way of speaking about gods and daimons and heroes and the world of Hades.
>
> ADEIMANTUS: We have.
>
> SOCRATES: Speech then about men would be the remainder.
>
> ADEIMANTUS: Obviously.[26]

All the names which designate the subjects of myth as discourse—whether they are cited by Plato[27] or not—exhibit an essential characteristic: they

26. *Rep.* III 392a3–9.
27. See Appendix 3.

are all proper names. Consequently, they refer not to classes ("gods, heroes, etc.") but to individuals ("Zeus, Oedipus, etc.") or to groups considered as individuals ("Muses, Trojans, etc."). Thus, the majority of these proper names, with rare exception, are masculine or feminine and refer to animate beings. In addition, all of these animate beings are endowed with a rational and therefore immortal soul. This explains why animals, plants, and inanimate objects are excluded from this inventory.

This exclusion does not mean that animals, plants, and inanimate objects do not play a role in myths. Indeed, it happens that these animate and inanimate things do intervene in decisive ways. However, their appearances always take as a model that of animate beings belonging to one of the five classes enumerated above, and not exclusively according to their mode of action as itemized by zoology, botany, physics, etc. The result of this is a permanent anthropomorphism.[28]

What can we say about the verbs that are woven together with the names whose characteristics we have just described? As a rule, they express actions similar to the correlates of those functions of which Vladimir Propp has established the typology in the case of the popular Russian folktale.[29]

If we were to draw up a typology of functions together with the inventory of proper names established by Plato, we would probably notice that just like the popular tale, myth is composed of a relatively small number of basic elements. However, the possible relations of these elements allow for the fabrication of an almost infinite number of stories.

Why however, does Plato, who carefully lists the subjects of mythical discourse, not do the same thing for the verbs which describe the actions performed by these subjects?

As a philosopher, Plato has something to say about gods, daimons, heroes, the inhabitants of Hades, and men, from his own point of view. Now, the actions described by the verbs used by the type of discourse called myth unfold in the sensible world which, for Plato, only exists insofar as it participates in the world of intelligible forms. That is why Plato does

---

28. The case of Aesop is of particular interest. In the *Phaedo,* Plato qualifies the type of discourse made by Aesop at times as *logos* (*Phdo.* 60d1) as in Herodotus (1.141) and Aristophanes (*Wasps* 1258, 1399; *Birds* 651), and at times as *muthos* (*Phdo.* 61b6) as in Aeschylus (*Myrmidons,* frag. 231 Mette). Aesop is also qualified as *logopoios,* as *muthopoios,* and even as *logomuthopoios.* On this, see B. E. Perry, *Studies in the Text History of the Life and Fables of Aesop* (Haverford: American Philological Association, 1936); *Aesopica* (Urbana: University of Illinois Press, 1952.)

29. See V. Propp, *Morphology of the Folktale,* 1st ed. trans. L. Scott with an introduction by Svatava Pirkova-Jakobson; 2d ed. rev. and ed. with a preface by L. A. Wagner, new introduction by A. Dundes (Austin and London: American Folklore Society/Indiana University Research Center for the Language Sciences, 1968). V. Propp, *Morphologie du conte* [1928], followed by *Les Transformations des contes merveilleux* [1928], with, in appendix, E. Mélétinski, *L'Étude structurale et la typologique du conte* [1969], trans. M. Derrida, T. Todorov, and C. Kahn (Paris: Seuil, 1970), 225.

not take them into account, and prefers to use verbs designating the relation between intelligible forms. Moreover, every message which is, over a long period of time, the object of an exclusively oral transmission, in which the poet—that specialist in the collective communication of the memorable—does not intervene, undergoes degradation. This deterioration may vary in severity, but it effects the actions accomplished more than the people who have accomplished them.[30]

This explains, to a degree, the fact that genealogies are indissociable from myths. Indeed genealogies constitute a sort of framework for myths. They must not, however, be mistaken for myths, as Marcel Detienne tends to do.[31] To be sure, the Egyptian priest says to Solon: "As for those genealogies *(ta genealogēthenta)* of yours which you just now recounted to us, Solon, they are no better than the myths of the children *(paidōn muthōn)*."[32] But this is only a declaration which bears upon a complex process which Plato describes in the following terms:

> CRITIAS On one occasion, wishing to draw them on to speak of antiquity, he began to tell myths *(muthologein)* about the most ancient things in our part of the world—about Phoroneus, who is called 'the first man,' and about Niobe, and after the deluge, of the survival of Deucalion and Pyrrha, and he traced the genealogy of their descendants *(kai tous ex autōn genealogein)* and reckoning up the dates, tried to compute how many years ago the events of which he was speaking happened.[33]

In sum, even if a myth is not related, it can be evoked at any time—as long as it has not been forgotten—to justify some or other genealogical relation.

Myth, irreducible to a series—whether ordered or not—of proper names, is also irreducible to a single phrase. Marcel Detienne is therefore wrong to hold that *muthos* in Plato can designate a proverb.[34] The only passage he cites to defend his position implies, on the contrary, a clear distinction between proverb and myth:

> ATHENIAN STRANGER The wise proverb[35] which forbids moving what is better left alone [the removal of buried treasure] has a wide range of applica-

---

30. See ch. 2.

31. The assurance of Marcel Detienne in the conclusion of his *The Creation of Mythology,* trans. Margaret Cook (Chicago and London: University of Chicago Press, 1986), 128, contrasts with the moderation of his interpretation at 88–89 of *Timaeus* 23b3–5 and 22a4–b3. This interpretation, moreover, represents a step backwards with regard to what one reads in "Une mythologie sans illusion," in J. B. Pontalis, ed., *Le Temps de la réflexion* 1 (Paris: Gallimard, 1980), 51.

32. *Tim.* 23b3–5.

33. *Tim.* 22a4–b3.

34. Detienne, *Creation of Mythology,* 90, n. 52 and 95, n. 95.

35. A proverb concerning what is sacred is often used by Plato; see in particular *Laws* III 684e1 and *Tht.* 181b1.

tion, and this is one of the cases to which it applies. Besides, one should be persuaded by the myths related on this subject *(peithesthai de khrē kai tois peri tauta legomenois muthois)* that such things are no blessing to a man's descendants.[36]

All the other examples of "maxims"[37] cited by Marcel Detienne can be explained by the particular usage that Plato makes of the term *muthos* in the *Laws* to designate the preamble that the legislator must give to each law.[38]

Each time Plato employs the term *muthos* in a "primary" sense,[39] he designates a discourse which includes more than one sentence. Now, just as a sentence cannot be reduced to the sum of the words of which it is composed, discourse presents an original unity similar to a long sentence and irreducible to the set of elements of which it is composed. From this perspective, myth appears, given the nature of its references, as an unfalsifiable discourse which can be characterized as a story because it relates events whose sequence does not respect a rational order.

To characterize myth as a story is the same as saying that it is not an argumentative discourse.[40] Even if it does not conform to a rational order, myth nevertheless always obeys an order which tries to bring analysis (structural among others) to the surface and which constitutes, beyond a doubt, one of the most powerful resources of oral memory.[41] Indeed, only a memory which refers to writing can remember a list of names without any narrative link, tables, formulas, etc.[42]

2. Reference

According to the definition that Plato gives in the *Sophist,* a falsifiable discourse bears upon an extralinguistic reality or referent. It is then possible to verify whether or not the linguistic sign which it constitutes truly corresponds to the referent to which it claims to refer. If the reply to the ques-

36. *Laws* XI 913b8–c3.
37. *Laws* IX 872c7–e4, 865d3–66a1.
38. On this point, see ch. 11.
39. See Appendix 1.
40. See ch. 10.
41. In his *Voyages aux îles du Grand Océan* (Paris, 1833), 1.393, J.-A. Moerenhout relates how a sacred singer from Raïatéa acquainted him with Polynesian cosmogony: "But I soon recognized the difficulty of writing all that; for he could only relate continuously and by declaiming; and, even then, his memory often betrayed him. If I stopped him to write it down, he no longer knew anything, he couldn't go on and had to start over again. It was only after numerous repetitions that I was able to write down on paper the following details." This passage is cited in part by Marcel Detienne, *Creation of Mythology,* 28.
42. See Jack Goody, "Mémoire et apprentissage dans les sociétés avec et sans écriture," *L'Homme* 1 (1977): 29–52.

tion asked by this kind of falsification is positive, then the discourse in question is true. If the reply is negative, then the same discourse is false. But, in order for such a falsification to be possible, the referent must be accessible. Within the framework of Platonic doctrine, two types of referents respond to this demand: intelligible forms and sensible things (which are situated in the present or in a recent past).

For Plato, the philosopher's discourse bears upon the intelligible forms apprehended by the intellect. These intelligible forms, which constitute true reality, are immutable. Thus the act of intellection which enables their apprehension as well as the discourse which externally expresses this act of intellection exhibit an absolute stability. They are always true because, like their referents which are situated outside time, they are indifferent to time.

On the other hand, sensible things, whose reality is dependent on their participation in the intelligible forms, are immediately situated in time. Consequently, the act of sensation which enables the apprehension of sensible things as well as the discourse which externally expresses this act of sensation are characterized by instability. For what is true at time t can become false at time $t + 1$; for example, "it is raining." Contrary to the discourse that focuses on intelligible forms, the discourse that bears upon sensible things is not indifferent to time. This is the case because its referent is located in a world subject to becoming. Such a situation therefore sets limits to the falsification of this type of discourse. Indeed, the adequacy or inadequacy of such a discourse to its referent can only be falsified if this referent can be perceived. For a referent to be perceptible, however, it must be situated, in relation to the percipient, in the present, or in a past recent enough for the individual in question to have had an experience of it, or to have been informed of it by someone who has had a direct experience of it.

The distant past—the knowledge of which rests exclusively on tradition—and the entire future cannot therefore be considered as valid referents for a discourse susceptible to falsification.

It is nevertheless obvious that Plato does not enclose his own discourse within the limits traced in the *Sophist*. Indeed, Plato mentions events that unfolded in a distant past, events he was only able to know through the intermediary of tradition. Above all, one of the most important components of his philosophy, that is, the realm of the immortal soul, is situated at an intermediate level between the world of forms and the world of sensible things.[43] These two types of referents are precisely what is designated

43. This is well illustrated by the ontological constitution of the world soul, after which the immortal part of the human soul is fashioned as a model. On this point, see L. Brisson, *Le Même et l'Autre*

by the five classes of names enumerated in books II and III of the *Republic:* gods, daimons, heroes, inhabitants of Hades, and men. Myths relate extraordinary events performed in a distant past by men living in the sensible world, and of which tradition has retained the memory. It is moreover between the intelligible world and the sensible world, at the level of the immortal soul, that gods, daimons, heroes, and the inhabitants of Hades are located. On the other hand, gods, daimons, and heroes are either immortals in the full sense, or immortalized offspring of immortals. Moreover, man is endowed with a soul of which a part is immortal and in this respect is akin to gods, daimons, and heroes. The soul's destiny before it takes up a body and after it leaves the body must therefore be explained; that is, according to ancient Greek popular belief, when it is in Hades. In the last analysis, myth covers more or less the same territory that is later claimed by history and theology—with theology perpetuating itself in its avatar, history.

Two consequences follow from this, with the first entailing the second. One is concerned with the relation that mythical discourse maintains with its referent. The other is concerned with the self-referential character of this type of discourse. Myth is an unfalsifiable discourse because its referent is located either at a level of reality inaccessible both to the intellect and to the senses, or at the level of sensible things, but in a past of which the author of this discourse can have no experience, whether directly or indirectly.

But how is this inaccessibility to be characterized? To hold that a referent is accessible to the intellect is, on the one hand, to indicate that this referent exists, and, on the other, that it is such and such. By contrast, to say that a referent is not accessible to the intellect and the senses is to indicate that it is not possible to determine if this referent is such and such, even taking for granted that it exists. In brief, in the first case the referent exists and can be precisely defined, whereas in the second the referent is not susceptible of any precise description, even if its existence must be taken for granted.

It is futile to list all the passages in which Plato takes for granted the existence of gods, daimons, heroes, and of an immortal part of the human soul, or to indicate all the other passages in which he demonstrates the existence of these same realities against all those who, in one way or another, raise doubts about them. One could mention, among others, book

---

dans la structure ontologique du "Timée" de Platon, 270ff. On the relation between the soul and myth in Plato, see W, Hirsch, *Platons Weg zum Mythos* (Köln, Berlin, and New York: De Gruyter, 1971).

X of the *Laws* for the existence of gods, daimons, and heroes, and the *Phaedo* in support of the existence of an immortal part of the human soul. Moreover, Plato does not seem to doubt the existence of facts dating back to a distant past, whether these concern the state and government of the world and men under the rule of Kronos[44] or the war between primeval Athens and Atlantis.[45] However, even if Plato does not doubt the existence of these referents, he must concede that there cannot be any definitive description either of the soul with respect to its immortality or of most of the extraordinary events that happened in the past. Why? Simply because these referents are accessible to neither the intellect nor the senses, assuming, of course, that the debate is not situated at the level of the intelligible in an attempt to define the intelligible form of a god, daimon, hero, or human soul in general.

How can this lacuna at the level of detailed description be dealt with? It can only be through a certain use of imitation. When the imitated reality is accessible to the senses, it is possible to verify if the imitation of it given by the discourse is adequate, that is, if there is resemblance between the copy and the model. All falsification however, becomes impossible as soon as the imitated reality is accessible neither to the senses nor to the intellect. Critias conducts a discourse of the first type, explicitly claimed to be a true discourse,[46] at the beginning of the *Timaeus* and in the dialogue named after him. By contrast, Timaeus conducts a discourse of the second type, explicitly introduced as a myth,[47] in the dialogue named after him.

But how do we imitate a model that escapes any definitive description? Is it even possible to imitate such a model? A practical response has been given to this problem, which however creates a scandal at the theoretical level. In order to imitate a reality which escapes all definitive description, we utilize a double imitation that substitutes for the first model another model which is accessible to the senses. By doing this, however, the shadow of the second model is projected onto the first. Hence the critique of Xenophanes (fl. 570–475). Not only are the gods decked out with the physical attributes of the human races that worship them: "But mortals consider that the gods are born, and that they have clothes and speech and bodies like their own."[48] And: "The Ethiopians say that their gods are snub-nosed

44. *Pol.* 271a5–b3.
45. *Tim.* 26c7–e5.
46. *Tim.* 26c7–d3, 26e4–5.
47. *Tim.* 29d2, 59c6, 68d2, 69b1.
48. DK 21B14. For the following quotations from Xenophanes, I will use the translation of G. S. Kirk, J. E. Raven, and M. Schofield in *The Presocratic Philosophers*, 2d ed. (Cambridge: Cambridge University Press, 1983), 168–69.

and black, the Thracians that theirs have light blue eyes and red hair."[49] And: "But if cattle and horses and lions had hands, or were able to draw with their hands and do the works that men can do, horses would draw the forms of the gods like horses, and cattle like cattle, and they would make their bodies such as they each had themselves."[50]

What is more: ethically, their behavior is that of the worst of men: Homer and Hesiod have attributed to the gods everything that is shameful and reproachable among men, stealing and committing adultery and deceiving each other."[51] Plato will take up this last criticism and make it his own.

In his critique of imitation as it functions in myth, Plato, like Xenophanes,[52] insists only on one aspect of a two-faced phenomenon. The spoken and/or acted image of a god, daimon, hero, inhabitant of Hades, or man of the past is only an appearance, insofar as it is by nature considerably different from its model. Nevertheless, this image, which consequently must be considered an appearing, remains the only means of evoking a reality which is by nature inaccessible both to intelligence and to the senses.[53]

Let us add an ethical remark to this epistemological one. The system of values defended by any myth presents a dynamic aspect which Xenophanes and Plato refuse to take into account. In myth, good and evil are presented from a dramatic point of view, within the domain of a series of events which is related by a story, and not from a dialectical point of view, in the form of an immutable system of oppositions which is made explicit by an argumentative discourse.

3. Falsification

A discourse can be characterized as falsifiable because its referent—which is either in the world of forms or in the world of sensible things—is accessi-

---

49. DK 21B16.

50. DK 21B15.

51. DK 21B11.

52. On the relation between Plato and Xenophanes, the following works may be consulted: D. Babut, "Xénophane, critique des poètes," *Antiquité classique* 43 (1974): 83–117; V. Guazzoni Foà, "Senofane e Parmenide in Platone," *Giornale di Metafisica* 16 (1961): 467–71; R. Mondolfo, "Platón y la interpretación de Jenófanes," *Revista de la Universidad nacional de Córdoba* 5 (1964): 79–80; P. Steinmetz, "Xenophanesstudien," *Rheinisches Museum* 109 (1966): 13–73; and more recently, J. H. Lesher, *Xenophanes of Colophon, Fragments. A Text and Translation with a Commentary, Phoenix* supplementary volume 30 (Toronto: University of Toronto Press, 1992).

53. See the article by J. P. Vernant, "Image et apparence dans la théorie platonicienne de la *mimēsis*," *Journal de psychologie normale et pathologique* 2 (1975): 133–60; reprinted under the title "Naissance d'images," in *Religions, histoires, raisons* (Paris: Maspero, 1979), 105–37.

ble either to the intellect or to the senses. In this case, truth or falsity are defined respectively as the correspondence or non-correspondence of this discourse to the referent upon which it bears. Truth presents no difficulties, but the same cannot be said for falsehood. Let us take this false statement, which serves as an example in the *Sophist:* "Theaetetus flies." At first view, it could be thought that what makes this statement false is its reference to a fact that does not exist, as indicated in this diagram:

False Statement refers to the Nonexistent Fact:	"Theaetetus flies" | Theaetetus flying

However, a statement that bears upon a nonexistent fact would not bear upon anything, simply because there is no such thing as a nonexistent fact, and therefore it would not be a meaningful statement.

Rather, a statement is false when it bears upon an existing fact that is different from the one it states:

False Statement refers to the Existing but Different Fact:	"Theaetetus flies" | Theaetetus sitting

This is an extremely brief explanation, which F. M. Cornford has developed in a much more elaborate form and which, since then, has provoked much discussion.[54]

In the case of myth, this explanation is no longer tenable, because the referent of this type of discourse is inaccessible both to the intellect and to the senses. It is therefore no longer possible to verify whether there is or is not a correspondence between a mythical discourse and its referent. It follows that myth should be situated beyond truth and falsehood; but this is not the case. Indeed, myth is explicitly deemed to be a false discourse in the following passage of book II of the *Republic:*

> SOCRATES And shall we not begin education in music earlier than in gymnastics?

---

54. On this subject, see first, F. M. Cornford, *Plato's Theory of Knowledge,* 311–17. Cornford's explanation has been criticized notably by J. C. Schultz, "An Anachronism in Cornford's *Plato's Theory of Knowledge,*" *Modern Schoolman* 43 (1965–66): 397–406. For a synthesis of contemporary work on the subject, see W. Detel, *Platons Beschreibung des falschen Satzes im "Theaitet" und "Sophistes,"* Hypomnemata 36 (Göttingen: Vandenhoeck & Ruprecht, 1972). For a more recent account, see L. M. de Rijk, *Plato's Sophist: A Philosophical Commentary* (Amsterdam: North-Holland Pub., 1986) and Nestor-Luis Cordero, *Platon, Sophiste* (Paris: Flammarion, 1993).

ADEIMANTUS Of course.

SOCRATES And under music you include discourses *(logous)*, do you not?

ADEIMANTUS I do.

SOCRATES And the discourses are of two kinds, the one true and the other false?

ADEIMANTUS Yes.

SOCRATES And education must make use of both, but first of the false?

ADEIMANTUS I don't understand your meaning.

SOCRATES Don't you understand that we begin by telling children myths *(muthous)*, and the myth is, taken as a whole, false, but there is truth in it also? And we make use of myth with children before gymnastics.

ADEIMANTUS That is so.[55]

This same accusation is found a little further on, but with more precision:

ADEIMANTUS . . . I don't apprehend which you mean by the greater [myths], either.

SOCRATES Those, I said, that Hesiod and Homer and the other poets related to us. These, I believe, composed false myths which they told and still tell to mankind.

ADEIMANTUS Of what sort? And with what in them do you find fault?

SOCRATES With that, I said, which one ought first and chiefly to blame, especially if the lie is not a pretty one.

ADEIMANTUS What is that?

SOCRATES When anyone imagines badly in his discourse the true nature of gods and heroes, like a painter whose portraits bear no resemblance to his models.[56]

And in book III of the *Republic* the accusation reappears in this context:

SOCRATES Then it seems we must exercise supervision also, in the manner of such myths as these, over those who undertake to supply them and request them not to dispraise in this undiscriminating fashion the life in Hades but rather praise it, since what they now tell us is neither true nor edifying to men who are destined to be warriors.[57]

Finally, in book VII of the *Republic* (522a7–8), Plato explicitly contrasts discourses which have a mythic character *(muthōdeis logoi)* and discourses which contain more truth *(alēthinōteroi logoi)*.

---

55. *Rep.* II 376e6–77a8.   57. *Rep.* III 386b8–c1.
56. *Rep.* II 377d2–e3.

Myth is already considered as a false discourse in the *Cratylus:*

HERMOGENES Then I am very sure that Cratylus was quite right in saying that I am no true son of Hermes, for I am not a good hand at discourses.

SOCRATES There is also reason, my friend, in Pan's being the double-formed son of Hermes.

HERMOGENES How do you make that out?

SOCRATES You are aware that discourse *(logos)* signifies all things *(pan)*, and it is always turning them round and round, and has two forms, true and false?

HERMOGENES Certainly.

SOCRATES Is not the truth that is in him the smooth or sacred form which dwells above among the gods, whereas falsehood dwells among men below, and is rough like the goat of tragedy *(trakhu kai tragikon)*, for tales and falsehoods have generally to do with the tragic or goatish life *(peri ton tragikon bion)*, and tragedy is the place of them?

HERMOCRATES Very true.

SOCRATES Then surely Pan, who is the declarer of all things *(pan)* and the perpetual mover *(aei polōn)* of all things, is rightly called *(aipolos)* [goatherd], he being the two-formed son of Hermes, smooth in his upper part, and rough and like a billy goat *(tragoeidēs)* in his lower regions. And, as the son of Hermes, he is discourse or the brother of discourse, and that brother should be like brother is no marvel.[58]

To understand Socrates laborious explanations, we must refer to the context.[59] Hermes has just been defined as the interpreter of thought through the intermediary of discourse *(logos)*. From this perspective, Pan, his son, must be considered either as discourse *(logos)*, or as the brother of discourse. Socrates then goes on to generalize the comparison that he had just

---

58. *Crat.* 408b6–d4.

59. I will only make two comments with respect to this particularly difficult passage. When Hermogenes says "I am very sure that Cratylus was quite right in saying that I was no true son of Hermes," he is referring to a statement made by Cratylus at the beginning of the dialogue (383c), clarified at 384c and taken up again at 407c and here. The allusion is obscure, but its meaning is clear in this case. Indeed, the etymology of the proper name "Hermogenes" means "of the race of Hermes." When one is "of the race of Hermes," who is the interpreter of thought through the medium of discourse, one should be able to employ all the tricks of discourse. However, this is not the case for Hermogenes. The rest of this passage pertains to the following series of terms: *trakhu* "bristling," *tragos* "billy goat," *tragōidia* "goat-song," that is, a religious song which accompanied the sacrifice of the billy goat at the festival of Dionysos and which constitutes the origin of tragedy, "tragedy," *tragikos* "goatish, tragic" and *tragoeidēs* "resembling a goat." In the final analysis, it is the etymology of the term *tragōidia* which serves as a background for this passage. On the subject in general, see now Timothy M. S. Baxter, *The Cratylus: Plato's Critique of Naming*, Philosophia antiqua 58 (Leiden: Brill, 1992).

initiated between Pan and discourse. Pan's nature is dual: the top of his body is that of a man with smooth skin, and the bottom that of a billy goat with skin bristling with hair. It is the same for discourse which can be either true or false. Thus, Socrates likens the top of Pan's body to true discourse, which is the attribute of gods (and a small number of men, that is, philosophers),[60] and he likens the bottom of Pan's body to false discourse, which is the lot of the vast majority of men. Now, through wordplay between that which has the aspect of a billy goat *(tragoeidēs),* that is, the bottom of the Pan's body to which false discourse corresponds; and that which pertains to tragedy *(tragikon)* where most myths are found, Socrates assimilates myth to false discourse. The context in which this assimilation is carried out is, moreover, very much in harmony with the denunciation of tragedy developed in the *Republic.*

In these four passages, myth is thus explicitly considered as a false discourse, although at the end of the first passage[61] Socrates concedes that myth also contains some truth.

Similarly, Socrates perceives in the mythical hymn *(muthikos humnos)*[62] in the *Phaedrus* a mixture of truth and falsehood with persuasive force. Related to this hymn are two discourses on Eros which Socrates performed as an exercise, taking Lysias' discourse as his model. Socrates, however, goes still further in the direction of the truth of the myth. At the end of the *Gorgias,* Socrates, who is opposed to Callicles on the nature of that which is just, relates a myth on the destiny of the soul after death. Before telling the myth, Socrates addresses Callicles in these terms:

> SOCRATES Give ears then, as they say, to a very fine discourse, which you, I suppose, will consider a myth *(muthon),* but I consider as actual truth [falsifiable discourse] *(logos),* for what I am going to tell you I shall recount as the actual truth.[63]

And after having told the myth, Socrates continues with the following observation which clarifies and attenuates, to a degree, what was stated before he began his story:

> SOCRATES Now perhaps all this seems to you like a myth told by an old woman and you despise it, and there would be nothing strange in despis-

60. Cf. *Tim.* 51e5–6.
61. Cf. *Rep.* II 377a4–6.

62. *Phdr.* 265c1.
63. *Gorg.* 523a1–3.

ing it if our searches could discover anywhere a better and truer account.[64]

At least in these last two cases, myth is thus considered overall as a true discourse.

In this case, however, how is it that myth, which appeared above as an unfalsifiable discourse, that is, as a discourse that can be neither true nor false, can be considered, in all these passages, sometimes as a true discourse and at other times as a false discourse?

This explanation can be found in a change of perspective. Truth and error no longer reside in the correspondence of a discourse with the referent to which it is supposed to refer, but in the agreement of a discourse—in the present case, myth—with another discourse raised to the level of a norm. This is true regardless of whether this discourse, that of the philosopher (and, more precisely, of course, that of Plato), bears upon the world of forms or upon the world of sensible things. Epistemology has given way to censorship.

In the *Republic,* Socrates describes the type of control that the founder of the city, who can only be the philosopher, must exert on the poet:

> SOCRATES Adeimantus, we are not poets, you and I at present, but founders of a state. And to founders it pertains to know the molds *(tupous)* on which poets must relate their myths *(muthologein)* and from which their poems must not be allowed to deviate each time they compose them, but the founders are not required themselves to compose myths.[65]

Tupos has been translated here by "mold," because, in the lost-wax process, this term designates the *forma impressa* or hollow mold, which Plato distinguishes in the *Theaetetus*[66] from the *apotupōma,* the *imago expressa,* or impression in relief.[67] In other words, the founder of the city provides the poets with the molds that they must employ to cast, out of the "wax" of sensible things, the artifacts that are myths. These molds *(tupoi)* are the laws *(nomoi)*[68] of which Plato gives us an example: (1) god is good and

64. *Gorg.* 527a5–8.

65. *Rep.* III 378e7–79a4.

66. *Tht.* 194b5.

67. This explanation is given in a note in A. Diès' translation of the *Theaetetus* (Paris: Les Belles Lettres, 1926), 236. See also Georges Roux, "Le sens de TUPOS," *Revue des études anciennes* 63 (1961): 5–14.

68. *Rep.* II 380c7, 387c7. On this point, see V. Goldschmidt, "Theologia" [1949], *Questions platoniciennes* (Paris: Vrin, 1970), 145–48.

therefore is only the cause of what is good;[69] (2) god is perfect and therefore can neither undergo nor impose any change.[70] It is obvious that these molds are directly derived from an analysis of the intelligible form of god.[71]

The truth or falsity of a myth therefore depends on its conformity with the philosopher's discourse on the intelligible forms in which the individual entities that are the subjects of this myth participate. Moreover, the truth or the falsity of a myth can also depend on its conformity with the discourse which proposes an explanatory model in the realm of cosmology. There are two examples of this in Plato. The first is a group of myths in the *Statesman*[72] and, the second, the myth of Phaethon in the *Timaeus*.[73]

There are three different myths in the *Statesman,* all presented as resulting from the same phenomenon: (1) that of Atreus and Thyestes, (2) that concerning the age of Kronos, and (3) that of the "earthborn race."

> STRANGER All these facts originate from the same event in cosmic history, and so do hosts of others yet more marvelous than these. However, as this great event took place so long ago, some of them have faded from man's memory; others survive but they have become scattered and have come to be told in a way which obscures their real connection with one another. No one has related the great event of history which gives the setting of all of them; it is this event which we must now recount.
>
> YOUNG SOCRATES Excellent, sir. Please go on, and leave nothing unsaid.[74]

This cosmological phenomenon is explained by reference to a mechanical model.[75] Meanwhile, in the *Timaeus,* the Egyptian priest who informs Solon states the following opinion about the myth of Phaethon:

> SOLON (relating the words of the Egyptian priest): There is a story which even you have preserved, that once upon a time Phaethon, the son of Helios, having yoked the steeds in his father's chariot, because he was not able to drive them in the path of this father, burned up all that was upon the earth, and was himself destroyed by a thunderbolt. Now this has the form of a myth, but really signifies a parallax of the bodies mov-

---

69. *Rep.* II 379b1.

70. *Rep.* II 381b4.

71. These passages are the subject of a lively debate. On the controversy, see G. Naddaf, "Plato's *Theologia* Revisited," *Méthexis* 9 (1996): 5–18.

72. *Pol.* 269b sq.

73. *Tim.* 22c–d.

74. *Pol.* 269b5–c3.

75. This has been explained quite well by P.-M. Schuhl, "Autour du fuseau d'Anankè" [1930], *La Fabulation platonicienne,* 2d ed. (Paris: Vrin, 1968), 71–78.

ing in the heavens around the earth, and a great conflagration of things upon the earth which recurs after long intervals.[76]

The truth of the myth of Phaethon is thus rejected in the name of the astronomical theory of the parallax.

In the case of the myth of Phaethon, as in the case of the myth of the *Statesman,* the procedure is the same. The truth or falsity of both of these myths depends on their conformity to a discourse of another type, that is, to be more precise, to a discourse which proposes a cosmological model; even if this cosmological discourse is itself likened to a myth.[77]

76. *Tim.* 22c3–d3.
77. See ch. 13.

TEN

THE OPPOSITION BETWEEN
MYTH AND ARGUMENTATIVE DISCOURSE

The *muthos/logos* dichotomy can be interpreted not only as the opposition between falsifiable discourse and unfalsifiable discourse—the principal aspects of which were just described—but also as the opposition between narrative discourse—or, more simply, a story—and argumentative discourse. Whereas the first contrast is founded on an external criterion, i.e., the relation between the discourse and the referent upon which it is supposed to bear, the second contrast depends on an internal criterion: the organization of its development. This second contrast makes sense only in a philosophical context, since both history and myth are kinds of stories.

A story relates events as they are supposed to have happened, without giving any explanation. Consequently, the linkage between its parts is contingent, at least from a superficial point of view, because, since Propp, several attempts have been made to uncover a logic of the story. Its only aim is to realize an emotional fusion between the hero of the story and its addressee through the intermediary of the storymaker and/or storyteller. On the other hand, argumentative discourse follows a rational order—however we choose to define 'reason.' The sequence of its parts is constructed according to the rules of logic, whose aim is to make its conclusion necessary. What the agent of such a discourse seeks is rational agreement with regard to this conclusion.

The opposition between myth and argumentative discourse is admirably illustrated by the construction of the *Statesman*. The aim of the *Statesman* is to find a definition of the statesman. The principal character is a Stranger from Elea, who represents a philosophical trend which exerted a great influence on Plato.[1] In order to obtain this definition, the Eleatic Stranger uses an argumentative discourse which utilizes one of the methods

---

1. On the relation between Plato and the Eleatics, see G. Prauss, *Platon und der logische Eleatismus* (Berlin: De Gruyter, 1966).

proper to dialectic: that of division. This method consists in dividing each intelligible form into two paths, in accordance with specific rules laid down at *Statesman* 262a–64b. One of these parts is again submitted to the same process and so on, in order that all the constituent elements of the sought-after definition may be obtained. In one place, a definition of the statesman as a shepherd of his people is proposed. However, the Stranger from Elea rejects this definition, having recourse to a myth which shows that the definition applies to a very distant past and not to the present. This is explained after the myth in question is related.[2] Further on, the same idea is once again taken up and developed with the help of an enlightening comparison with painting.[3] This is what the Stranger from Elea declares before relating his myth:

STRANGER We must begin all over again from another starting point and travel by another road.

YOUNG SOCRATES What kind of road must this be?

STRANGER We have to bring in some pleasant stories to relieve the strain. There is a mass of ancient myth a large part of which we must now use for our purposes; after that we must go on as before, dividing always and choosing one part only, until we can arrive at the summit of our climb and the object of our journey. Shall we begin?

YOUNG SOCRATES Yes, certainly.

STRANGER Come then, listen closely to my myth as a child would. After all, you are not so very many years too old for stories.[4]

There is an astonishing similarity between the presentation of myth in the *Statesman* and in the *Protagoras*.

Indeed, Protagoras replies in the following way to Socrates before relating his myth:

SOCRATES . . . If then you can demonstrate more plainly to us that virtue is something that can be taught, please don't hoard your wisdom but give us this demonstration *(epideixon)*.

PROTAGORAS I shall not be a miser, Socrates. Now shall I, as an old man speaking to his juniors, put my explanation in the form of a myth, or give it as a reasoned argument?
(Many of the audience answered that he should relate it in whichever form he pleased.)

PROTAGORAS Then I think it will be pleasanter to tell you a myth.[5]

2. *Pol.* 274e1–4.   4. *Pol.* 268d5–e6.
3. *Pol.* 277a3–c6.   5. *Prot.* 320b8–c7.

The philosophical context here is completely different from the *States-man.*

Indeed, Protagoras makes no reference to the intelligible world of forms. And this is the case quite simply because Protagoras is one of the sophists who, in the passage of the *Timaeus* cited below, is alluded to in these terms: "it appears to some, that true opinion and intelligence in no way differ."[6] Further, this is the thesis, explicitly attributed to Protagoras, which is subjected to a detailed critique in the *Theaetetus.*

In the dialogue which bears his name, Protagoras—the sophist for whom Plato has the most respect—recounts a myth,[7] and then develops an argumentative discourse,[8] in order to set forth, by different means, the same theme: that virtue can be taught, and that it is the sophist who is best qualified to deliver such instruction. In the three decisive moments of this twofold development, that is, at the beginning of the myth,[9] at the end of the myth,[10] and at the end of the argument which follows it,[11] Protagoras returns to the opposition myth/argumentative discourse.

The myth related by Protagoras refers to a very distant past, which witnessed the appearance of beasts and men, to whom the gods allotted different qualities.[12] By contrast, the argumentative discourse which follows it describes certain social and political practices in fifth and fourth century Greece, and tries to justify them by limiting itself to observed human behavior. Thus, in neither case do we abandon the sensible world even if, in the first case, the events in question are only the objects of tradition, whereas, in the second, the facts in question are verifiable through the intermediary of the senses.

Socrates refers to the same opposition between myth and argumentative discourse at the beginning of the *Phaedo:*

> SOCRATES When I had finished my hymn, I reflected that a poet, if he is to
> be worthy of the name, ought to make myths and not arguments *(ennoē-*
> *sas hoti ton poiētēn deoi, eiper melloi poiētēs einai, poiein muthous all'ou*
> *logous),* and I was not good at telling myths *(kai autos ouk ē muthologikos).*
> So I availed myself of some of the myths *(muthous)* which were ready to

6. *Tim.* 51d5–6.
7. *Prot.* 320c–24d.
8. *Prot.* 324d–28d.
9. *Prot.* 320c2–4.
10. *Prot.* 324d6–7.
11. *Prot.* 328c3–4.
12. On the Protagoras myth, see Luc Brisson, "Le Mythe de Protagoras: Essai d'analyse structurale," *Quaderni Urbinati di Cultura classica* 20 (1975): 7–37.

hand, those of Aesop, and familiar to me, and I versified the first of them that suggested themselves.[13]

This opposition, formulated in an elliptical way, needs to be clarified. Myth and argumentative discourse appear as the results of fabrication in the realm of discourse. Now, since the poet is the maker of myth, the philosopher must be the maker of argumentative discourse. The fabrication of myths must remain a pastime for the philosopher.

In the *Phaedo,* Plato describes what Socrates last moment must have been like and tries to explain why his master died a noble and fearless death. He bases himself upon a myth which teaches that human beings have an immortal and indestructible soul which is the seat of memory and individuality. Further, this myth teaches that the soul will survive when it is separated from the body which it moves, and that it will enjoy a privileged position if, during previous existences, the individual in question lived a life directed by rational activity.[14] Socrates tries to prove that the human soul is immortal and indestructible by using the deductive method, that is, the *logos:* argument by opposites,[15] argument by reminiscence,[16] argument by affinity,[17] and a second argument by opposites.[18] The deductive method, however, is quickly confronted with absolute limits. Two Pythagoreans, who are Socrates' interlocutors, go so far as to question the validity of the axioms which constitute the departure point for the deduction: Simmias suggests the image of a lyre[19] and Cebes that of a weaver.[20] Since Socrates has only a few moments left to live, he does not have time to question the validity of the axioms which he accepts, and he encourages his disciples to continue the task. Socrates himself relates the continuation of the myth *(muthos)* which served as the departure point for the discussion[21] and then drinks the hemlock. By this gesture, Socrates testifies that he is persuaded by this myth, which allows him to firmly believe in the immortality and indestructibility of the soul, which the deductive method has shown itself to be demonstrating. Moreover, before undertaking his account, Socrates recalls the usefulness of this myth.[22] Indeed, for Plato, the interest of myth resides neither in its truth value nor in its argumentative power, but in its usefulness at the level of ethics and politics. We must still examine in what this utility consists.

13. *Phdo.* 61b3–7.
14. *Phdo.* 81b–d.
15. *Phdo.* 70c–72e.
16. *Phdo.* 72e–77a.
17. *Phdo.* 78b–84b.

18. *Phdo.* 102a–107a.
19. *Phdo.* 85b–86e.
20. *Phdo.* 86e–88b.
21. *Phdo.* 107d–15a.
22. *Phdo.* 110b1–4.

ELEVEN

THE UTILITY OF MYTH

Myth has two disadvantages for a philosopher such as Plato. It is a unfalsifiable discourse which can often be assimilated to a false discourse. It is also a story whose elements are linked in a contingent way, unlike argumentative discourse, whose inner organization manifests necessity. However, these two disadvantages are compensated by two advantages which give myth a real utility, which is displayed in such adjectives as *ōphelimos, lusitelēs, khrēsimos,* and *kalos,* which Plato uses to qualify *muthos.* But what are these advantages?

Even if myth is an unfalsifiable discourse, it still constitutes the means by which the basic knowledge shared by all the members of a community is communicated. The community ensures that this knowledge is transmitted from generation to generation. And, even if myth is not characterized by necessity, as is the case for argumentative discourse, myth, as a story, constitutes nonetheless a privileged instrument for modifying the behavior of the inferior part of the human soul. The action proper to myth can be presented as extraordinary, like the effect of a charm or spell, or as ordinary, like the effect of persuasion in general. There are two types of constraint—in ethics, for the individual, and in politics, for the community—which are indispensable for ensuring that our behavior conforms to rules and laws, whatever the particular rules or laws may be: a physical constraint, exerted on the body through violence, and a moral constraint, exerted on the soul through persuasion. Plato does not dismiss physical constraint, but he prefers moral constraint. Consequently, whenever it is possible, Plato appeals to persuasion rather than violence. Now, myth constitutes an instrument of persuasion which is all the more effective in that its audience, within the framework of a given community, is universal. This enables myth to play for ordinary people a role similar to that of an intelligible form for the philosopher. It serves as a model to which we can refer, in order to determine the behavior which we should adopt in any given case. It follows, therefore, that in both ethics and politics, myth can take the place of philosophical discourse. There is an example of this on the ethical level in the *Phaedo:*

> SOCRATES Of course, no man of reason *(nous)* ought to insist that the facts are exactly as I have described them. But that either this or something very like it is a true account of our souls and their future inhabitations— since we have clear evidence that the soul is immortal—this, I think, is both a reasonable contention and a belief worth risking, for the risk is a noble one *(kalos gar ho kindunos).* We should use such accounts as if to cast a spell on ourselves *(hōsper epaidein heautōi),* and that is why I have already drawn out my myth so long.[1]

As Socrates indicates, the myth he has just told[2] is not addressed to reason *(nous),* which approaches the problem of immortality from a completely different angle, namely that of rational proof.[3] Moreover, what this story relates about the nature and destiny of the soul inspires some doubt, simply because the discourse is unfalsifiable. Nevertheless, Socrates insists on telling this myth because he considers it a particularly useful incantation. Myth relieves us of the fear of death through persuasion,[4] and, at the same time, it reminds us of the priority of the rational part of the soul—which alone is truly immortal—over the appetitive part.[5] Consequently, the interpretation which J. Salviat provides of the expression *kalos gar ho kindunos* seems to be a good one.[6] The adjective *kalos* must be understood not in an aesthetic sense as "beautiful" but in an evaluative sense, meaning "advantageous."

It is easy to move to the political from the ethical, insofar as collective behavior is conditioned, in the final analysis, by individual behavior. This is why the beliefs about destiny of the soul after death have a direct repercussion on the warrior's valor:

> SOCRATES Then it seems we must exercise supervision also, in the matter of such myths as these, over those who undertake to supply them and request them not to dispraise in this undiscriminating fashion the life in Hades but rather praise it, since what they now tell us is neither true nor useful *(oute alēthē oute ōphelima)* to men who are destined to be warriors.[7]

1. *Phdo.* 114d1–7.
2. *Phdo.* 107d–14c.
3. *Phdo.* 102a–107b.
4. *Phdo.* 77d–78a.
5. *Phdo.* 114d–15a.
6. J. Salviat, "*Kalos gar ho kindunos,* risque et mythe dans le *Phédon,*" *Revue des études grecques* 78 (1965): 23–39.
7. *Rep.* III 389b7–9.

The same myth can thus present usefulness on the ethical level as well as on the political. On the political level as well, however, it is to be noted that the usefulness of myth is independent of its status with respect to truth or falsity:

> SOCRATES And also in the account of these myths *(en . . . tais muthologias)* of which we were just now speaking, owing to our ignorance of the truth about antiquity we liken the false to the true as far as we may and so make it useful *(khrēsimon).*[8]

In book III of the *Republic,* one finds the following justification of the utilization of falsehood, that is, of lying, in both foreign and domestic politics: "The rulers of the city may, if anyone, fitly lie on account of enemies or citizens for the benefit of the state *(ep'ōpheleiai);* no other may have anything to do with it."[9] In the following passage, Socrates explains the appropriate use of the "noble lie"—viz., the myths of authochtony[10] and of the three classes[11]—whose purpose is to account simultaneously for both the unity and the diversity of the citizens within the ideal city described in the *Republic:*

> SOCRATES How, then, might we contrive one of those opportune falsehoods of which we were just now speaking,[12] as if by one noble lie *(gennaion ti)* to persuade if possible the rulers themselves, but failing that the rest of the city?
>
> GLAUCON What kind of falsehood do you mean?
>
> SOCRATES Nothing unprecedented, but a sort of Phoenician tale, something that has happened now in many parts of the world, as the poets have induced men to believe, but that has not happened and perhaps would not be likely to happen in our day and demanding no little persuasion to make it believable.[13]

The myth of autochthony alluded to here reappears in the same context and plays the same role in book II of the *Laws:*

> ATHENIAN And, even had it not been so—as our present argument has shown that it is—could a legislator of even moderate merits *(ophelos),* supposing him to have ventured on any falsehood for the sake of its good effect *(ep'agathōi)* on the young, have devised a more useful *(lusitelesteron)* falsehood than this, or one more potent to induce us to practice all justice freely, and without compulsion *(mē biai all'hekontas)?*

---

8. *Rep.* II 382c10–d3.
9. *Rep.* III 389b7–9.
10. *Rep.* III 414d–e.
11. *Rep.* III 415a–d.
12. *Rep.* III 414d–e.
13. *Rep.* III 414b8–c7.

CLINIAS Why, as to truth, sir, truth is a glorious thing and an enduring thing, but it seems no easy matter to convince men of it.

STRANGER Well, what about the myth *(muthologēma)* of the man from Sidon—was it easy to convince anyone of that? Now there are many such myths.[14]

In both cases, then, the myth of autochthony is brought up in respect to the foundation of Thebes by Cadmus to which the following two expressions allude: "A Phoenician" *(Phoinikikon ti)* and "the man from Sidon" *(tou Sidōniou)*. Indeed, according to certain versions of the myth, Cadmus was the son of Phoenix or Agenor, kings of Tyre and Sidon. Cadmus was led by a cow to the site of the future Thebes after having been advised to abandon the pursuit of his sister Europa by the Delphic oracle. He decided to make a sacrifice to Athena and sent his men to look for water at a nearby spring, but the snake who guarded the spring killed most of them. Cadmus came to their rescue and killed the snake. Athena then appeared to him and recommended that he sow the teeth of the snake. Cadmus did so, and immediately armed men, the Spartoi, sprung from the earth. Since they were threatening, he decided to get rid of them, so Cadmus threw stones in the middle of the group. Not knowing who hit them, the Spartoi mutually accused one another. The quarrel quickly turned into a massacre, which only five survived: Echion, Hyperenor, Chthonios, Peloros, and Oudaeos. They became the first ancestors of the Thebans.

To use this myth is obviously to conduct a false discourse, because autochthony is contrary to what is known about the reproduction of human beings, at least in the actual state of things. There was a time, however, when things were different. In the *Statesman,* the Eleatic Stranger situates this "race of the sons of the earth," whose existence he refuses to doubt, under the reign of Kronos.[15] Yet, this myth is obviously useful, even if it is now similar to a false discourse. It can be used to persuade[16] the citizens that they are all brothers, and that their first duty is to protect their mother, that is, the earth from which they emerged and upon which they live.

Thus, Plato does not hesitate to take up a story, whose falsehood in the current circumstances he elsewhere denounces, but which presents the advantage of being known by everyone. Plato's goal in doing so is that the behavior of the citizens of the city—whether the ones described in the *Republic* or in the *Laws*—may be in accord with the necessities of commu-

14. *Laws* II 663d3–e6.
15. *Pol.* 271a5–b3.
16. *Rep.* III 414c1, c5–6, c7; *Laws* II 663e4, e6.

nal life, and in particular, with the defense of their territory. Furthermore, starting with the fourth book of the *Laws,* we notice a wholly new use of myth which takes over from the general practice we have described: here, myth is used as a preamble to laws which are about to be proclaimed.

In book IV of the *Laws,*[17] Plato reflects on the practice of the legislator, comparing the legislator with the poet and physician. The discourse of the legislator, unlike that of the poet, must be noncontradictory. In other words, the legislator can only have one discourse on the same subject, whereas the poet does not hesitate to put into play two contradictory discourses on the same subject. Plato reminds us that this is the reason why the legislator must not allow the poet to compose whatever he wishes.[18] Nevertheless, even if the legislator is only allowed to maintain a single discourse on the same subject, this discourse is not necessarily simple. In this regard, Plato mentions two physicians whose behavior radically differs.[19] The first gives his patients no explanation of the sickness by which they are afflicted, but brutally lays down a prescription, and then moves on to his next patient. The second, on the other hand, first consults with the patient and his friends, then takes the time to give to the patient an explanation which accounts for his prescription. In the same way, the legislator's discourse can be either simple or double. If it is simple, it is short because it is only composed of two elements: the prescription of the law and the penalties to be incurred by whoever fails to submit to the law. If it is double, it is at least twice as long because he prefaces the prescription of the law with a preamble *(proomion).* The preamble introduces, along with the violence attached to the penalty for failure to obey the law, the persuasion destined to assure at the outset obedience to this law. In brief, the legislator has two methods to assure that the prescribed law is respected: first, persuasion, which is what the preamble attempts to mobilize, and second, violence, which is attached to the penalty incurred by whomever does not submit to it. Plato, however insists on relying on persuasion rather than on repression because to use the latter is to admit defeat, which is implied by lack of respect for the law.

For Plato, a preamble is above all an exhortation *(paramuthia).*[20] By

17. *Laws* IV 719b–c.

18. *Laws* IV 719b–c.

19. A controversy has begun and continues on the distinction between these two different types of physicians. On the subject, see F. Kudlien, *Die Sklaven in der griechischen Medizin der klassischen und hellenistischen Zeit* (Wiesbaden: F. Steiner, 1968), chap. 3; R. Joly, "Esclaves et médecins dans la Grèce antique," *Sudhoffs Archiv für Geschichte der Medizin und der Naturwissenschaften* 53 (1969): 1–14; J. Jouanna, "Le Médecin, modèle du législateur dans les *Lois* de Platon," *Ktema* 3 (1978): 77–92.

20. *Paramuthia, Laws* IV 720a1; *paramuthion, Laws* VI 773e5, IX 880a7, X 885b5, XI 923c2.

means of a pun, Plato likens the exhortation *(paramuthia* or *paramuthion)* to a "myth which precedes the law" *(ho pro tou nomou muthos).*[21] This comparison[22] is supported by the last fourteen occurrences of the word *muthos* in the *Laws.*[23] In nine cases, this word refers to the traditional myths of ancient Greece, and in five other cases it refers to discourses which are perhaps not myths as such but which maintain explicit links with some of these myths.

In the last analysis, the particular use that Plato makes of myth in these fourteen cases is only a specialization of the general practice described above. To persuade the citizens to respect such or such a law, the legislator begins by recalling a myth which illustrates the behavior required by the law. For a law that stipulates that girls must take part in the same physical exercises as the young men, the Athenian Stranger invokes ancient myths *(muthous palaious)*[24]—probably those concerning the Amazons—to support this prescription. The recourse to this well-known example enables him to convince the multitude to accept more readily this law, which went against the general practice in ancient Greece.[25]

Even though myth is an unfalsifiable discourse which is not argumentative, it is all the more effective in that it transmits a basic knowledge which is shared by all the members of the community. Consequently, within this community, it can play the role of an instrument of persuasion with a universal impact. Since it is the only alternative to violence, myth allows, within the human soul, for the preeminence of reason over the mortal part and it ensures, in the city, that the multitude submit to the prescriptions of the philosophers, that is, the legislators or founders of the city. In both cases, myth plays the role of a paradigm, and it is by means not of education but of persuasion that all those who are not philosophers—that is, the majority of human beings—are led to embrace this paradigm in order to adapt their behavior to it.

21. *Laws* XI 927c7–8.
22. On this point, see Herwig Görgemanns, *Beiträge zur Interpretation von Platons "Nomoi,"* Zetemata, Heft 25 (Munich: Beck, 1960), 30–71, esp. 59, n. 3; Silvia Gastaldi, "Legge e retorica: I proemi delle *Leggi* di Platone," *Quaderni di Storia* 10 (1984): 69–109.
23. See Appendix 4.
24. *Laws* VII 804e4.
25. Cf. *Laws* VII 804e; *Rep.* V 451c sq.

TWELVE

THE REPUDIATION OF
ALLEGORICAL INTERPRETATION

The usefulness that Plato attributes to myth cannot be dependent upon any allegorical interpretation. The repudiation of such interpretation is justified in the following passage in book II of the *Republic:*

> SOCRATES But Hera's fetterings by her son and the hurling out of heaven of Hephaestus by his father when he was trying to save his mother from a beating, and the battles of the gods in Homer's verse are things that we must not admit into our city either wrought in allegory or without allegory *(out'en huponoiais oute aneu huponoiōn)*. For the young are not able to distinguish what is and what is not allegory *(hoti te huponoia kai ho mē),* but whatever opinions are taken into mind at that age are wont to prove indelible and unalterable.[1] For which reason, maybe, we should do our utmost that the first myths that they hear should be so composed as to bring the fairest lessons of virtue to their ears *(hoti kallista memuthologēmena pros aretēn akouein).*[2]

The three examples of the word *huponoia* in this passage are the only ones found in the whole Platonic corpus.

Although Plato rarely uses this word, it is nonetheless very interesting. As J. Pépin points out,[3] *huponoia* has a meaning which is later expressed by *allēgoria.*[4] According to its etymology, *huponoia* is a substantive which corresponds to the verb *huponoein*. Now, *huponoein* (literally, "to see or to think beneath"), is simply to distinguish a (deep) hidden meaning behind the obvious (superficial) meaning of a discourse. The only two examples

---

1. Cf. *Tim.* 26b2–c3.
2. *Rep.* II 378d3–e3.
3. J. Pépin, *Mythe et allégorie: Les origines grecques et les contestations judéo-chrétiennes,* 2d ed. (Paris: Études augustiniennes, 1976), esp. 85–92. On Plato's attitude with regard to allegory, see J. Tate, "Plato and Allegorical Interpretation," *Classical Quarterly* 23 (1929): 142–54; Mauro Tulli, "Il giudizio di Platone sull'esegesi allegorica," in *Ricerche di Filologica classica III: Interpretazioni antiche e moderne di testi greci* (Pisa: Biblioteca di Studi Antici 53, 1987), 45–52.
4. Moreover, Plutarch makes an explicit link between the two words in *De audiendis poetis* 4.19e.

of *huponoein* in the Platonic corpus confirm this definition. The first is found in the *Gorgias:*

> SOCRATES I suspected *(hupōpteuon)* too, Gorgias, that you meant this kind of persuasion, with such a province; it is merely that you may not be surprised if a little later I ask you the same kind of question, though the answer seems clear to me. Yet I may repeat it—for, as I said, I am questioning you, not for your own sake, but in order that the argument may be carried forward consecutively, and that we may not form the habit of suspecting *(huponoountes)* and anticipating each other's views, but that you may complete your own statements as you please, in accordance with your initial plan.[5]

It is worth noting that Socrates designates the suspicion not only by using *huponoein* but also by using *hupopteuein* "to see beneath."

The other example of *huponoein* is found in book III of the *Laws.* Speaking about men who, having survived past catastrophes, are not familiar with city life, the Athenian Stranger concludes as follows:

> ATHENIAN Thus they were good men, partly for this reason, and partly from their proverbial simplicity *(dia tēn legomenēn euētheian);* they were so simple of character *(euētheis ontes)* that when they heard things called fair or foul, they obediently took the statements for infallible truths. No one was sufficiently subtle to suspect deception *(huponoein),* as men do today; what they were told about gods or men they believed to be true, and lived by it. Thus they came to be just the kind of men you and I have been describing.[6]

This text has a twofold ambiguity.

First, the adjective *euēthēs* and the noun *euētheia* express both goodness and stupidity of character.[7] By using these two terms, Plato wants to indicate that the goodness of these men is due largely to their stupidity. The mountain dwellers of which Plato speaks at *Timaeus* 22b6–23b3 must be included in this group. These mountain dwellers who survived the Flood remain illiterate and ignorant of the Muses, because they are not city dwellers. Indeed, it is only in a city that people have a sufficient amount of leisure to devote themselves to writing and music (in the broad sense of the term). In these circumstances, such men obviously cannot suspect that, beneath what they are told concerning gods and men, there may lie some

---

5. *Gorg.* 454b8–c5.
6. *Laws* III 679c2–8.
7. Claude Gaudin, "EUĒTHEIA: La théorie platonicienne de l'innocence," *Revue philosophique de la France et de l'étranger* 159 (1981): 145–68.

falsehood. For to suspect *(huponoein)* implies a knowledge *(sophia)* and a science *(epistēmē)* which they lack. It is this verb which brings about the second ambiguity in this passage. To be sure, here *huponoein* probably refers to the allegorical interpretation of myths that the sophists, in particular, were practicing at this time. The words *sophia* and *epistēmē* reinforce this hypothesis. Plato's critique, however, goes further than this. With respect to myths, the men of this time are seen to be not only incapable of any allegorical interpretation but even of that discernment of the true and the false which is considered as indispensable in the *Republic* and the *Laws.*

With respect to myth, then, Plato adopts a position which is intermediary between a naive attitude and a scholarly attitude. The naive attitude is that of the survivors of the great natural catastrophes, who not only refrain from any allegorical interpretation but even of any discernment of truth from falsity. The scholarly attitude, on the other hand, is reflected by those who want to transform falsehood into truth by practicing an allegorical interpretation. Indeed, as we saw in the passage of the *Republic* quoted above,[8] Plato rejects any recourse to an allegorical interpretation without, however, forbidding himself from discerning between the true and the false.

Here we hit upon a fundamental aspect of the attitude of knowledge and science with regard to myth in ancient Greece.[9] This attitude originated in ancient Greece in the sixth century B.C., when people began to ask questions about *phusis* ("nature") outside of the framework of traditional religion.[10] First of all, scientific knowledge detected falsity in myth, and this then opened two paths. Either scientific knowledge purely and simply rejected what was false and kept only that aspect of myth which could be considered as true. Generally speaking, this did not amount to much.[11] Alternatively, scientific knowledge tried to transform the false into the true through a process of allegorical interpretation.

The latter position goes far back into the past of ancient Greece. Ac-

---

8. *Rep.* II 378d3–e3.

9. In chapter 1 ("Ambiguous Borderlines") of *The Creation of Mythology,* M. Detienne has clearly shown that the modern attitude of science with respect to myth strangely resembles that of Plato's and Parmenides' contemporaries.

10. For a detailed analysis of the Greek concept of *phusis,* see Gerard Naddaf, *L'Origine et l'évolution du concept grec de "phusis"* (Lewiston, N.Y.: Mellen, 1992). A second revised French edition of this work is forthcoming with Les Éditions Klincksieck in Paris and an English edition with the State University of New York Press.

11. This is Plato's position, which is certainly derived from Xenophanes, a position which is quite firm in the *Republic,* but softened somewhat in the *Laws.* For Xenophanes, see the three fragments quoted above in chapter 9, sect. 2.

cording to Jean Pépin, Pythagoras (*fl.* 532–31) and Heraclitus (*fl.* 504–501) prepared the way for allegorical interpretation. However, the first true practitioner may have been Theagenes of Rhegium, the oldest historian of Homeric literature. Whereas Theagenes of Rhegium practiced a physical allegory, Anaxagoras (c. 500–428) devoted himself to ethical allegory. His disciples, Metrodorus of Lampsacus and Diogenes of Apollonia, also practiced allegorical interpretation but preferred physical allegory. By the end of the fifth century, the atomist Democritus (*fl.* 440–35) was practicing both physical and psychological allegory. After these beginnings, allegory was finally adopted by the sophists and, in particular, by Prodicus of Ceos.

In brief, as early as the sixth century B.C., the attacks launched against myth by such "philosophers" as Xenophanes, had provoked a reaction. In order to defend myths against accusations of falsehood in the areas of ethics and of physics, some thinkers tried to interpret them by distinguishing a profound meaning beneath their superficial meaning (which could indeed give rise to accusations of falsehood). They did this by assimilating gods and heroes to physical elements, dispositions of the soul, or virtues and vices.

Plato's contemporaries, Antisthenes and Diogenes, one of whose favorite procedures was etymology, practiced a moralizing allegory by turning Hercules and Ulysses, Medea and Circe into Cynic heroes. Thus, they annexed certain myths to their own philosophy.

It was in reaction to these excesses of the Cynics and Sophists with regard to allegory that Plato is reacting at the beginning of the *Phaedrus:*[12]

PHAEDRUS Tell me, Socrates, isn't it somewhere about here that they say Boreas seized Orithyia from the river Ilissos?

SOCRATES Yes, it is the story.

PHAEDRUS Was this the actual spot? Certainly the water looks charmingly pure and clear; it's just the place for girls to be playing beside the stream.

SOCRATES No, it was about a quarter of a mile further down, where you cross to the sanctuary of Agra; there is, I believe, an altar dedicated to Boreas close by.

PHAEDRUS I have never really noticed it, but pray tell me, Socrates, do you believe that myth to be true?

SOCRATES I should be quite in fashion if I disbelieved it, as the men of science *(sophoi)* do. I might proceed to give a scientific account *(sophizo-*

12. On the other hand, in the passage of the *Republic* cited above (378d–e3), Plato is probably referring to the Pythagoreans. See P. Boyancé, *Le Culte des Muses chez les philosophes grecs: Études d'histoire et de psychologie religieuses* ([1936], Paris: de Boccard, 1972), 121–31.

menos) of how the maiden, while at play with Pharmacia, was blown by a gust of Boreas down from the rocks hard by, and having thus met her death was said to have been seized by Boreas, though it may have happened on the Areopagus, according to another version of the occurrence. For my part, Phaedrus, I regard such theories as no doubt attractive, but as the invention of clever, industrious people who are not exactly to be envied, for the simple reason that they must then go on and tell us the real truth about the appearance of centaurs and the Chimera, not to mention a whole host of other such creatures, Gorgons and Pegasuses and countless other remarkable monsters of legend flocking in on them. If our sceptic, with his somewhat crude science *(agroikōi tini sophiai khrōmenos),* means to reduce every one of them to the standard of probability, he'll need a great deal of time for it. I myself have certainly no time for the business, and I'll tell you why my friend. I can't as yet "know myself," as the inscription at Delphi enjoins, and so long as that ignorance remains it seems to me ridiculous to inquire into extraneous matters. Consequently I don't bother about such things, but accept the current beliefs about them, and direct my inquiries, as I have just said, rather to myself, to discover whether I am really a more complex creature and more puffed up with pride than Typhon, or a simpler, gentler being whom heaven has blessed with a quiet, un-Typhonic nature.[13]

Socrates evokes here several procedures used by allegorical interpretation. A whimsical usage of etymology is at the starting point of an allegory of the physical type: Orithyia is the "mountain runner" *(orē thein),* and Boreas, the boreal wind. There is also an allegory of the moral type: Typhon represents in particular a smoky soul (in Greek, *tuphos* expresses the idea of vapor or smoke). From this point, it is only a small step—which we may safely take[14]—to assuming that Plato is criticizing Antisthenes, who may, moreover, be represented by Cratylus in the dialogue named after the latter.[15]

Plato thus repudiates all practice of allegory, whatever the procedure employed. But what reasons does he invoke to justify this repudiation? In the *Republic,* he emphasizes that the children for whom the myths are mainly intended do not have the means to distinguish between what is allegorical and what is not. In the *Phaedrus,* he insists that the task that a

13. *Phdr.* 229b4–30a6.
14. See J. Pépin, *Mythe et allégorie,* 113–14.
15. On the adversaries whom Plato maybe attacking in the person of Cratylus, see K. Gaiser, *Name und Sache in Platons "Kratylos,"* Abhandlungen der Heidelberger Akademie der Wissenschaften, Philosophisch-historische Klasse, Jahrgang 1974 (Heidelberg: Carl Winter/Universitätsverlag, 1974), 11–12. Against the position that sees the image of Antisthenes behind that of Cratylus, see Timothy M. S. Baxter, *The Cratylus: Plato's Critique of Naming,* Philosophia antiqua 58 (Leiden: Brill, 1992).

universal interpretation of the allegorical type would demand would be enormous if it were applied to everything within the myths told in ancient Greece that would require such interpretations. Is this, however, a definitive reply? No. The first of the aforementioned reasons is acceptable. Myth is above all intended for children, and they are not capable of distinguishing what belongs to allegory and what does not. The second, however, is only partly convincing. It is impossible to allegorically interpret a single mythological element without applying the same procedure to all the other very numerous elements which cause difficulties. But why back away from such a task, however gigantic, if one accepts the hypothesis that myths, in the final analysis, really conceal the truth? It is precisely this postulate which Plato rejects, since for him truth can only be revealed in philosophical discourse.

A myth's truth value or lack thereof is only secondary, insofar as a myth is true or false according to whether or not it accords with the discourse conducted by the philosopher on the same subject. Why, then, try to transform the falsity of a myth into truth? Truth must rather be sought where it lies, that is, in philosophical discourse. Above all, that knowledge or science which appears in ancient Greece in the sixth century, and which Plato calls by the name of "philosophy,"[16] must not be used to transform the falsehood of myth into a truth. Indeed, such a practice would in fact reverse the order of status by making philosophy an instrument of the interpretation of myths, which in turn would be seen as the genuine receptacles of truth.

16. W. Burkert, "Platon oder Pythagoras? Zum Ursprung des Wortes 'Philosophie'," *Hermes* 88 (1960): 159–77; Luc Brisson, "Mythes, écriture, philosophie," in J. F. Mattéi, ed., *La naissance de la raison en Grèce,* Actes du Congrès de Nice, May 1987 (Paris: PUF, 1990), 49–59.

Thirteen

Plato's Derivative Use of the Term "Muthos"

As we have seen, *muthos* can designate that type of discourse which, in the first part of this book, we have described as a fact of collective communication. Plato submits this discourse to a thorough critique, which we have examined in detail in the preceding chapter. There are, however, eighteen occurrences of *muthos* in the Platonic corpus which designate various other types of discourse,[1] which I should now like to review.

This derivative usage of *muthos* can be characterized as follows: Plato employs the term *muthos* to designate types of discourse that are habitually designated by other words, and he does so because of a partial similarity between the definition of myth and the definition of these other types of discourse. In other words, we must explain the metaphorical usage that Plato makes of the word *muthos*.[2]

When Plato employs the term *muthos* in a derivative sense, the types of discourse designated by this term fall into two classes: rhetorical and philosophical. Indeed, two occurrences of this word refer to a rhetorical exercise: the first speech in which Socrates imitates Lysias in the *Phaedrus*.[3] As an exercise, a discourse of this kind can be likened to a game or a fiction: that is, to a linguistic performance which does not bear upon any extralinguistic reality. Rather, it is its own reference, which is the source of its obvious similarity with myth.

But it is in a philosophical context that Plato employs the sixteen other occurrences of *muthos*. Five of these occurrences refer to philosophical doctrines which Plato challenges. In the *Theaetetus,* Plato characterizes the doctrine of Protagoras as a *muthos*.[4] Just before this passage, Plato likens another materialist doctrine, perhaps the one developed in the school of

---

1. See Appendix 1.
2. On this subject, see Luc Brisson, "Sémantique de la métaphore," *Dialogue* 15 (1976): 256–81.
3. *Phdr.* 237a9, 241e8.
4. *Tht.* 164d9, e3.

Aristippus, to a *muthos*.[5] Finally, in the *Sophist,* each of the doctrines relative to the number of basic realities is straight away considered to be a *muthos*.[6] By using the term *muthos* to designate all these philosophical doctrines, Plato issues a precise critique with respect to them. These doctrines are false. As false discourse, they bear upon a reality other than the one they describe. Consequently, they must be considered as semblances, that is, as images that do not conform to the realities that they are supposed to represent.[7] Now, myths too can be considered as semblances—whence the likening of these false philosophical doctrines to myths.

What we have here is *only* a partial likeness, for the falsehood of a myth, which is not a unfalsifiable discourse,[8] cannot be of the same order as that of a philosophical doctrine, which, according to Plato, *is* susceptible of real falsification. Plato does not, however, restrict this derivative use of the term *muthos* to describe the doctrines he is fighting. In eleven other cases, he uses the same term to describe his own discourse. On the one hand, four of these examples refer to the cosmological postulates on the constitution of the sensible world set forth in the *Timaeus*.[9] In three cases, however, we find the expression *eikōs muthos*.[10] This deserves a closer examination. As G. Vlastos rightly remarks, the fundamental element in this expression is the attribute *eikōs*.[11] To be convinced of this, we need only note the following: in seven places in the *Timaeus,* Plato describes Timaeus' discourse on the constitution of the sensible world as an *eikōs logos*.[12] Moreover, *eikōs, eikotōs,* etc., are also found in six others places in the *Timaeus* with a similar meaning.[13] All this is explained by the fact that what is developed in the *Timaeus* is a discourse on the constitution of the sensible world.

The meaning of this last remark is clarified by the following passage

---

5. *Tht.* 156c4.

6. *Soph.* 242c8, d6.

7. See *Soph.* 266d8–e1 for a definition of a semblance.

8. See ch. 9, sect. 3.

9. *Tim.* 29d2, 59c6, 68d2, 69b1.

10. *Tim.* 29d2, 59c6, 68d2.

11. G. Vlastos, "The Disorderly Motion in the *Timaeus*" [1939], *Studies in Plato's Metaphysics* (London: Routledge & Kegan Paul/New York: Humanities Press, 1965), 382. Pierre Hadot tries to show in his article "Physique et poésie dans le *Timée* de Platon," *Revue de Théologie et de Philosophie* 115 (1983): 113–33, how the expression *eikōs logos* describes a particular type of literary genre of which the *Timaeus* is the first example: it is the likely story which tells the story of the birth of the universe. For a reply, see Luc Brisson, "Le discours comme univers et l'univers comme discours: Platon et ses interprètes néoplatoniciens," *Le texte et ses représentations,* 127.

12. *Tim.* 30b7, 48d2, 53d5–6, 55d5, 56a1, 57d6, 90e8.

13. *Tim.* 34c3, 44d1, 48c1, 49b6, 56d1, 72d7.

of the *Timaeus,* in which Plato distinguishes two types of discourse according to the nature of their objects:

> TIMAEUS Concerning a copy *(peri te eikonos),* then, and its model *(kai peri tou paradeigmatos)* we must make this distinction: a discourse of that which is abiding and stable and discoverable by the aid of reason will itself be abiding and unchangeable (so far as it is possible and it lies in the nature of a discourse to be incontrovertible and irrefutable, there must be no falling short of that); while a discourse of what is made as a copy of that other *(tous de tou pros men ekeino apeikasthentos),* but is only a copy *(ontos de eikonos),* will itself be but a copy, standing to discourse of the former kind in proportion *(eikotas ana logon te ekeinōn ontas):* as reality is to becoming *(hotiper pros genesin ousia),* so is truth to belief *(touto pros pistin alētheia).*[14]

In this perspective, *eikōs logos* must be understood as follows: "a discourse which bears upon the copies of the intelligible forms," that is, upon sensible things. If this is the case, then *eikōs muthos* must mean: "a myth which bears upon the copies of the intelligible forms," that is, sensible things.

This paraphrase needs to be explained. Only the present state of sensible things, which are copies of intelligible forms, are susceptible of being perceived by the senses, and as being described by a falsifiable discourse which is designated by the expression *eikōs logos.* The state of sensible things before and during their constitution escapes any direct or even indirect perception. No falsifiable discourse can account for it. Consequently, it can only be explained through a discourse which presents an explanatory model, whose validity cannot possibly be falsified. This is why Plato employs the expression *eikōs muthos* to describe this type of discourse. Indeed, what we have here is clearly a discourse which is unfalsifiable with regard to sensible things, or, more precisely, to the state of affairs before and during the constitution of the copies of the intelligible forms, that is, of sensible things.

The seven occurrences of *muthos* that remain to be explained appear in contexts which are relative to politics. Two of these occurrences refer to the cities described by Socrates in the *Republic* and by the Athenian Stranger in the *Laws,* respectively.[15] Here is what Critias says at the beginning of the *Timaeus,* when he contrasts the city which Socrates had described the previous day—which was similar to that described in the *Republic*—to that of primeval Athens, one of whose glorious deeds was written down in Egypt, and then told to Solon by a priest in Saïs:

14. *Tim.* 29b3–c3. Cornford trans.
15. *Tim.* 26c8; *Laws* VI 752a2.

CRITIAS The city and citizens, which you yesterday described to us as a myth, we will now transfer to the world of reality. It shall be the ancient city of Athens and, the citizens whom you imagined *(tous politias hous dienoou),* we will suppose that they were our veritable ancestors of whom the priest spoke *(phēsomen ekeinous tous alēthinous einai progonous hēmin, hous elegen ho hiereus).*[16]

Socrates' discourse on the ideal city is likened to a myth because the tradition concerning primeval Athens, which corresponded to this model in reality (*Tim.* 25d7–c5) has vanished, at least in ancient Greece. Consequently, this ideal city no longer has any existence except in the mind of the person describing its constitution; thus one can only hope for its realization in the future. The interest of this derivative use of the term *muthos* resides in the introduction of this future dimension into the realm of myth which, until now, has been restricted to a distant past.

The following passage from the *Laws* must be interpreted in the same sense:

ATHENIAN Still, when you are once in the ring, as they say, the time for excuses is past, and that is the case just now with you, and with me too. You with your nine colleagues, as I understand, have pledged yourselves to the Cretan people to throw your souls into the work of the foundation, and I, on my side, am pledged to help you with your present myth *(muthologian).* And, to be sure, since I am telling a myth, I should not like to leave it without its head; it would look monstrously ugly if it roamed at large in that condition.

CLINIAS Indeed, this is hardly possible.[17]

The myth of which the Athenian Stranger speaks is the discourse he is holding on the colony that the Cretans have charged him with. In this respect, the procedure of the Athenian Stranger in the *Laws* is akin to that of Socrates mentioned by Critias at the beginning of the *Timaeus.*[18] In both cases, a political model is elaborated which is intended to regulate the foundation of a real city in a future of unspecified proximity. Now, even if, from a temporal point of view, this procedure reverses that which consists in elaborating a cosmological model intended to account for the state of sensible things before and during their constitution, nevertheless, from a referential point of view, there is an equivalence between them. For although the references proper to these two types of discourse do not pertain

16. *Tim.* 26c7–d3.
17. *Laws* VI 751d7–752a5.

18. *Tim.* 26c7–d3.

to the world of intelligible forms, still they cannot be apprehended by the senses, insofar as they are situated either in the distant past or the future.

In brief, the comparison of the cosmological model described in the *Timaeus* and the political models described in the *Republic* and the *Laws* to a myth is based on the similarity at the level of the relation that these different types of discourse maintain with a referent which, in each case, is not susceptible of any real apprehension.

There is one last case which covers five occurrences found in the *Laws*.[19] These occurrences can only be explained by the role Plato ascribes to myth in this dialogue, in which, by reactivating the old meaning of *muthos*,[20] Plato makes myth function as a preamble to the laws.

From this perspective, as has already been noted,[21] the Athenian Stranger insists on the persuasive character of myth by likening it to the exhortation constituted by the preamble to a law. In the cases which have just been mentioned, the Athenian Stranger employs the term *muthos* to characterize a discourse which plays the role of a preamble to a law, even though this term no longer refers to the sphere of traditional myths in ancient Greece. Consequently, *muthos* becomes a simple synonym of "preamble" or "exhortation," that is, of a discourse intended to persuade the citizen to obey such and such a law. The most illuminating example of this is surely *Laws* VIII 841c6–7, where a preamble is explicitly compared to a *muthos:* "It may be that my present proposals are no more than a myth *(kathaper isōs en muthōi)*." In the four other cases, on the other hand, there is a metaphorical designation which conceals to a certain extent the semantic operation at work. Nevertheless, it must be noted that the context in which the eighteen occurrences appear in which Plato makes a derivative use of *muthos* is always marked by an explicit reference to the domain of myth strictly speaking: in the *Phaedrus* Socrates' discourse focuses on Eros;[22] in the *Theaetetus* the report of the doctrines of Protagoras[23] and of the materialists[24] mentioned previously takes place in an atmosphere which Plato describes in terms borrowed from the vocabulary of the mysteries;[25] in the *Sophist,* the doctrines on the number of basic realities,[26] which Plato presents back-to-back, are presented as inspired by the Muses and as

---

19. *Laws* VI 771c7, 773b4, VII 790c3, 812a2, VIII 841c6.
20. On this point, see Appendix 4.
21. See ch. 11.
22. *Phdr.* 237a9, 241e8.
23. *Tht.* 164d9, e3.
24. *Tht.* 156c4.
25. To be convinced, one only has to reread *Tht.* 155e–56a.
26. *Soph.* 242c8, d6.

haunted by such mythical characters as Aphrodite; finally, in the *Timaeus*,[27] the city described by Socrates on the previous day is compared to primeval Athens, which resisted the general military offensive by Atlantis. And, in his description of the colony in *Laws* VI,[28] the Athenian Stranger explicitly mentions the adventure of Theseus,[29] who accompanied the seven or ten Athenians who had to be delivered to the Minotaur each year.

In the *Laws,* traditional mythology is also present in the context of the five occurrences where *muthos* is taken in the sense of *para-muthia, -muthion.* In *Laws* VI 771c7, *muthos* appears in a passage concerning the territorial and social division of the city into twelve sections, with each one attributed to one of the twelve great divinities. In *Laws* VI 773b4, it would not be surprising if *muthos* referred to the marriage of Hera to Zeus. As far as the occurrence of *muthos* in *Laws* VII 790c3 is concerned, it is to be noted that the Athenian Stranger speaks of the Corybantes immediately after.[30] To be sure, the occurrence of *muthos* at *Laws* VII 812a2 does not seem to refer to any mythical element in particular. However, it is worth noting that this *muthos* refers to literary studies, of which the essential part bears upon myth. Finally, at *Laws* VIII 841c6, what the Athenian Stranger has just said is compared to a *muthos,* that is, a traditional myth. In the *Timaeus, muthos* describes a discourse which develops a cosmogony including the parody of a theogony.[31]

Consequently, these eighteen occurrences in which Plato makes a derivative use of the term *muthos* are found in contexts which themselves explicitly refer, in general, to the realm of myths that were told in ancient Greece or that Plato tells, whether or not he takes responsibility for them, that is, to the type of discourse designated by the term *muthos* when it is used in a primary sense. The difference between the primary and the derivative sense of the word *muthos* is thereby greatly attenuated.

It is largely upon his refusal to distinguish between the primary and derivative uses of the term *muthos* that Marcel Detienne bases the arguments that enable him to conclude that "myth" refers to objects that are so heterogeneous that, in the end, myth as such ceases to exist.[32] Is this refusal the result of a theoretical presupposition?

27. *Tim.* 26c8.
28. *Laws* 751d7–52a5.
29. *Laws* VI 751e1–2, III 702e5.
30. *Laws* VII 790c5–e4.
31. *Tim.* 29d2, 59c6, 68d2, 69b1.
32. Marcel Detienne, *The Creation of Mythology.*

CONCLUSION

Myth does not exist. That is what Marcel Detienne claims.[1] As such, he is part of a current cultural mode that some have amusingly called "inexistentialism."[2] The dissolution of myth into mythology, which can no longer pretend to the status of "science of myths," is thus fulfilled.

Myth is no longer a literary genre, and any attempt to distinguish myth from a tale, a fable, or a legend is always condemned to failure. Nor is myth a kind of story that can be approached *qua* signifier or *qua* signified. Indeed, on the one hand, there is no linguistic trait which provides for an indisputable identification of a myth. Furthermore, no one agrees on the kind of "story" that a myth must relate, if indeed, it is a "story" which a myth relates. Marcel Detienne rejects the correlation of myth and story when he argues that even proverbs and genealogies, which have nothing to do with stories, are characterizable as myth.

But how does one define a mythology without myths? Mythology can be neither a kind of knowledge, nor a particular kind of symbolic activity, but the anonymous memory of a community which does not use writing, a memory in which each member of the community recognizes himself as soon as the memorable is repeated—its repetition entailing its transformation. That which mythology, whose territory begins to be restricted beginning in the sixth century B.C. but to which Plato is the first to name, loses in specificity with regard to myth, it gains in extension to the point of including everything that some or other oral civilization conserves in memory.

Marcel Detienne's argumentation is based, in the final analysis, on this

1. Marcel Detienne, *The Creation of Mythology,* in particular, chapter 7, "Untraceable Myth," 124–33.

2. Marcel Gauchet, "De l'inexistentialisme," *Le Débat,* May 1980, 23–24; Pierre Vidal-Naquet, "Un Eichmann de papier," *Esprit,* September 1980, 8; rpt. in *Les Juifs, la mémoire et le présent* (Paris: Maspero, 1981), 197–98.

negation: myth is not a story. Since myth is not a story, it loses the order which assures its specificity as a memory transmitted from generation to generation, and on which analysis can be based. This order, which is not a rational order, is what structures the story as a set of sentences having its own meaning, which cannot be reduced to the sum total of the meanings of the individual sentences. Moreover, it is this order which enables us to speak of the "story" related in a myth.

Marcel Detienne invokes Plato in particular to support his thesis.[3] But Plato likens myth to a story each time he employs the word *muthos* in its primary sense. In this respect, three clarifications are in order. Genealogies constitute the framework of the story which, even if it is not in fact related, can be evoked at any moment to justify such or such a relation (see ch. 9, sect. 1). In addition, Plato never characterizes a proverb as "myth," even though there is no valid reason to think that proverbs and myth are not closely connected. And finally, whatever Detienne says, there is nothing to indicate that the old men of the *Laws* "mythologize" without making stories. On the contrary, everything leads to believe that they do "tell" myths (see Appendix 2). In any case, the distinction between the primary and derivative uses of a word must be taken into consideration. This alone enables the satisfactory interpretation of several examples of *muthos* in the Platonic corpus (see ch. 13). It is largely for having refused to take these into account that Detienne comes to see in myth something very different from a story.

To maintain that a myth is a story permits its reestablishment as an elementary unit of meaning for mythology, but it does not resolve, in the least, the problem posed by its definition. We still must know, however, under what conditions a definition of myth is possible.

Myth, then, cannot be defined either as a literary genre characterized by the themes it develops, by the type of interest it arouses, or by the effects it produces; or even as a type of story with immutable and universally recognized boundaries. But to admit this is simply to recognize that it is impossible to apply to the domain of orality distinctions which are peculiar to a domain where writing ensures the accumulation of literary productions into a whole, upon which the classificatory activity of the learned is

---

3. There is only one exception to this domain, a fragment from Anacreon where the word *muthiētēs* appears (*Poetae melici graci,* no. 353, ed. D. L. Page, 1963, frag. 21B, ed. B. Gentili, 1958). But this fragment is difficult to interpret because it is without a context (for a commentary, see G. Perrotta and B. Gentili, *Polinnia: Poesia greca arcaica* [Messina and Florence: G. D'Anna, 1965], 230–31) and therefore in no way constitutes a decisive example in support of Marcel Detienne's thesis.

then deployed. The failure of any attempt to define a myth as a precise literary object reveals the point of view of the observer.

Mythology works not on an object which is given to it, but rather on an object which it gives to itself in a twofold movement of negation, as Plato indicates in the *Timaeus* (23a5–b3). To undertake research on the memorable is to take an outside critical look at what constitutes the identity of a given collectivity and ensures for it a true unanimity. Above all, it is to put into writing that which is exclusively destined to be heard. But to recognize that mythology largely constructs the object on which it focuses does not disqualify it as "science," since most sciences proceed in this way: what is an atom, for example? The recognition of this state of things simply indicates that there can be only an operational definition of myth, that is, a definition through procedures which enables its identification and description. Both parts of this book are dedicated to this twofold task. As a whole, it confines itself to Plato's use of the word *muthos,* its derivatives, and the compounds in which *muthos* appears as the first term. It is nevertheless to this usage that the word "myth" necessarily refers when it is employed as a predicate to characterize a certain kind of discourse.

In Plato, *muthos,* which until then was essentially a "speech" noun, did not come to designate a nonfalsifiable and a nonargumentative discourse until the emergence of a *logos* which claimed to be a falsifiable and/or argumentative discourse. *Muthos* is not a falsifiable discourse because its normal referents, gods, daimons, heroes, inhabitants of Hades, and men of the past, remain inaccessible both to sense perception and to intelligence. Nor is it an argumentative discourse, because these referents are described and shown as if they were concrete beings through systematic recourse to imitation. Despite the inferior status with which he endows it, Plato recognizes that *muthos* has a particular usefulness in the realm of ethics and politics, where it constitutes, for the philosopher and the legislator, a remarkable instrument of persuasion independently of any allegorical interpretation.

The theoretical analysis developed in the second part of this book deals in fact with a social practice of which Plato elsewhere gives a description (ethnological, in a way) which is systematized in the first part of this book by a reference to the theory of communication. Myth thus appears as a discourse through which is communicated everything that a given community conserves in memory and transmits orally from generation to generation, whether or not through the intermediary of a professional and whether or not this discourse was developed by a technician of oral communication like the poet. As the result of redoubled imitation, myth, since it represents a reality inaccessible both to the intellect and the senses, is destined to model or modify in a more or less spectacular way the behavior of the souls of those who listen to it.

An operational definition treats an object not as a substance but as a nexus of relations. Hence, it insists on the active role of the subject who defines the object. Now, this plays a greater role in the humanities than in the exact sciences. Indeed, in the humanities, the subject takes itself as an object, whence the constant interaction between the two poles in accordance with more or less conscious interests. But the relative occultation of the object in favor of the subject whose activity is then revealed is not the same as its dissolution. It simply indicates that the object in question will never appear in its absolute identity, thus ensuring a perfect univocity to the word which designates it. But what object can comply with such exorbitant demands? It is, in the first place, because he demanded such an epiphany from myth that Detienne was forced to resign himself to proclaiming the disappearance of myth into the waters of mythology.

But there is more. Not only is the meaning of the word *muthos* not univocal, but its range is not immediately universal.[4] For to say that "x is a myth" in a context other than that of ancient Greece is the same as saying "x is a myth like z in ancient Greece." This remark, which has more to do with pragmatics than semantics, reveals the following fact. The word *muthos* refers not to a natural object (water, fire, trees, rocks, etc.) which is found almost anywhere and to which, consequently, a word corresponds in each language, but to a cultural object specific to ancient Greece. Now it is in accordance with this particular referent that all the other cultural objects to which the word "myth" refers are recognized and named, when the term is employed in a context other than that which is its own in ancient Greece. This procedure is based on a certain number of genuine resemblances between what one calls a "myth" in ancient Greece and what one considers as such elsewhere. But, from the outset, irreducible differences appear between the two domains. Once again, the point of view of the outside observer is called into question; such an observer is the heir— and, therefore, the prisoner—of a specific cultural context. This point of view presents certain limits, which, however, can be compensated by a series of recoveries that any observer (anthropologist, ethnologist, etc.) who is conscious of the matter and concerned with preserving the identity of that which is observed, tries to put to work, even though he knows that perfection in this domain, as in many others, cannot be attained. The use

4. On this, see Pierre Smith, "Positions du mythe," *Le Temps de la Réflexion* 1 (1980): 61–81.

of the word "myth" outside the context which was originally its own therefore demands a constant labor of adaptation. The need for a mediation in this domain, however, is by no means equivalent to an impossibility.

Even if the word which designates it presents neither a univocal meaning nor an immediately universal range, myth is not therefore necessarily condemned to dissolution. On the contrary, the call made by Lévi-Strauss for the perception of myth as myth by all readers throughout the world demands to be transcended. Any spontaneous confidence vouchsafed to obviousness, intuition, and language is loaded with demands which lead straight to a general suspicion. Such a confidence can serve to obtain a temporary consensus on such and such a point; but it never replaces a definition, however provisional, however imperfect.

Data on the Occurrences of "Muthos" in the Platonic Corpus

According to L. Brandwood's index,[1] which gives a complete inventory of the occurrences of all the terms appearing in the works of Plato, with the exception of the definite article *ho* and the conjunction *kai,* there are 101 occurrences of the term *muthos.*

Of these 101 occurrences, 8 are found in quotations, 87 in works which, beyond a doubt, are by Plato, and 6 in works attributed to Plato, but whose authenticity is nowadays either considered as doubtful or rejected by the majority of specialists.

The interest of this inventory resides in the fact that it provides us, to a certain degree, with an idea of the evolution of the meaning of this lexeme. First, here is a list of the 8 occurrences of *muthos* that are found in quotations made by Plato, classified according to their respective source.[2] In these 8 occurrences, *muthos* designates the "thought which expresses itself," "opinion," and this corresponds to what H. Fournier states regarding the evolution of the meaning of *muthos.*[3]

AUTHOR QUOTED	WORK QUOTED	LOCATION IN PLATO
Adespota elegiaca	frag. 1 (West IEG II)	*Dem.* 383c1
Euripides	*Melanippe* (frag. 484 Nauck)	*Symp.* 177a4
Homer	*Illiad* 4.412	*Rep.* III 389e6
	Illiad 9.309	*Hipp.* II 365a2
	Odyssey 20.17	*Phdo.* 94d8
	Odyssey 20.17	*Rep.* III 390d4
	Odyssey 20.1	*Rep.* IV 441b6
Theognis	Frag. 437 (West IEG I	*Men.* 96a1

In Plato, this meaning of *muthos* is modified, and the term comes to designate a very particular type of discourse. Here is a list of the 87 occurrences of *muthos* that are found in works that are unanimously attributed to Plato: *Crat.* 408c8; *Gorg.* 505c10, 523a2, 527a5; *Laws* I 636c7, d3, d5, 645b1, II 664a6, III 682a8, 683d3, 699d8, IV 712a4, 713a6, c1, 719c1, VI 752a2, 771c7, VII 773b4, 790c3, 804e4, 812a2, VIII 840c1, 841c6, IX 865d5, 872e1, X 887d2, 903b1, XI 913c2, 927c8, XII944a2; *Phdo.* 60c2, 61b4, b6, 110b1, b4, 114d7; *Phdr.* 237a9, 241e8, 253c7; *Phlb.* 14a4; *Pol.* 268d9, e4, 272c7, d5, 274e1, 275b1,

---

1. L. Brandwood, *A Word Index to Plato* (Leeds: Maney & Son, 1976).
2. See ibid., 991–1003.
3. H. Fournier, *Les Verbes "dire" en grec ancien* (Paris: Klincksieck, 1946), 215–16.

277b5, b7; *Prot.* 320c3, c7, 324d6, 328c3, 361d2; *Rep.* I 330d7, 350e3, II 376d9, 377a4, a6, b6, c1, c4, c7, d5, 378e5, 379a4, 381e3, III 386b8, 391e12, 398b7, 415a2, c7, VIII 565d6, X 621b8; *Soph.* 242c8, d6; *Tht.* 156c4, 164d9, e3; *Tim.* 22c7, 23b5, 26c8, e4, 29d2, 59c6, 68d2, 69b1.

This list must be analysed from different points of view. When these occurrences are classified according to their frequency in a particular dialogue, the following result is obtained:

RANK	DIALOGUE	FREQUENCY
1	*Laws*	27
2	*Rep.*	20
3	*Pol.*	8
4	*Tim.*	8
5	*Phdo.*	6
6	*Prot.*	5
7	*Gorg.*	5
8	*Phdr.*	3
9	*Tht.*	3
10	*Soph.*	2
11	*Crat.*	1
12	*Phlb.*	1

Occurrences of *muthos* are thus found only in 12 of the 26 dialogues which are considered to be authentic. Further, 54 percent of these same occurrences are located either in the *Laws* (31 percent) or in the *Republic* (23 percent). In the latter, 16 of the 20 occurrences of *muthos* are concentrated in books II and III, which bear upon the role of music in the education of the future Guardians.

Before examining more closely these 87 occurrences, here is a list of the 6 occurrences of *muthos* that are found in the works of Plato whose authenticity is contested: *Alc.* I 123a1; *Epin.* 975a6, 980a5; *Epist.* VII 344d3, XII 359d9; *Min.* 318d11. These occurrences will not be taken into consideration in what follows.

Let us return now to the 87 occurrences of *muthos* in the works of Plato generally considered as authentic. This group can be divided into a certain number of subgroups according to the following criteria. The first of these criteria corresponds to the following question: what type of discourse does the term *muthos* refer to in each of the 87 occurrences in this group?

Sixty-nine of these 87 occurrences refer to what even one with a very limited knowledge of ancient Greek civilization would qualify as "myth." I am appealing here to spontaneous usage, that is, to a kind of linguistic reflex which the English word "myth" introduces when employed in a precise context, namely, that of ancient Greece. This is not an attempt to limit ourselves to this spontaneous usage, in order to spare ourselves the trouble of defining such a type of discourse; rather, the goal is to obtain the largest possible consensus on the classification of the material on which this analysis will focus. In this perspective, 69 of these 87 occurrences of *muthos* refer to what one spontaneously calls "Greek myth." The use that Plato makes of *muthos* in these 69 occurrences is characterized as "primary."

Of these 69 occurrences, whereas 27 refer to myths which Plato tells, either recognizing them as his own or attributing them to someone else, 42 refer to myths which were told in ancient Greece: they can be found in any dictionary of Greek mythology. Just as when we appealed to the spontaneous usage off the word "myth," so when we have recourse to a dictionary of Greek mythology, our goal is to obtain beforehand an agreement—as wide as can be—on the classification of the material our analysis shall study.

Twenty of these 42 occurrencess only refer in a general way to myths told in ancient Greece: *Crat.* 408c8; *Gorg.* 505c10; *Laws* III 699d8, VIII 840c1; *Phlb.* 14a4; *Pol.* 272c7; *Rep.* I 350e3, II 376d9, 377a4, a6, b6, c1, c4, c7, 378e5, 379a4, III 391e12, 398b7; *Tim.* 23b5.

On the other hand, the 22 other occurrences refer to the following particular myths:

the activity of the souls of the dead, *Laws* XI 927c8;
the Amazons, *Laws* VII 804e4;
the *Biaiothanatoi* (victims of a violent death), *Laws* IX 865d5;
the foundation of Troy, *Laws* III 682a8, and of Lacedaemon, Argos, and Messene,
    Laws III 683d3;
the gods who roam at night under a number of different shapes, *Rep.* II 381e3;
Ganymede, *Laws* I 636c7, d3, d5;
Hades, *Rep.* I 330d7, III 386b8;
Nestor, *Laws* IV 712a4;
the fates of parricides, *Laws* IX 872e1;
Patrocles and the weapons of Achilles, *Laws* XII 944a2;
Phaethon, *Tim.* 22c7;
the poet inspired by the Muses, *Laws* IV 719c1;
the discovery of a treasure, *Laws* XI 913c2;
Zeus Lycaeus, *Rep.* VIII 565d6.

Four other occurrences must be added to these 18, of which three refer to one or more myths told by Aesop: *Phdo.* 60c2, 61b4, b6; and one to the myths told by Homer and Hesiod: *Rep.* II 377d5.

There remain 27 occurrences of *muthos* which refer to the myths Plato tells as his own or which he attribues to someone else. Here is the list:

the Atlantis myth, *Tim.* 26e4;
the myth of autochthony, *Rep.* III 415a2; *Laws* II 664a6;
the class myth, *Rep.* III 415c7;
the Er myth, *Rep.* X 621b8;
the myth of the earth's surface, *Phdo.* 110b1, b4, 114d7;
the myth of the judgment of the dead, *Gorg.* 523a2, 527a5;
the myth on the nature and destiny of the soul, *Phdr.* 253c7;
Protagoras' myth of the gift of political wisdom, *Prot.* 320c3, c7, 324d6, 328c3,
    361d2;
the providence myth, *Laws* X 903b1.
the puppet myth, *Laws* I 645b1;
the myth of the reversal of the world's rotation, *Pol.* 268d9, e4, 272d5, 274e1,
    275b1, 277b 5, b7; and again in *Laws* IV 713a6, c1.

These myths are indissociable from a certain number of traditional myths in ancient Greece: they either take them over as they are, or else transpose them in accordance with precise requirements which are relative to the context in which they appear.

It is worth noting that Plato uses the term *muthos* 18 times to refer to types of discourse other than the ones which characterize the myths told in ancient Greece or those which he himself develops in his works as his own or as those of others. The use Plato makes of these 18 occurrences may be characterized as "derivative."

Plato thus likens to a *muthos* the rhetorical exercise which Socrates carries out in *Phaedrus* 237a9, 241e8. Further, Plato considers as a *muthos* not only the doctrines of other philosophers (*Tht.* 156c4, 164d9, e3; *Soph.* 242c8, d6) but also his own. Indeed, Plato calls *muthos* the discourse he develops in *Timaeus* 29d2, 59c6, 68d2, 69b1. He also calls *muthos* the discourses that Socrates (*Tim.* 26c8) and the Athenian Stranger (*Laws* VI 752a2) hold on the political constitution of the ideal state. Finally, in the *Laws,* by playing on words, Plato employs the term *muthos* to designate the preambles which are to serve as exhortations to the laws: *Laws* VI 771c7, 773b4, VII 790c3, 812a2, VIII 841c6.

Having classified the occurrences of *muthos* according to the sense of discourse it designates, I would now like to identify the interlocutors who employ this same term in Plato's dialogues. Here is the list by the order of frequency with which they use the word *muthos:*

Socrates, 34 + [2] attributed to Callicles: *Crat.* 408c8; *Gorg.* 505c10, [*Gorg.* 523a2], [*Gorg.* 527a5]; *Phdo.* 60c2, 61b4, b6, 110b1, 114d7; *Phdr.* 237a9, 241e8, 253c7; *Phlb.* 14a4; *Prot.* 361d2; *Rep.* II 376d9, 377a4, a6, b6, c1, c4, c7, d5, 378e5, 379a4, 381e3, III 386b8, *Rep.* 391e12, 398b7, 415a2, c7, VIII 565d6, X 621b8; *Tht.* 156c4, 164d9, e3; *Tim.* 26e4.

Athenian Stranger, 27: *Laws* I 636c7, d3, d5, 645b1, 664a6, III 682a8, 683d3, 699d8, IV 712a4, 713a6, c1, 719c1, VI 752a2, 771c7, 773b4, VII 790c3, 804e4, 812a2, VIII 840c1, 841c6, IX 865d5, 872e1, X 887d2, 903b1, XI 913c2, 927c 8, XII 944a2.

Eleatic Stranger, 10: *Pol.* 268d9, e4, 272c7, d5, 274e1, 275b1, 277b5, b7; *Soph.* 242c8, d6.

Protagoras, 4: *Prot.* 320c3, c7, 324d6, 328c3.

Timaeus, 4: *Tim.* 29d2, 59c6, 68d2, 69b1.

Critias, 1 + [2] attributed to an Egyptian priest: [*Tim.* 22c7], [*Tim.* 23b5], *Tim.* 26c8.

Cephalus, 1: *Rep.* I 330d7.

Simmias, 1: *Phdo.* 110b4.

Thrasymachus, 1: *Rep.* I 350e3.

One will note that 79 + [2], that is, 93 percent, of the 87 occurrences of the term *muthos* are due to the primary interlocutors in the dialogues mentioned, whereas 4 + [2], that is, only 7 percent, are attributed to secondary interlocutors (Critias, Cephalus, Simmias, and Thrasymachus). This ratio corresponds to that which prevails in the totality of Plato's dialogues between the duration of the discourse of the primary interlocutors and that of the discourse of the secondary interlocutors.[4]

---

4. As an example, I would like to point out that in the second part of the *Parmenides,* Parmenides' discourse includes 10,538 words and that of the young Aristotle, who replies, 985, which is a ratio of 91.6 percent to 8.4 percent; see L. Brisson, "La Répartition des négations dans la seconde partie du *Parménide* de Platon," *Revue de l'Organisation internationale pour l'étude des langues anciennes par ordinateur* 1 (1978): 45–49.

THE DERIVATIVES OF "MUTHOS" AND
THE COMPOUNDS OF WHICH "MUTHOS"
CONSTITUTES THE FIRST TERM
IN THE PLATONIC CORPUS

In Plato, there are only two derivatives of *muthos: muthikos* and *muthōdēs,* and each one is found only once.[1] The suffix *-ikos*—which is particularly prominent in philosophical vocabulary—indicates the fact of belonging to the class which is designated by the noun to which it applies: thus the adjective *muthikos* (*Phdr.* 265c1) can be translated as "what belongs to the class of myths," "what concerns myth." The suffix *-ōdēs*—which cannot be accounted for phonetically—expresses a resemblance with what is designated by the noun to which it applies: thus the adjective *muthōdēs* (*Rep.* VII 522a7) can be translated as "what resembles a myth," "what presents the character of a myth." Because of their uniqueness and obvious meaning, the occurrences of these derivatives of *muthos* will be dealt with at the same time as those of *muthos.*

Muthos constitutes the first term of all the compounds to be examined in this appendix, and this is the case simply because in the Platonic corpus, only *diamuthologeō* is not constructed in this way.[2]

It is worth noting that all the compounds of which *muthos* is the first term can be distributed into two groups which are linked, on the one hand, to *muthopoios* and, on the other, to *muthologos.*

In fact, the situation is even simpler, for there is only one example of *muthopoios* (*Rep.* II 377b11), whose second term is *-poios,* a thematic derivative of *poieō,* "to make." This

---

1. The primary reference work used in this appendix is Pierre Chantraine, *La Formation des noms en grec ancien* (Paris: Champion, 1933). For the list of the occurrences of these words in the Platonic corpus, see L. Brandwood, *A Word Index to Plato.*

2. This verbal compound was constructed from *muthologeō* with the help of the preverbal *dia-,* which indicates both a relation between at least two people and the fact that an action is sustained. It is obvious therefore that in its three occurrences in Plato, *diamuthologeō* designates an elaborate discussion between several people. In the *Apology* (39e5) and the *Phaedo* (70b6), this discussion focuses on the destiny of the soul after death. In book I of the *Laws* (I 632e4), *diamuthologeō* appears in a passage which outlines the plan of what follows and which must be developed according to the model of what was already stated. Now the first pages of the *Laws* focus on the legislation established by Minos and Lycurgus under the inspiration of Zeus and Apollo. Further, at the beginning of book III (680d3), the description of the city of Magnesia is likened to a *muthologia.* In these three cases, *diamuthologeō* therefore conserves the meaning of *muthologeō*, which the preverbal *dia-* modifies in its own way. Moreover, it is worth noting the presence of *paramuthia* (*Phdo.* 70b2) and *paramuthion* (*Laws* I 632e5) near to *diamuthologeō* in two of the three cases.

term does not exist on its own, but always appears as the second term of compounds. In Plato, there is no occurrence of the verbal compound *muthopoieō* to which *muthopoios* should correspond from a nominal viewpoint. But the only occurrence of *muthopoios*— which, as one might expect, designates the "myth-maker"—appears in a context which explicitly indicates this correspondence, for it includes the syntagma [*muthon*] *poieō:*

> SOCRATES We must begin, then, it seems by a censorship over our myth-makers *(muthopoiois)*, and if they make a myth well *(kalon [muthon] poiēsōsin)*, we must accept it and, if not, we must reject it.[3]

If we consider that Plato mentions Homer, Hesiod, and other poets, a few lines later,[4] we must understand that the "myth-maker" par excellence is the poet.

The interest of the compound is thus limited: on the one hand, it is a *hapax legomenon* in Plato, and, on the other, its meaning is unique. This is not the case for *muthologos* and its derivatives. But, before examining this other nominal compound, *logopoieō* must be mentioned. This word is derived from *logopoios*, which has as a derivative *logopoiikos*.

We find in *Euthydemus* 289d–e, two of the three occurrences of *logopoieō*, three of the four occurrences of *logopoios*, and the only example of *logopoiikos* in the complete works of Plato. After this passage, the art of the *logopoios*, or "speech-maker," is defined as follows:

> SOCRATES . . . [The speech-maker's art] is really the charming of juries and parliaments and any sort of crowds and so happens to be an exhortation *(paramuthia)*.[5]

The discourses in question may be different, but all are concerned with collective communication and not individual communication.

This is precisely the domain in which the type of discourse called myth is situated. This is why we can liken to a myth the discourse designated by *logos*, which appears as the first term in the verbal compound *logopoieō* in *Republic* II 378d3 and in *Laws* I 636d1, and of the nominal compound *logopoios* in *Republic* III 392a13. In *Republic* II 378d3, it is the poets who "make discourses," and the examples which illustrate what Plato means leave little doubt that these discourses are myths:

> SOCRATES And we must compel the poets to make their discourses *(logopoiein)* with respect to these principles. But Hera's fetterings by her son and the hurling out of heaven of Hephaestus by his father when he was trying to save his mother from a beating, and the battles of the gods that Homer has made *(pepoiēken)* . . .[6]

Things are even more explicit in *Laws* I 636c7–d1, where the Athenian Stranger says: "And you know it is our universal accusation against the Cretans that they were the inventors of the myth of Ganymede because it was they who made this discourse *(hōs logopoiēsantōn toutōn)*." Finally, in *Republic* III 392a13–b1, poets and speech-makers are mentioned side by side: "Because I presume we are going to say that so it is that both poets and myth-makers *(kai poiētai kai logopoioi)* speak wrongly about men in matters of greatest importance." In this case, we could substitute *muthopoios* for *logopoios* just as, in the previous example, we could have substituted *muthopoieō* for *logopoieō*, even if this verbal compound does not appear as such in Plato.

---

3. *Rep.* II 377b11–c2.
4. *Rep.* II 377d3–5.

5. *Euthd.* 290a3–4.
6. *Rep.* II 378d2–5.

But let us leave *muthopoios* and look at *muthologos,* which is composed of *muthos* as the first term and *logos* as the second. *Logos* is derived from the root **leg-.* In roots where all vocalic degrees are allowed, the thematic derivative includes the *o* vowel of the root. And since the accent is on the root, *logos* must be considered, as a simple term, as an action noun. However, compound agent nouns correspond to simple action nouns. Hence the meaning of the compound *muthologos:* "one who tells a myth or myths," or more simply, the "myth(s)-teller."

What, then, can we say about *muthologos,* of which four occurrences are found in Plato? In three of the four examples of *muthologos*—that is, in *Republic* III 392d2, 398a8–b1, and *Laws* XII 941b5—*muthologos* is gramatically linked to *poiētēs.* This clearly shows how the poet is connected to the "mythteller," and the three cases bring to mind *Republic* III 392a13, where the poets and the "makers of discourse," that is, myths, are cited side by side. This link turns out to be necessary, especially if seen from the point of view of an oral civilization where the fabrication of a story is indissociable from its narration.

In the final occurrence of *muthologos* in Plato, at *Laws* II 664d3, only the narrative aspect persists. Indeed, we are told that those over sixty who do not belong to any of the three choruses mentioned are assigned the unique task of telling myths, and nothing allows us to suppose that they fabricate them themselves.[7]

However, it would be a mistake to conclude that *muthologos* and *poiētēs* are identical on the basis of the three other examples of *muthologos.* Indeed, when *poiētēs* is employed in the context of discourse, it refers, like *poieō,* from which it is derived, to a fabrication which is carried out at the level of form as well as of its content. *Muthologos,* however, refers to a fabrication which is carried out only at the level of the content of the discourse. Therefore, it is not redundant to connect *poiētē* to *muthologos,* for a *muthologos* is one who tells a myth or myths, whether s/he fabricates them or not. Such fabrication pertains exclusively to the content and not to the form of the discourse in question, as is the case with *poiētēs.*

The derivative *muthologikos,* which is found only once in Plato, at *Phaedo* 61b5, refers precisely to this meaning of *muthologos.* Since the suffix *-ikos* signifies "belonging to," *muthologikos* must be understood as an adjective signifying the fact of belonging to the class of *muthologoi,* that is, to the class of "those who tell myths." Socrates, for his part, holds that he does not belong to this class although he does range Aesop within it. We must therefore suppose that *muthologos* here means not only "one who tells a myth or myths," but also "one who fabricates a myth or myths." Further, since Socrates wants to set the myths made by Aesop to verse, it is obvious that the fabrication in question bears upon the content and not upon the form of the type of discourse constituted by myth. In sum, if Socrates does not consider himself *muthologikos,* it is not because he does not tell myths but rather because he does not fabricate myths which, moreover, he would like to set to verse.

We must also examine another important derivative of *muthologos, muthologia.* In ancient Greek, the suffix *-ia* is used to form abstract and feminine substantives. This is the

---

7. The semantic analysis of these four examples of *muthologos* in the Platonic corpus, which corroborates what was said in chapters 3 and 4, clearly shows the tendentious interpretation which Marcel Detienne proposes of *Laws* II 664d1–4 (*Creation of Mythology,* 86–102 and 158–61). Indeed, there is nothing to indicate that the old "mythologues" of the *Laws* are the guardians of a "mythology without myth" which "occupies the whole field of politics." Such a commentary subordinates the passage to the imperatives of a general thesis, yet the passage is an integral part of a whole which by no means justifies such a conclusion.

case with *muthologia,* of which there are eight occurrences in Plato's works: *Rep.* II 382d1, 394b9; *Phdr.* 243a4; *Pol.* 304d1; *Crit.* 110a3; *Laws* III 680d3, VI 752a1; *Hipp.* I 298a4. There is a lot to say about this nominal compound, which could be translated by the paraphrase: "the fact of telling a myth or myths."

Just as *muthologos* is linked to *poiētēs,* there is a passage in Plato where *muthologia* is linked to *poiēsis,* namely, *Rep.* III 394b9–c1. Now in ancient Greek, the suffix -*sis* is also used to form abstract and feminine substantives. In fact, Attic -*si,* like its western Greek counterpart -*ti,* goes back to the Indo-European suffix -*ti,* which provides, for the most part, verbal abstracts designating agents or instruments. In ancient Greek, we do find some nouns with their suffix in -*sis* which designate agents or instruments; but most of the roots suffixed in this way correspond to action nouns. This is the group to which *poiēsis*—whose meaning was described above—belongs. In this context, how must we interpret the syntagma *poiēsis kai muthologia?* As we already saw, *poiēsis* designates the kind of fabrication to which the English term "poetry" corresponds; it pertains not only to the content of the discourse, but also to its form. On the basis of the parallel *poiētēs kai muthologos,* I would suppose that *muthologia* would rather have a tendency to indicate the action of a person who tells a myth or myths, whether he fabricates them or not. In the present case, it is obvious that it is not only a question of telling myths, but also, and especially, of fabricating them.

This idea of fabrication is found again in the following passage of the *Phaedrus,* where Socrates declares, in an allusion to the palinode of Stesichorus concerning Helen: "For those who offend in telling a myth *(peri muthologian),* there is an ancient mode of purification known to Stesichorus, though not to Homer" *(Phdr.* 243a3–5). Stesichorus, a poet of the seventh/sixth century B.C., had spoken harshly of Helen in one of his poems. He was punished, like Homer, with blindness, but he recovered his sight after retracting his words by explaining that it was not Helen, but her phantom of whom he had spoken harshly. In this context, to tell a myth is also and above all to fabricate it. The same idea of fabrication is also found in *Republic* II 382d1 and *Laws* III 680d3, VI 752a1. Matters are less clear with regard to *Hippias* I 298a4. And in the case of *Statesman* 304d1, where the fact of telling one or more myths *(muthologia)* is contrasted with teaching *(didakhē),* it seems that only the narrative aspect is taken into consideration:

> STRANGER Which is the art to which we must assign the task of persuading the general mass of the population by telling them suitable myths *(dia muthologias)* rather than by giving them formal instruction *(dia didakhēs)?*
>
> YOUNG SOCRATES I should say that it is obvious that this is the province to be assigned to rhetoric *(rhētorikhēi).*[8]

In the end, the syntagma *poiēsis kai muthologia* is truly parallel to the syntagma *poiētēs kai muthologos.* Indeed, in the paraphrase "the fact of telling one or more myths," which I employ to translate *muthologia,* we must distinguish not only a narrative aspect but also, and especially, the idea of fabrication. This fabrication bears upon the content which characterizes a particular type of discourse, and not to its form, which is evoked by the term *poiēsis.*

It is worth noting that in two of the cases mentioned, *Republic* II 382d1 and *Hippias* I 298a4, *muthologia* is in the plural. This is easily explained if one understands by *muthologia*

8. *Pol.* 304c10–d3.

the "telling of a myth or myths," and not the totality of myths proper to a civilization, to which the English word "mythology" refers.

There is, however, a passage in the *Critias* where the twofold English meaning of "mythology" seems to apply to the term *muthologia*, that is, (1) the totality of myths proper to a civilization, and (2) the science which studies the origin, development, and meaning of myths:

> CRITIAS They produced from the soil a race of good men and taught them the order of their polity; their names have been preserved, but their deeds forgotten by reason of the destructions of their successors and the lapse of time. For the remnant of survivors, as has, indeed, been already said, was ever left unlettered among its mountains, and had heard no more than the names of the country's rulers and a few of their deeds. So they were well pleased to give the names to their sons, but as for the virtues and laws of older generations, they knew nothing of them beyond some dim reports, but were, for many generations, themselves and their children, in want of bare necessities. So they gave their minds to their own needs and made their discourses of them, forgetting the story of faraway, early days. For the fact of telling myths and the inquiry into ancient things *(muthologia gar anazētēsis te tōn palaiōn)* both visit cities in train of leisure, when they see men already provided with the necessities of life, and not before.[9]

Here, as elsewhere in general, *muthologia* can be translated by "the fact of telling a myth or myths." This paraphrase implies not only a narrative aspect, but also the idea of fabrication in the order of discourse at the level of the content. Critias contrasts this practice, which is current within the framework of the city and which consists of telling myths, with the situation which prevailed previously, among the mountaineers—who fabricated only discourses which bear exclusively upon the necessities of life.

However, the fact that *muthologia* is linked by the particule *te* to *anazētēsis tōn palaiōn*, the "inquiry into ancient things," provokes, in turn, a modification of the meaning of *muthologia*. These myths that are told and fabricated pertain to the past, as is the case in *Republic* III 392d2–3. But since this past is not well known, to speak of it satisfactorily one must initially inquire into what it truly was. From this perspective, *muthologia* means not only the fabrication and narration of particular myths but also the inquiry into what these myths narrate. We thus come nearer to the twofold meaning of "mythology."

Further, it is worth noting that this "inquiry into ancient things," when associated with the "action of telling myths," appears in the city not only with leisure, but also with literacy.[10] *Muthologia* is again associated with *poiesis* through the mediation of music. However, *muthologia* comes to designate a more complex action, when it is coordinated with an "inquiry into ancient things" and when it appears in a context where writing is being developed. It then implies a sorting out of diverse versions of the same myth, in order to construct a reference version that can be put into writing. Although this is not explicit, the context strongly suggests it.

This being said, it must be acknowledged that the most important derivative of *muthologos* is the denominative *muthologeō*, of which fifteen occurrences are found in the works of Plato generally considered as authentic:

9. *Crit.* 109d2–110a6.
10. *Tim.* 23a5–b3.

REFERENCE	VOICE	SUBJECT	GOVERNMENT	MEANING
Gorg. 493a5	active	(Timocreon)	accusative	f/n
Gorg. 493d3	active	Socrates	accusative	n
Laws III 682e5	active	Lacedaemonians	accusative	f/n
Phdo. 61e2	active	indefinite	*peri* + gen.	f/n
Phdr. 276e3	active	(Sophist)	*peri* + gen.	f/n
Rep. II 359d6	active	indefinite	accusative	f/n
Rep. II 376d9	active	indefinite	*en* + *muthōi*	f/n
Rep. II 378e3	passive			f/n
Rep. II 379a2	active	poets		f/n
Rep. II 380c2	active	indefinite		f/n
Rep. II 392b6	active	poets + *logopoioi*	accusative	f/n
Rep. III 415a3	active	city founders		f/n
Rep. VI 501e4	active	(Socrates)	accusative	f/n
Rep. IX 588c2	passive		infinitive	f/n
Tim. 22b1	active	Solon	*hōs* + indicative	n

Abbreviations: f = fabrication; n = narration.

Two other occurrences of the same term are found in works of Plato whose authenticity is contested: *Hipp.* I 286a2, *Epist.* VIII 352e1.

Of the fifteen occurrences in the first group, nine are found in the *Republic,* of which nearly 50 percent are in books II and III. In 13 out of 15 cases, *mutholoeō* is in the active. In general, its object is in the accusative. In two cases (*Phdo.* 61e2, *Phdr.* 276e3), however, *muthologeō* is introduced by *peri* and the genitive. It is also interesting to note the pleonastic character of the construction *en muthōi muthologountes* (*Rep.* II 376d9). Finally, *muthologeō* can govern a proposition introduced by the infinitive (*Rep.* IX 588c2) or *hōs* and the indicative (*Tim.* 22b1).

In nearly all cases, *muthologeō* means "to tell (or speak of) in (or in the form of) a myth": a paraphrase which refers not only to the narration but also to the fabrication of the myth in question. This ambiguity is more or less noticeable, except in two cases (*Gorg.* 493d3, *Tim.* 22b1), where *muthologeō* appears to have only a narrative aspect.

The necessity of taking the idea of fabrication into consideration in most of the occurrences of *muthologeō* in Plato becomes evident if we consider the subjects of this verb. In *Gorgias* 493a5, the subject is Timocreon, a poet of the fifth century B.C.; in *Republic* II 379a2, poets; in *Republic* II 392a6, the subjects are poets and makers of discourse.

The last item of evidence is particularly interesting. Indeed, we have the pair of subjects, poets and makers of discourse, corresponding to the pair of verbs: to sing and to tell in a myth. Here, myth again corresponds to the content of the discourse fabricated by the poet, whereas the form of this same discourse—placed in relation to song—falls within the domain of poetry. In the same order of ideas, one may note that the discourse which constitutes the object of this action can be in prose or verse (*Rep.* II 380c1–2). Further, poets must carry out their activity according to certain rules, which are laws (*Rep.* II 379a1–4). In the same passage, *dei muthologein* is taken up by *poiēteon muthous,* thus leaving no doubt about the concept of fabrication indicated by this verbal compound. Finally, in *Laws* III 682e5, we find the syntagma *muthologeite te kai diaperainete,* as if Plato wanted to bring out the idea of fabrication connected with *muthologeō* by coordinating with it a verb which exclusively indicates a narrative aspect, that is, *diaperaino,* "to relate to the end."

The same semantic ambiguity is found in *muthologeō* as in *muthologos* and *muthologia.* Indeed, "to tell (or speak of) something in (the form of) a myth," is also, in most cases, to fabricate a myth about something, with this fabrication pertaining to the content of this discourse.

It is, moreover, appropriate to note one example of *multhologēteon* (*Rep.* II 378c4), a verbal adjective indicating obligation and formed from *muthologeō*, and three examples of *diamuthologeō* (*Ap.* 39e5, *Phdo.* 70b6, *Laws* I 632e4), a verbal compound of which *mutholo-geō* constitutes the second term.

The final nominal compound to investigate is *muthologēma*. Greek widely developed the old Indo-European suffix *m* + nasal in the category of neuters: *-ma* corresponds to the Latin *-men,* to the Sanskrit *-man,* and to the Indo-European *-mn.* This suffix is added to a verbal theme to constitute verbal derivatives expressing the result of an action. This is also the case, as P. Chantraine notes, for denominatives in *-eō,* which have their derivatives in *-ēma.* Now, *muthologēma* allows us to verify what has just been said, at the morphological level as well as the semantic level. Indeed, it seems that in both its two occurrences (*Phdr.* 229c5, *Laws* II 663e5) *muthologēma,* which is derived from *mutholoeō,* designates "the result of the action of telling something in a myth," that is, "what is told in a myth." Let us examine both of these two cases.

At the beginning of the *Phaedrus, muthologēma* refers to the myth of the abduction of Orithyia by Boreas:

PHAEDRUS Tell me, Socrates, isn't it somewhere about here that they say Boreas seized Orithyia from the river?

SOCRATES Yes, that is the story.

PHAEDRUS Was this the actual spot? Certainly the water looks charmingly pure and clear; it's just the place for girls to be playing beside the stream.

SOCRATES No, it was about a quarter of a mile lower down, where you cross to the sanctuary of Agra; there is, I believe, an altar dedicated to Boreas close by.

PHAEDRUS I have never really noticed it, but pray tell me Socrates, do you believe that what one relates in this myth *(touto to muthologēma)* is true?

There are thus at least two versions of this myth of the abduction of Orithyia by Boreas. Further, what follows informs us that this same myth was the object of an allegorical interpretation. In other words, *muthologēma* designates a myth already subjected to a certain elaborative and/or interpretative study.

We find the same thing in the *Laws,* where *muthologēma* refers to the myth of the Spartoi who sprang from the teeth sowed by Cadmus—a myth already referred to in the *Republic* (III 414d–e):

ATHENIAN Well, and that most improbable myth of the man from Sidon *(to men tou Sidōniou muthologēma)*—was it easy to convince anyone of that? Now there are many such myths.

CLINIAS Myths? Of what sort?

ATHENIAN Why, they say teeth were sown in the ground and armed men sprang up from them. And yet the example is striking proof for a lawgiver that the youthful mind will be persuaded of anything, if one will take the trouble to persuade it. Thus he need only tax his invention to discover what conviction would be most beneficial to a city, and then contrive all manner of devices to ensure that the whole of such a community shall treat the topic in one single and selfsame life-long tone, alike in song, in myth, and in discourse.[11]

As in the *Phaedrus, muthologēma* here refers to a precise myth. This myth, moreover, was the object of a particular elaboration, to convince the citizens of their common origin and hence to justify their duty of defending the earth from which they were born.

In brief, *muthologēma* indicates more than the result of the action designated by the verb *muthologeō.* In Plato, this word also means that the myth in question has been subject to a labor of elaboration and/or interpretation.

Insofar as it indicates the result of the action designated by the verb *muthologeō,* however, *muthologēma* is akin to *poiēma,* even if this is not explicitly stated by Plato. From this point of view, the following series of correspondences can be obtained:

muthologos	*poiētēs*
muthologikos	*poiētikos*
muthologia	*poiēsis*
muthologeō	*poieō*
muthologēma	*poiēma*

Whereas the words in the right column designate a fabrication which pertains not only to the content but also to the form of the discourse, the words in the left column take up again the idea of fabrication in the order of discourse, but only on the level of the content. At the same time, they also express the new idea of narration. And this is the case simply because in an oral civilization, to fabricate a discourse, and in particular a myth, is necessarily to tell it.

Finally, the compounds constructed from *mutheomai,* "to say, to tell," deserve to be mentioned. This verb, which is derived from *muthos,* is only found in the poets. This explains why its only occurrence in the Platonic corpus is found in a quote from the *Iliad* (*Crat.* 428c4–5 = *Il.* 9.644–45).

On the other hand, in the works of Plato about whose authenticity there is no doubt, there are a considerable number of occurrences of the following compounds, of which *mutheomai* directly or indirectly constitutes the second term: namely, *paramutheomai,* "to exhort, encourage etc.": *Crit.* 108c7; *Euthd.* 277d4; 288c4; *Ion* 540c5; *Laws* I 625b6, II 666a2, IX 854a6, XI 928a1, XII 944b3; *Mnx.* 237a1, 247c5; *Phdo.* 83a3, 115d5; *Pol.* 268b3; *Prot.* 346b4; *Rep.* IV 442a2, V 451b1, 476e1, VI 499e2; *Soph.* 230a2; *paramuthēteon* (verbal adjective of the latter), *Laws* X 899d6; *paramuthia,* "exhortation, encouragement, etc.": *Euthd.* 290a4; *Laws* IV 720a1; *Phdo.* 70b2; *Rep.* V 450d9; *Soph* 224a4; *paramuthion,* "exhoration, encouragement, etc.": *Crit.* 115b4; *Euthd.* 272b8; *Laws* I 632e5, IV 704d8, 705a8, VI 773e5, IX 880a7, X 885b3, XI 923c2; *Phdr.* 240d4; *Rep.* I 329e5; and *aparamuthētō,* "unable to be exhorted": *Laws* V 731d3.

Since all these compounds conserve the primary sense of *muthos,* "thought expressing itself, opinion," they have not been taken into consideration in this book, with two exceptions: *paramuthia* and *paramuthion* (see chapters 11 and 13).

11. *Laws* II 663e5–664a7.

PROPER NAMES OF CHARACTERS AND BEINGS MENTIONED BY PLATO AND IN TRADITIONAL ANCIENT GREEK MYTHS

In the works of Plato generally considered as authentic, there are 260 proper names relative to characters or beings which play a role in a certain number of myths in ancient Greece. Here is the list. For the occurrences of these names, one can refer to L. Brandwood, *A Word Index to Plato.*

Abaris	Aphrodite	Centaurs	Elasippus
Achelous	= Ouranian	Cerberus	Endymion
Acheron	= Pandemonian	Cercyon	Epeus
Acherusia	Apollo	Chaos	Ephialtes
Achilles	Ardiaeus	Charites	Epimetheus
Admetus	Ares	Charybdis	Er
Adrastia	Aristodemus	Chimera	Erato
Aeacus	Artemis	Chiron	Erectheus
Aegina	Asclepius	Chryses	Erichthonius
Aegyptus	Astres = Stars	Chrysippus	Eriphyle
Aeneas	Astyanax	Clito	Eros
Agamemnon	Atalanta	Clotho	Erinyes
Aidos	Ate	Cocytus	Erysichthon
Ajax	Athena	Codrus	Eumelus = Gadirus
Alcestis	Atlas	Curetes	Eumolpus
Alcinous	=Titan	Creon	Eurypyle
Amazons	= King of	Cresphontes	Eurysthenes
Ameles	Atlantis	Cronos	Evaemon
Ammon	Atreus	Cylopea	Evenor
= Thamous	Atropos		
= Zeus	Autochthon	Daedalus	Gadrius = Eumelus
Ampheres	Autolycus	Dardanus	Gaia (Ge)
Amphion	Azaes	Demeter	Ganymede
Amphitryon		Deucalion	Geryon
Amycus	Boreas	Diaprepes	Giants
Amyntor	Briareus	Dike	Glaucus
Ananke		Diomedes	Gorgons
Andromache	Cadmus	Dione	Gyges
Antaeus	Calliope	Dionysus	
Antenor	Ceneus	Dioscuri	Hades
Antilochus	Cecrops	Doris	Harmonia

Hecamede	Metion	Pelops	Sisyphus
Hector	Metis	Penelope	Spercheus
Hecuba	Minos	Penia	Sphinx
Helen	Mnemosyne	Persephone	Styx
Helios = Sun	Mneseus	Phaethon	
Hephaestus	Mormolyce	Pharmacia	Tantalus
Hera	Musaeus	Phemius	Tartarus
Heracles	Muses	Pherrephatta	Telamon
Hermes	Myrina	= Persephone	Telephus
Hestia	Myrtilus	Phix = Sphinx	Temenus
Hippocentaurs		Phoenix	Terpsichore
Hippodamia	Neith = Athena	Phorcys	Tethys
Hippolytus	Nemesis	Phoroneus	Thalia
Hydra	Neoptolemus	Pirithous	Thamus = Ammon
	Nereids	Pluto	Thamyras
Iapetus	Nestor	Polydeuces	Thaumas
Ilithyia	Ninos (Assyria)	Polhymnia	Themis
Inachus	Niobe	Poros	Theoclymenus
Iolaus		Poseidon	Theodore (of Samos)
Ion	Oceanus	Priam	Thersites
Iphicles	Oeagrus	Procles	Theseus
Iris	Oedipus	Prometheus	Thetis
Isis	Olympus	Proteus	Theuth
	Orestes	Pyriphlegethon	Thyestes
Lachesis	Orithyia	Pyrrha	Tiresias
Laius	Orpheus		Titans
Lethe	Otus	Rhadamanthus	Tityus
Leto	Ouranos	Rhea	Triptolemus
Leucippe			Tyche
Ligurians = Muses	Palamedes	Sarpedon	Typhon
Lotophages	Pallas = Athena	Satyrs	
	Pan	Scamander	Ulysses
Macareus	Pandorus	Scamandrius	Urania
Machaon	Panopeus	= Astyanax	
Marsyas	Parcae	Scylla	Xanthus
Medea	Patrocles	Selene = Moon	
Melanippe	Pegasus	Sileni	Zalmoxis
Menelaus	Peleus	Simois	Zethus
Menoetius	Pelias	Sirens	Zeus
Mestor			

There are 16 cases found in works considered by most specialists as inauthentic.

Achaemenes	Europa	Ormazes	Polyidos
Agamedes	Eurysaces	Perseus	Talos
Amphiaraos	Laomedon	Phtia	Tityos
Athamas	Lynceus	Pleiades	Trophonios

There could be added to this list a number of other names of different peoples who descend from the heros who founded the cities and who play a role in myths. Further, Plato also mentions numerous important themes found in the traditional mythology of ancient Greece: the races (of gold, silver, bronze, and iron), the Isles of the Blessed, the judgement after death, the sow of Crommyon, the gardens of Adonis, etc. Finally, it must be noted that the numerous allusions to characters or mythological beings whose names were not explicitly cited by Plato have not been taken into account.

Myth and Preamble in the Laws

	PLACE	LAW	PREAMBLE	MYTH(S)
1	VI 771c7	Organization of religious festivals (771c–d5)	Division of the 5,040 families into 12 parts corresponding to the 12 principal deities (771a5–c7)	Contextual reference to myths relative to the 12 principal deities
2	VI 773b4	Marriage (772d5–e6); cf. IV 721b1–3	Justifications (772e7–73e4, cf. also IV 721b6–d6)	Probable reference to the "paradigmatic" marriage of Zeus and Hera
3	VII 790c3	Education of the body: no true law (790a8–b6)	Description of these cares for the first year of childhood (788a1–90c3)	Contextual reference to the practices of the Corybants (790c5–e4)
4	VII 804e4	Education of women (804d6–e1)	Justification through examples (804e1–806d2)	Direct reference to the Amazons
5	VII 812a2	Literary studies (809e2–10c4)	Condemnation of traditional literary instruction (810c5–12a3)	Contextual reference to the myths which constitute the essential part of literary studies
6	VII 840c1	Lawful use of sexuality (841c8–e4)	Problems relative to sexuality (835c1–41c8)	Myths conveyed by tradition in ancient Greece
7	VIII 841c6	Lawful use of sexuality (841c8–e4)	A part of the preamble on supervision in sexual affairs (839e5–41c8)	841b2–c2 is compared to a myth
8	IX 865d5	Murder (865d3–5, 865e6 sq.)	Telling of a myth to justify the law (865d5–e6)	Myth concerning the return to earth of those who experienced a violent death

(continues)

	PLACE	LAW	PREAMBLE	MYTH(S)
9	IX 872e1	Patricide (873b1–c1)	Telling of a myth to justify the law (872c7–73b1)	Myths originating from priests in antiquity (872e1–73a3)
10	X 887d2	Existence of the gods (907d4–909d2)	Preamble relative to the existence of the gods (887c5–99d3)	Myths conveyed by tradition in ancient Greece
11	X 903b1	Divine providence (907d4–909d2)	Preamble relative to divine providence (899d4–905d1)	The golden age under the rule of Kronos and the demiurge of the *Timaeus*
12	XI 913c2	Discovery of a treasure (913c3–d8)	Preamble on the consequences for the posterity of those who seize a treasure that they have discovered (913a1–c3)	Myths conveyed by tradition in ancient Greece (913c1–3)
13	XI 927c8	Orphans (927c7–928d4)	Preamble as a warning against injustice with respect to orphans (926e9–927c7)	Myth on life after death (927a1–c3)
14	XII 944a2	Abandoning arms (944b4–45b1)	Preamble on the reasons for abandoning one's arms (943d4–44b4)	Patrocles and the arms of Achilles (944a2–8; cf. the allusion to Caeneus at 944d5–7)

The works cited in each section are listed by date of publication.

PLATO'S GENERAL ATTITUDE TOWARD MYTH

Crome, C. *De mythis platonicis imprimis de necyiis.* Düsseldorf, 1835.

Jahn, A. *Dissertatio platonica.* Berne: Jennium, 1839.

Schwanitz, G. *Die Mythen des Plato.* Leipzig: Fleischer, 1852.

Deuschle, J. *Die platonischen Mythen.* Hanau: König, 1854.

Fischer, A. *De mythis platonicis.* Munich, 1865.

Westcott, B. F. "The Myths of Plato," *Contemporary Review* 2 (1866): 199–211, 469–81.

Hirzel, R. *Über das Rhetorische und seine Bedeutung bei Plato.* Munich, 1871.

Volquardsen, C. R. *Platons Theorie vom Mythus und seine Mythen.* Schleswig, 1871.

Forster, E. *Die platonischen Mythen.* Rastatt, 1873.

Gregoriades, P. *Peri tōn muthōn para Platōni* [in modern Greek]. Göttingen: Vandenhoeck & Ruprecht, 1879.

Thiemann, K. *Die platonische Eschatologie.* Berlin, 1892.

Döring, A. "Die eschatologischen Mythen Platos," *Archiv für Geschichte der Philosophie* 6 (1893): 475–90.

Couturat, L. *De Platonicis mythis.* Paris: Alcan, 1896.

Brochard, V. "Les Mythes dans la philosophie de Platon," *Année philosophique* 11 (1901): 1–13; reprinted in *Études de philosophie ancienne et de philosophie moderne,* 46–59. Paris: Alcan, 1912.

Plato. *The Myths of Plato.* Translated with introductory and other observations by J. A. Stewart. London: Macmillan, 1905. Reprint, London: Centaur, and Carbondale: Southern Illinois Univ. Press, 1960; New York: Barnes & Noble, 1970.

Willi, W. *Versuche einer Grundlegung der platonischen Mythopoiie.* Zurich: Füssli, 1925.

Calogero, G. "Miti ed amori platonici." *Cultura* 6 (1926–27): 533–42.

Reinhardt, K. *Platons Mythen.* Bonn: Cohen, 1927.

Friedländer, P. *Platon,* vol. 1: *Eidos, Paideia, Dialogos.* Berlin and Leipzig: De Gruyter, 1928. New and updated edition, *Platon,* vol. 1: *Seinswahrheit und Lebenswirklichkeit.* Berlin: De Gruyter, 1954. Published in English, *Plato,* vol. 1: *An Introduction.* Translated by Hans Meyerhoff. New York: Pantheon Books, 1958. See 171–210.

Frutiger, P. *Les Mythes de Platon.* Paris: Alcan, 1930.

Hildebrandt, K. *Platon: Logos und Mythos* [1930]. 2d ed. revised and updated, Berlin: De Gruyter, 1959.

Popelova, J. "Mythi platonici quid valeant." *Acta secundi Congressus Philologorum Classicorum Slavorum Pragae,* 185–97. Prague, 1931.

Buisman, J. R. *Mythen en allegorieën in Plato's kennis-en zijnsleer.* Amsterdam and Paris, 1932.

Stöcklein, P. *Über die philosophische Bedeutung von Platons Mythen. Phililogus* Suppl. Bd. 30, Heft 3. Leipzig: Dieterich, 1937.

Imbelloni, J. "Atlantis: Teoría platónica del mito." *Nosotros* (Buenos Aires) 3 (1938): 123–40.

Levi, A. "I miti platoni sull'anima e sui suoi destini." *Rivista di Filosofia* 30 (1939): 137–66.

Bassi, D. "La mitologia in Platone." *Rendiconti dell'Istituto Lombardo (Classe di Lettere, Scienze morali e storiche)* 73 (1939–40): 457–84.

Levi, A. "I miti platonici." *Rivista critica di storia della filosofia* 1 (1946): 197–225.

Untersteiner, M. *La fisiologia del mito,* 351–64, 375–84. Milan: Bocca, 1946.

Schuhl, Pierre-Maxime. *La Fabulation platonicienne* [1947]. 2d ed. revised and updated to include articles appearing between 1930 and 1968, Paris: Vrin, 1968.

Edelstein, L. "The Function of Myth in Plato's Philosophy." *Journal of the History of Ideas* 10 (1949): 463–81.

Buffière, F. *Les Mythes d'Homère et la pensée grecque.* Paris: Les Belles Lettres, 1956.

Pfeil, H. "Die Weisheit der Antike und der Moderne Mensch, aufgezeigt an Platons Mythen." In F. Hörmann, ed., *Vom Menschen in der Antike,* 143–73. Munich: Bayerischer Schulbuch-Verlag, 1957.

Loewenclau, Ilse von. "Mythos und Logos." *Studium generale* 11 (1958): 731–41.

Chatte, Reme C. "Los mitos en el *Fedro* y el *Banquete," Rivista de educación* 4, no. 10 (1960): 1–22.

Mathieu. V. "Convergenza verso il bene e mito schematico in Platone." *Rendiconti della Classe di Scienze morali, storiche e filologiche dell'Accademia dei Lincei* 15 (1960): 102–22.

Pieper. J. "Über die Wahrheit der platonischen Mythen." In Klaus Oehler and Richard Schaeffer, eds., *G. Krüger zum 60. Geburtstag,* 289–96. Frankfort: Klostermann, 1962.

Müller, G. "Die Mythen der platonischen Dialogue." *Nachrichten der Giessener Hochschulgesellschaft* 32 (1963): 77–92.

Pfeil, H. *Das platonische Menschenbild, aufgezeigt an Platons Mythen.* Mit Beifügung ausgewählter Platon-Text. Aschaffenburg: Pattloch, 1963.

Anton, J. P., "Plato's Philosophical Use of Myth." *Greek Orthodox Review,* 9 (1963–64): 161–80.

Brunet, C. "Mythes et Croyances." *Revue de métaphysique et de morale* 69 (1964): 276–88.

García, Calvo A. "Dialéctica y mito." *Actas del II. Congreso español de estudios clásicos,* Madrid-Barcelona, 4–10 April 1961, 300–317. Publicaciones de la Sociedad espánola de estudios clásicos 5. Madrid, 1964.

Pagliano, M. "Introduzione all'*Eutifrone.*" *Vichiana* 1 (1964): 376–89.

Romano, F. *Logos e mythos nella psicologia di Platone.* Padua: Cedam, 1964.

Pieper, J. *Über die platonischen Mythen.* Munich: Kösel, 1965.

Dörrie, H. "Der Mythos im Verständnis der Antike II: Von Euripides bis Seneca," *Gymnasium* 73 (1966): 44–62.

Escudero, C. "Mito y filosofia: El mito platónico y su significado." *Perficit* n. s. 1 (1967–68): 243–302, 307–45.

Gregory, M. J. "Myth and Transcendence in Plato." *Thought* 43 (1968): 273–96.

Paisse, J.-M. "Réminiscence et Mythes platoniciens." *Les Études classiques* 37 (1969): 19–43.

Theodorakopoulos, I. N. "El mito platónico." *Folia humanistica* 7 (1969): 243–49.

Sease, V. W. "The Myth in Plato's Theory of Ideas." *The South-Western Journal of Philosophy* 1 (1970): 186–97.

Gaffney, S. K. "Dialectic, the Myths of Plato, Metaphor and the Transcendent in the World." *Proceedings of the American Catholic Philosophical Association* 45 (1971): 77–85.

Hirsch, W. *Platons Weg zum Mythos.* Berlin and New York: De Gruyter, 1971.

Wartofsky, M. W., The *Republic* as myth, the dilemma of philosophy and politics." *The Philosophical Forum* (De Kalb, Ill.) 10 (1971): 249–66.

Hitchcock, D. L. *The Role of Myth and its Relation to Rational Argument in Plato's Dialogues.* Ph.D. diss., Claremont Graduate School, 1974.

Stormer, G. P. "Plato's Theory of Myth." *Personalist* 55 (1974): 216–23.

Moors, Kent Francis. *Myth and Opinion in Plato's "Republic."* Ph.D. diss., Northern Illinois University, 1976.

Callahan, J. F. "Dialectic, Myth and History in the Philosophy of Plato." In *Interpretations of Plato,* ed. H. F. North, 64–85. A Swarthmore Symposium. *Mnemosyne* Suppl. 50, Leiden: Brill, 1977.

Roy, D. H. *The Political Status and Function of Plato's Myths.* Ph.D. diss., University of Notre Dame, 1977.

Sabbatucci, D. "Aspetti del rapporto *mythos-logos* nella cultura greca." In *Il mito greco,* 57–62. Atti del Convegno internazionale Urbino, 7–12 maggio 1973, a cura di B. Gentili and G. Paioni. Rome: ed. dell'Ateneo e Bizzarri, 1977.

Takho-Godi, A. "Realistic and Symbolic Interpretation of Myth in Plato and Porphyry" (in Russian). *Byzantine Studies: A Collection on the Occasion of the 80th Birthday of S. G. Kaukhčišvili* (in Russian), 37–46. Tbilisi: Mecnijereba, 1978.

Segal, Ch. "The Myth was Saved: Reflections on Homer and the Mythology of Plato's *Republic.*" *Hermes* 106 (1978): 315–56.

Zaslavsky, Robert. *Platonic Myth and Platonic Writing.* Ph.D. diss., The New School for Social Research, 1978. Reprinted Washington D.C.: University Press of America, 1981.

Takho-Godi, A. "Platonic Myth as Reality and Image" (in Russian). In *Plato and his Time* (in Russian), 58–82. Moscow: Nauka, 1979.

Wright, R. "How Credible are Plato's Myths?" In G. W. Bowersock, W. Burkert, and M. Putnam, eds., *Akktouros: Hellenic Studies Presented to B. M. Knox on the Occasion of his 65th Birthday,* 364–71. Berlin and New York: De Gruyter, 1979.

Detienne, M. *L'Invention de la mythologie.* Paris: Gallimard, 1981. *The Creation of Mythology.* Translated by Margaret Cook. Chicago: University of Chicago Press, 1986. Chapter 5 is entitled "La cité défendue par ses mythologues." This chapter is a new version of an article entitled "Les Mythologues de la cité." *Revue Française de Psychanalyse* 43 (1979): 355–74. This article was integrated in another article entitled "Une Mythologie sans illusion." *Le Temps de la réflexion* 1 (1980): 27–60.

Kremer-Marietti, Angèle. "Platon et le mythe." *Revue de l'Enseignement Philosophique* 31 (1980–81): 34–58.

Cobb-Steven, Veda. "*Mythos* and *Logos* in Plato's *Phaedo.*" *Analecta Husserliana* 12 (1982): 391–405.

Moors, Kent Francis. *Platonic Myth: An Introductory Study.* Washington D.C.: University Press of America, 1982.

Smith, Janet Elizabeth. "Plato's Myths as 'Likely Accounts,' Worthy of Belief." *Apeiron* 19 (1985): 24–42.

Carchia, Gianni. "Critica e salvazione del mito in Platone." *Aut Aut* 216 (1986): 41–64.

Nilles, J. C. "Approche mythique du Bien, du *phytourgos* et du démiurge." *Revue Internationale de Philosophie* 40 (1986): 115–39.

Smith, Janet Elizabeth. "Plato's Use of Myth in the Education of Philosophic Man." *Phoenix* 40 (1986): 20–34.

Detienne, Marcel. "La double écriture de la mythologie: Entre le *Timée* et le *Critias.*" In *Métamorphoses du myth en Grèce ancienne,* ed. Claude Calame, 17–33. Religions en perspectives, no. 4. Geneva: Labor & Fides, 1988. Reprinted in *L'écriture d'Orphée,* 167–86. Paris: Gallimard, 1989.

Capizzi, Antonio. "Il nesso mythos-logos in Platone." *Discorsi* 9 (1989): 309–325.

Mattéi, Jean-François. "The Theater of Myth in Plato." In Charles L. Griswold, Jr., ed., *Platonic Writings, Platonic Readings,* 66–83. New York and London: Routledge, Chapman, and Hall, 1988. "Le théâtre du mythe chez Platon." In *L'ordre du monde: Platon-Nietzsche-Heidegger,* 48–69. Paris: PUF, 1989.

Moors, Kent Francis. "*Muthologia* and the Limits of Opinion: Presented Myth in Plato's *Republic.*" In *Proceedings of the Boston Area Colloquium in Ancient Philosophy,* vol. 4, ed. John J. Cleary and Daniel C. Shartin, 213–47. Lanham, Md.: University Press of America, 1989. Commentary by D. A. Hyland, 248–55.

Stewart, Robert Scott. "The epistemological function of Platonic myth." *Philosophy and Rhetoric* 22 (1989): 260–80.

Kobusch, Theo. "Die Wiederkehr des Mythos: Zur Funktion des Mythos in Platons Denken und in der Philosophie des Gegenwart." In *Mythos: Erzählende Weltdeutung im Spannungsfeld von Ritual, Geschichte und Rationalität,* ed. Gerhard Binder and Bernd Effe, 13–32. Bochumer Altertumswissenschaftliches Colloquium, no. 2. Bochum: Trier Wiss. Verlag, 1990.

Lafrance, Yvon. "Myth et raison dans la théorie platonicienne des idées." In *La naissance de la raison en Grèce,* ed. Jean-François Mattéi, 315–24. Actes du Congrès de Nice (May 1967). Paris: PUF, 1990.

McMinn, J. B. "Plato's Mantic Myths in the Service of Socrates' Maieutic Art." *Kernos* 3 (1990): 219–34.

Ruiz Yamuza, Emilia. *El mito como estructura formal en Platón.* Publicaciones de la Universidad de Sevilla, Serie. Filosofía y Letras 86. Madrid: Publ. de la Uni. de Sevilla, 1986.

Tarrant, Harold A. S. "Myth as a Tool of Persuasion in Plato." *Antichthon* 24 (1990): 19–31.

Cerri, Giovanni. *Platone sociologo della comunicazione.* Prefazione di Bruno Gentili. Milan: La Cultura, Il Saggiatore, 1991.

Droz, Geneviève. *Les mythes platoniciens.* Inédit Sagesse. Paris: Seuil, 1992.

Lledo, Emilio. *El surco del tiempo: Meditaciones sobre el mito Platónico de la escritura y la memoria.* Barcelona: Editorial Crítica, 1992.

McCabe, Mary Margaret. "Myth, Allegory, and Argument in Plato." *Apeiron* 25 (1992): 47–67.

Arrighetti, Graziano. "Plato between Myth, Poetry, and History." In Siegfried Jäkel, ed., *Power and Spirit,* 43–61. Turku: Turun Xliopisto, 1993.

Vallejo Campos, Alvaro. *Mito y persuasión en Platón.* Rivista de Filosofía, Suplementos 2. Seville, 1993.

Mattéi, Jean-François. *Plato et le miroir: De l'âge d'or à l'Atlantide.* Paris: PUF, 1996. A Collection of essays, most previously published, on Plato's attitude toward myth and on the different Platonic myths.

Schefer, Christina. *Platon und Apollon: Vom Logos züruck Mythos.* International Plato Studies, 7. Sankt Augustin: Academia Verlag, 1996.

On "Platonic" Myths
Aristophanes' Myth (*Symposium* 189d–93d)

Bollack, Jean. "Le mythe d'Aristophane dans le *Banquet* de Platon." Summary in *Revue des Études Grecques* 75 (1962): ix–x.

Dover, K. J. "Aristophanes' speech in Plato's *Symposium.*" *Journal of Hellenic Studies* 86 (1966): 41–50.

Brisson, Luc. "Bisexualité et médiation en Grèce ancienne." *Nouvelle Revue de Psychanalyse* 7 (1973): 27–48.

Hani, Jean. "Le mythe de l'androgyne dans le *Banquet* de Platon." *Euphrosyne* 11 (1981–82): 89–101.

Atlantis (*Critias; Timaeus* 21e–26d)

For a general presentation and a complete bibliography, see Plato, *Timée/Critias,* translation, introduction, and notes by Luc Brisson, with the collaboration of Michel Patillon for the translation. GF 618. Paris: Flammarion, 1992.

Naddaf, Gerard. "The Atlantis Myth: An Introduction to Plato's Later Philosophy of History." *Phoenix* 48 (1994): 189–209.

Pradeau, Jean-François. *Le monde de la politique: Sur le récit atlante de Platon,* Timée (17–27) *et* Critias. International Plato Studies, 8. Sankt Augustin: Academia Verlag, 1997.

The Winged Chariot (*Phaedrus* 246a–49d)

For a general presentation and a complete bibliography, see Plato, *Phèdre,* translation, introduction, and notes by Luc Brisson. Paris: Flammarion, 1989; revised and updated edition, 1992.

Autochthony (*Republic* III 414d–e)

Hall, R. W. "On the myth of the metals in the *Republic.*" *Apeiron* 1, no. 2 (1967): 28–32.

Hahm, D. E. "Plato's 'Noble Lie' and Political Brotherhood." *Classica & Mediaevalia* 30 (1969 [1974]): 211–17.

Broze, Michèle. "Mensonge et justice chez Platon." *Revue Internationale de Philosophie* 40 (1986): 38–48.

Loraux, Nicole. "Variations grecques sur l'origine: Gloire du Même, prestige de l'Autre." *Cahiers de l'Ecole des Sciences philosophiques et religieuses* (Paris) 2 (1987): 69–94.

Hartman, Margaret. "The Hesiodic Roots of Plato's Myth of Metals." *Helios* 15 (1988): 103–14.

Moors, Kent. "Chthonic themes in Plato's *Republic.*" *Diálogos* (Puerto Rico) 25, no. 55 (1990): 29–77.

The Cave (*Republic* VI 514a–17a)

This myth (or this allegory) is indissociable from two other allegories: that of the sun as the image of the Good (*Republic* VI 506d–9d), and that of the "divided line" (*Republic* VI 509c–11e). For a complete and annotated bibliography of the editions, translations, and interpretations of these famous passages of the *Republic,* see Yvon Lafrance, *Pour interpréter Platon: La ligne en République VI 509d–511e. Bilan analytique des études (1804–1984).* Collection Noêsis/Collection d'études anciennes. Montréal: Bellarmin; Paris: Les Belles Lettres, 1987.

Aubenque, Pierre. "De l'égalité des segments intermédiaires dans la ligne de la *République.*" *SOPHIHS MAIHTORES: Chercheurs de sagesse,* Hommage à Jean Pépin, 37–44. Paris: Études Augustiniennes.

The Cicadas (*Phaedrus* 259b–d)

For a general presentation and a complete bibliography, see Plato, *Phèdre,* translation, introduction, and notes by Luc Brisson. Paris: Flammarion, 1989; revised and updated edition, 1992.

Pinnoy, Morits. "Platonica minora: due miti originali nel *Fedro* di Platone." *Quaderni Urbinati di Cultura Classica* 37 (1991): 29–43. On the myth of the Cicadas and the myth of Theuth.

Gottfried, Bruce. "Pan, Cicadas, and Plato's Use of Myth in the *Phaedrus.*" In Gerald A. Press, ed., *Plato's Dialogues: New Studies and Interpretations,* 179–95. Savage, Maryland: Rowman & Littlefield, 1993.

Er (*Republic* X 614a–21d)

Schuhl, Pierre-Maxime. "Autour du fuseau d'*Ananké*" [1930]. In *La Fabulation Platonicienne* [1947], 2d ed. rev., 71–78; 79–98. Bibliothèque d'Histoire de la Philosophie. Paris: Vrin, 1968.

Vernant, Jean-Pierre. "Le fleuve *Amélès* et la *Mélétè Thanatou*" [1960]. Reprinted in *Mythe et pensée chez les Grecs,* 79–94. Paris: Maspero, 1965. There are reprints of this article in various collections.

Lincoln, Bruce. "Waters of Memory, Waters of Forgetfulness." *Fabula* 23 (1982): 19–34.

Russel, J. R. "The Platonic Myth of Er, Armenian Ara and Iranian Arday Wiraz." *Revue des Études Arméniennes* 18 (1984): 477–85.

Thayer, H. S. "The Myth of Er." *History of Philosophy Quarterly* 5 (1988): 369–84.

Schills, Griet. "Plato's Myth of Er: The Light and the Spindle." *Antiquité Classique* 62 (1993): 101–14.

The Eschatological Myth in *Gorgias* (493a–b)

Blank, David L. "The Fate of the Ignorant in Plato's *Gorgias.*" Hermes 119 (1991): 22–36.

The Eschatological Myth of the *Laws* (*Laws* X 903b–5b)

Schuhl, Pierre-Maxime. "Une machine à peser les âmes" [1947]. In *La Fabulation Platonicienne* [1947], 2d ed. rev., 95–98. Bibliothèque d'Histoire de la Philosophie, Paris: Vrin, 1968.

Schuhl, Pierre-Maxime. "Un cauchemar de Platon." [1953]. In *Études platoniciennes,* 85–89. Bibliothèque de Philosophie contemporaine. Paris: PUF, 1960.

Kucharski, Paul. "Observations sur le myth des *Lois,* 903b–905d" [1954]. In *Aspects de la spéculation platonicienne,* 73–96. Publications de la Sorbonne, Série Études 1. Paris/Louvain: Béatrice-Nauwelaerts, 1971.

Gaiser, Konrad. "Miti di Platone sull'esempio di *Leggi* X 903b–905d." *Platone come scrittore filosofico: Saggi sull'ermeuneutica dei dialoghi platonici,* Con una premessa di Marcello Gigante, 125–152. Lezione della Scuola di Studi Superiori i Napoli 2. Napoli: Bibliopolis, 1984.

The Eschatological Myth in the *Phaedo*

Sedley, David. "Theology and Myth in the *Phaedo.*" In John J. Cleary, ed., *Boston Area Colloquium in Ancient Philosophy,* vol. 5, 359–83. Commentary by Gail Fine, 384–98. Lanham, Maryland: University Press of America, 1991.

Gyges (*Republic* II 359d–60b)

Schuhl, Pierre-Maxime. "Platon et le cheval de Troie." [1935, 1936]. In *La Fabulation Platonicienne* [1947], 2d ed. rev., 63–70. Bibliothèque d'Histoire de la Philosophie. Paris: Vrin, 1968.

Hanfmann, G. M. A.. "Lydiaka." *Harvard Studies in Classical Philology* 63 (1958): 65–88.

Fauth, W. "Zum Motivbestand der platonichen Gygeslegende." *Rheinisches Museum* 113 (1970): 1–4.

The Human Puppets (*Laws* I 644d–45c)

Eliade, Mircea. "Mythes et symboles de la corde." *Eranos-Jahrbuch* 29 (1960): 109–37.

Rankin, H. D. "Plato and Man the Puppet." *Eranos* 60 (1963): 127–31.

Burkert, Walter. "Götterspiel und Götterburleske in altorientalischen und griechischen Mythen." *Eranos-Jahrbuch* 51 (1982): 335–67.

Eros as related by Diotima (*Symposium* 203a–c)

Wippern, Jürgen. "Eros und Unsterblichkeit in der Diotima-Rede des *Sympsions.*" In Hellmut Flashar und Konrad Gaiser, eds., *Festgabe für Wolfgang Schadewaldt,* 123–29. Pfullingen: Neske, 1965.

Wippern Jürgen. "Zur unterrichtlichen Lektüre der Diotima-Rede in Platons *Symposions.*" *Der altsprachliche Unterricht* 5 (1966): 35–59.

Irigaray, Luce. *Éthique de la différence sexuelle.* Paris: Minuit, 1985. See pp. 27–39.

The Myth in the *Statesman* (268d–75a)

Schuhl, Pierre-Maxime. "Sur le mythe du *Politique*" [1932]. In *La Fabulation Platon-icienne* [1947], 2d ed. rev., 79–98. Bibliothèque d'Histoire de la Philosophie. Paris: Vrin, 1968.

Herter, Hans. "Gott und die Welt bei Platon. Eine Studie zum Mythos des *Politikos*" [1958]. In his *Kleine Schriften*, ed. Heinrich Dörrie, 316–29. Collectanea 7. New York and Hildesheim: Olms, 1973.

Robinson, T. M. "Demiurge and World Soul in Plato's *Politicus*." *American Journal of Philosophy* 88 (1967): 57–66.

Brisson, Luc. *La structure ontologique du* Timée *de Platon*. Paris: Klincksieck, 1974, chap. 7; rev. and updated edition, Sankt Augustin: Academia Verlag, 1994.

Vidal-Naquet, Pierre. "Le mythe du *Politique*, les ambiguïtés de l'âge d'or et de l'histoire" [1975]. In *Le chasseur noir: Formes de pensée et formes de société dans le monde grec*, 69–94. Paris: Maspero, 1981; 2d ed., 1983.

Mohr, Richard D.. "The formation of the cosmos in the *Statesman* myth." *Phoenix* 32 (1978): 250–52.

Rosen, Stanley. "Le myth platonicien du monde renversé." *Actes du Groupe de Recherches sur l'expression littéraire et les sciences humaines*, 7–28. Publications de la Faculté des Lettres et Sciences Humaines de Nice, no. 24. Paris: Les Belles Lettres, 1983. "Plato's Myth of the Reversed Cosmos." In *The Quarrel Between Philosophy and Poetry: Studies in Ancient Thought*, 56–77. New York and London: Routledge, 1988.

Mohr, Richard D. "Disorderly Motion in Plato's *Statesman*" [1981]. Reprinted in *The Platonic Cosmology*, 141–57. Philosophia antiqua 42. Leiden: Brill, 1985.

Brague, Rémi. "L'isolation du sage: Sur un aspect du mythe du *Politique*." In *Du temps chez Platon et Aristote*, 73–95. Quatre Études. Paris: PUF, 1982.

Dillens, Anne Marie. "De la philosophie au mythe: A propos de lambeaux de légendes rassemblés dans le *Politique* de Platon." In *Qu'est-ce que Dieu? Philosophie/Théologie, Hommage à l'abbé Daniel Coppieters de Gibsons (1929–1983)*, 207–25. Brussels: Publications des Facultés Universitaires Saint-Louis, 1985.

Dumont, Jean-Paul. "Temps, image et existence chez Platon: Le paradoxe du *Politique*." In *Politique dans l'Antiquité: Images, mythes et fantasmes*, 89–111. A collection of studies by Jean-Paul Dumont and L. Bescond, Publication of the Research Centre "Catégories de la Pensée Antique." Lille: Presses de l'Univ. De Lille, 1986.

Tulli, Mauro. "Età di Crono e ricerca sulla natura nel *Politico* di Platone." *Studi Classi e Orientali* 40 (1990): 97–115.

Brisson, Luc. "Interprétation du mythe du *Politique*." In Christopher J. Rowe, ed., *Reading the* Statesman: *Proceedings of the Third Symposium Platonicum*, 349–63. International Plato Studies, 4. Sankt Augustin: Academia Verlag, 1995.

Broze, Michèle. "Le politique et ses falsifications." *Revue de Philosophie Ancienne* 13 (1995): 31–53.

Nightingale, Andrea Wilson. "Plato on the Origins of Evil: The *Statesman* Myth Reconsidered." *Ancient Philosophy* 16 (1996): 65–91.

Protagoras' Myth (*Protagoras* 320c–22d)

Wolz, H. G. "The Protagoras Myth and the Philosopher-Kings." *Review of Metaphysics* 17 (1963–64): 214–34.

Capizzi, A. "Li 'mito di Protagora' e la polemica sulla democrazia." *Cultura* 8 (1970): 552–71.

Brisson, Luc. "Le myth de Protagoras: Essai d'analyse structurale." *Quaderni Urbinati di Cultura Classica,* 20 (1975): 7–37. Critiqued from a marxist point of view by Alessandro Lami, "Gli epigoni: il mito di Protagora strutturalmente analizzato." In *Filogogia e marxismo: Contro le mistificazioni,* a cura di Vincenzo di Benedetto and Alessandro Lami, 169–176. Forme materiali e idelogie del monde classico 17. Napoli: Liguori, 1980.

Lami, Alessandro. "Il mito del *Protagora* ed il primato della politica." *Critica Storica* 12 (1975): 169–76.

Miller, Clyde Lee. "The Prometheus Story in Plato's *Protagoras.*" *Interpretation: A Journal of Political Philosophy* 7, no. 2 (1978): 22–32.

Edwards, Mark J. "Protagorean and Socratic Myth." *Symbolae Osloenses* 67 (1992): 89–102.

Theuth (*Phaedrus* 274c–75b)

For a general presentation and a complete bibliography, see Plato, *Phèdre,* translation, introduction, and notes by Luc Brisson. GF 488. Paris: Flammarion, 1989; rev. and updated ed., 1992.

The *Timaeus* as a Myth (*Timaeus*)

For a general presentation and a complete bibliography, see Plato, *Timée/Critias,* translation, introduction, and notes by Luc Brisson, with the collaboration of Michel Patillon for the translation. GF 618. Paris: Flammarion, 1992.

Baltes, Matthias. "*Gegonen* (Platon, *Tim.* 28b7): Is die Welt real entstanden oder nicht?" In K. A. Algra, P. W. van der Horst, and D. T. Runia, eds., *Polyhistor: Studies in the History and Historiography of Ancient Philosophy,* 76–96. In honor of Jaap Mansfeld. Philosophia Antiqua, 69. Leiden: Brill, 1996.

Calvo, Thomas, and Luc Brisson. *Interpreting the* Timaeus-Critias: *Proceedings of the Fourth Symposium Platonicum.* International Plato Studies, 9. Sankt Augustin: Academia Verlag, 1997.

On Some Mythical Figures Mentioned in the Platonic Corpus

APHRODITE

Pirenne-Delforge, Vinciane. "Épithètes culturelles et interprétation philosophique: A propos d'Aphrodite Ourania et Pandémos à Athènes." *Antiquité Classique* 57 (1988): 142–57.

APOLLO

Gallini, C. "Il Dio che scioglie." *Annali della Facoltà di Lettere, Filosofia e Magistero della Università di Cagliari* 28 (1960): 529–58.

Montrasio, Fernando. "Le etimologie del nome di Apollo nel *Cratilo.*" *Rivista Critica di Storia della Filosofia* 43 (1988): 227–59.

ARION (THE HORSE)

Matthews, Victor J. "The Parentage of the Horse Arion: A Reason for Plato liking Anti-machus." *Eranos* 85 (1987): 1–7.

ASCLEPIUS

Santilli, Paul C. "Socrates and Asclepius: The final words." *International Studies in Philosophy* 22 (1990): 29–39.

DIONYSOS

Vicaire, Paul. "Platon et Dionysos." *Bulletin de l'Association Guillaume Budé,* 1958, 15–16.

Vicaire, Paul. "Les Grecs et le mystère de l'inspiration poétique." *Bulletin de l'Association Guillaume Budé,* 1963, 68–85.

DIOSCURI

Griffith, John G. "Static Electricity in Agathon's Speech in Plato's *Symposium*." *Classical Review* 40 (1990): 547–48.

EROS

Vernant, Jean-Pierre. "Un, deux, trois: Eros." *Mélanges Pierre Lévêque I: Religion,* 293–302. Annales Littéraires de l'Université de Bessançon. Paris: Les Belles Lettres, 1988.

HERCULES

Loraux, Nicole. "Socrate, Platon, Héraklès: Sur un paradigme héroïque du philosophe" [1985]. In *Les expériences de Tirésias: Le féminin et l'homme grec,* 202–14. NRF Essais. Paris: Gallimard, 1989.

LYNCEUS

Fritz, Kurt von. " Der vermeintliche Augenarzt Lynkeus in Platon *Siebtem Brief*" [1971]. In *Schriften zur griechischen Logik,* vol. 1: *Logik und Erkenntnistheorie,* 175–214. Problemata Fromman-Holzboog. Stuttgart: Frommann-Holzboog, 1978.

PROMETHEUS

Kofman, Sarah. "Prometheus, The First Philosopher." *Sub-stance* 15 (1986): 26–35.